284

Scandals in the Highest Office

Also by Hope Ridings Miller:

Embassy Row: The Life and Times of Diplomatic Washington
Great Houses of Washington, D.C.

Hope Ridings Miller

Scandals

in the

Highest Office

Facts and Fictions
in the Private Lives of Our Presidents

Random House
New York

All rights reserved under International and Pan-American Copyright
Conventions. Published in the United States by Random House, Inc., New
York, and simultaneously in Canada by Random House of Canada
Limited, Toronto.

Library of Congress Cataloging in Publication Data

Miller, Hope Ridings.
Scandals in the highest office.
Bibliography: p.
1.   Presidents—United States—Biography.
2.   Corruption (in politics)—United States.   I.   Title.
E176.1.M647   973'.0992 [B]   73-5022
ISBN 0-394-46873-2

Manufactured in the United States of America
First Edition

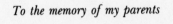

To the memory of my parents

Contents

Scandals in the Highest Office

Introduction

Shakespeare's line, "The greatest scandals wait on greatest state," has been attested again and again in American history in the character attacks on several of our chiefs of state. Some of these onslaughts were entirely fabricated; some were based on "certain truths"; *all* were politically motivated.

Maligned Presidents as a rule have publicly ignored aspersions on their rectitude, but Theodore Roosevelt was an exception. When a newspaper item intimated that he was a drunkard, he brought suit against the editor and issued a statement that reads, in part:

> Any man familiar with public life realizes the foul gossip that ripples beneath the surface about almost any public man and especially about every President.
>
> It is only occasionally printed in reputable papers and set forth in explicit form. But it is hinted in private. And if it is left unrefuted after a man's death it lasts as a stain

which is then too late to remove. From Lincoln to Garfield to Cleveland and McKinley, this gossip has circulated and still circulates . . .

In the case of Mr. Cleveland, for instance, it took the form of accusing him of actions so atrocious that even to think of them makes one indignant. And in this case I know that there was not the smallest shadow of foundation for the charges . . .

T.R. clearly was referring to Presidents who were abused by gossip that they were addicted to alcohol; but that imputation was the least with which Lincoln and Cleveland constantly had to contend, and not the only one that assailed McKinley's good name. In the case of James A. Garfield, whispers that he was "a heavy drinker" were discredited early in his presidential campaign. The serious threats to his chance for victory were allegations that he was paid for expediting a paving contract while he was the Republican leader in Congress, and that he was implicated in the Crédit Mobilier scandal. With a reverse twist on scandalmongery, his campaign managers made use of the Chicago's *Tribune*'s plaint that the "so-called exemplary" Democratic candidate, Winfield Scott Hancock, did "nothing but eat and drink and enjoy himself sensually." Garfield won the election by a small majority. Tales of his dishonest dealings subsided before he was inaugurated, and less than four months later, they were submerged by the emotional wave that swept the country when he was mortally wounded by a frustrated office seeker.

Perhaps purposely, T.R. did not mention two of his controversial predecessors, Andrew Johnson and Ulysses S. Grant; yet their adversities in the highest office were unnecessarily compounded by talk that they were habitually intoxicated. President Johnson was said to be "rarely sober" before that canard came up, repeatedly, in his trial by the Senate, after the house had voted eleven articles calling for his impeachment. A defense witness early in the official proceeding started to relate an extenuating remark that Johnson had made to him, privately, at five o'clock on the previous afternoon. Benjamin F. Butler abruptly stopped the testimony and insinuated that the President at such an hour would be too drunk to speak coherently. The slur echoed throughout the protracted case, but the import would have been ineffectual without the political censure that pervaded the trial. A Southern Democrat, nominated as Lincoln's running mate to bring bipartisan support to the Republican incumbent in 1864, Johnson was anathema to the Radical Republicans in Congress from the moment he moved up to the presidency. His attempts thereafter to carry out Lincoln's plans for leniency toward the defeated South would have brought on the plot to remove him, even if he had been a teetotaler. Still, persistent gossip about his intemperance intensified the drive against him, and although he finally escaped impeachment by a single vote slight of a two-thirds majority, his administration went down as one of the most calamitous in our history.

Grant, whom the Republicans nominated to succeed Johnson, had hardly launched his campaign when a press account described him "a soaker behind the door and in the dark." With that as an opener, Democrats went on to charges that he was also a thief, citing a report that he stole silver from a Southern gentlewoman's home after he dined there in the course of the Civil War. Following his inauguration, talk purporting that he was personally dishonest stopped; but throughout his first term he was repeatedly pictured as a hopeless inebriate, duped by crooked appointees and other financial manipulators. Despite all that, he was renominated—and backed by big money, was easily reelected. Even though his second term was as riddled with graft as the first, he might have been put up for a third—which he wanted—but for incessant complaints that liquor had rendered him incapable of properly handling his official duties.

If Theodore Roosevelt's defense of his besmeared predecessors had taken into account those who were persecuted by charges far more derogatory than alcoholism, Washington, Jefferson and Jackson would have been included. Furthermore, any spoken or written criticism of T.R. himself was mild, indeed, compared with the defilement of other outstanding Presidents who would follow him. T.R., at worst, was never called an adulterer.

The American political disposition seems to combine a desire to regard every chief executive as the embodiment of perfection with a tendency to relish inferences that he is, or has been, morally errant—particularly with women. Even the most incredible whispers to that effect will find receptive ears and avid distributors. There are always individuals with political reasons for degrading the President of the United States, and countless others who spread evil stories as an exercise in reducing the highest officeholder to the lowest common denominator. Moreover, personal behavior which in other parts of the world would be considered inconsequential, or, at least, a public official's private business, has been given enormous importance in our country. Perhaps this excessive attention to morals is a result of our Puritan background or a peculiarity of our democratic system, which denies any privacy at all to those whom we ourselves have elevated. Perhaps, on the other hand, Americans in general are pleased by implications that the men who lead them are unusually virile and active in sexual matters as well as in matters of state.

Anyway, scandals in high places seem to have little permanent effect. Within this century, Woodrow Wilson's eminence survived relentless whispers that he was a womanizer. Even the sensational, posthumous revealments about Warren G. Harding would not have irreparably dishonored his name if his administration had not been permeated with political and economic corruption. Smashing majorities retained Franklin

Delano Roosevelt in the presidency three times, despite sporadic talk about his heady amours; and recent disclosures about his enduring love for his wife's one-time social secretary have actually added a romantic dimension to his historic image.

In the more tolerant climate that followed World War II, rumors about Dwight David Eisenhower's wartime attachment to a British WAC did not impair his popularity. Moral standards were even more relaxed when gossip purported that John Fitzgerald Kennedy and, later, Lyndon Baines Johnson constantly philandered, before and during their White House years. People who wanted to believe any, or all, of the spicy talk did—and passed it on; but many of those who heard it put it down as the kind of twaddle that circulates around, though not always out of, Washington about almost any man who holds the supreme post.

From the day that Jefferson was the first to take the highest official oath on Capitol Hill, the morbid practice of producing and preserving seamy tales about our national leaders has obsessed scandalmongers in and around the District of Columbia. Charles Willis Thompson, correspondent for the New York *World*, stressed that point, as it applied to earlier years, in his book, *Presidents I Have Known and Two Near Presidents* (1929), as follows:

> When I went to live in Washington, Negroes were pointed out to me on the streets with the information "That man belongs to the____family. You know—the illegitimate descendants of George Washington."
>
> After I had lived there a while, I became accustomed to hearing this sort of remark about every President. Sometimes with meticulous details, such as that President Arthur's mistress was the daughter of a certain Supreme Court Justice. That Harrison suffered a heart attack in a house of prostitution, and so on.

7

President Wilson's friendship with Mrs. Peck was the handle for numberless utterly impossible stories and all related on the authority of "somebody in the position to know."

In succeeding chapters, we will examine the scandals that harassed Presidents Washington, Arthur and Wilson. But the Harrison story has turned out to be too nebulous to trace with the same accuracy. Two Harrisons—William Henry ("Old Tippecanoe") and his grandson Benjamin—held the presidency, and rumors through the decades have conflicted in identifying which one was supposedly stricken in a brothel. Moreover, in the light of reliable biography, it is incredible that either of these men ever patronized such a place.

A possible explanation for the persistence of the wicked legend is that it could have been a confused outgrowth of scandal about the Benjamin Harrison who was William Henry's father. A prominent figure in Revolutionary America, he was berated by a fellow member of the Continental Congress for having written a lewd letter to General Washington, hoping to amuse him. As we shall see, after it was intercepted by a British patrol, it was widely publicized with a forged insertion, indicating that the intended recipient was as grossly sensual as the writer. Harrison was branded at the time as "a man of low morals," and whispers ran that he was intimate with slave women on his Virginia plantation and frequented Philadelphia houses of ill fame. The disparagements had no lasting effect on his prestige; he was later elected governor of Virginia. But the salacious letter he supposedly wrote to the supreme commander had repercussions on George Washington's reputation even after he became President.

The delineation of scandal, with its inevitable quotient of conjectures, presumptions, mangled facts and flagrant falsehoods, is not conventional history. But in the sense of Washington Irving's definition of history ("a register of the crimes

8

and miseries that man has inflicted on man"), the slanders and libels that were hurled at succeeding chief executives have become significant parts of their life stories. Furthermore, in some instances, the traducements indirectly brought about changes in government.

Every man who holds high public office, particularly the presidency, must accept, along with the honor, the reality that his entire life is open to constant scrutiny. In a way, the people are entitled to know everything they can find out about the individuals whom they empower. Our laws of libel and certain Supreme Court decisions have made it clear that any elected official has less right to privacy than other citizens. The serious questions raised by the slanders, libels and probative stories about the personal weaknesses of Presidents have to do with how the import affected the discharge of official duty. The evidence seems to show that even the worst calumny did not impair the public performance—or destroy the historic conception—of any truly great national leader in our history.

I

Shafts
at the Superhero

No famous American has ever been so slandered in life—and so idolized after death—as George Washington.

During the War of Independence, British and Tory publications branded him as a licentious dolt from whom his Tory mistress filched secret documents, and then as a traitor who was loyal to the British Crown while commanding the Continental army. Officers in his own forces tried to oust him for incompetence, and one charged him with moral turpitude. The Anti-Federalist press reprinted the earlier libels after he became President and also castigated him as a perfidious schemer angling to be monarch over the plain people he despised.

Although he resented criticism of any kind, Washington publicly seemed to accept the worst abuse with silent fortitude; but after each onslaught he apparently stewed inwardly, and he often boiled over to intimates. Had he been alive when the

publication of his letters to a married woman aroused invidious conjectures, he would have been indignant, but he had
lived to see a good deal of gossip about him discredited, and
during his final years the conception of him as the embodiment of all virtues already had begun to emerge.

That image was venerated for decades on a steadily rising
pedestal, until the idea that he had ever been a mortal with
ordinary frailties was lost in the ascension. The deification is
illustrated in Brumidi's mural, "The Apotheosis of Washington," on the canopy of the United States Capitol. Six thousand
square feet in area, the spectacle features the Father of the
Nation, flanked by Liberty and Justice, with a retinue of female
forms representing the thirteen original states and personifi-
cations of war, agriculture, commerce, mechanics and the arts
and sciences. The glorified portrayal is, of course, in keeping
with the illusion that was exploited shortly after Washington
died—in Mason Locke Weems' copybook version of a youth
who could not tell a lie, growing up to be a peerless soldier
who fathered our country and then presided over it with infinite wisdom.

Other early biographers also fostered the legend that Washington, in the words of Jared Sparks, "was not like other men,"
and that impression inspired celebrated men in nineteenth-
century England to eulogize him excessively. Gladstone described him as "the purest figure in history"; Byron rated him
"next to the Divinity"; and Thackeray wrote of his having "a
life without stain, a frame without a flaw."

Two famous nineteenth-century Americans, however, were
skeptical about overpraise of our first President. "Every hero
becomes a bore at last," Emerson warned. "They cry up the
virtues of George Washington—'Damn George Washington!'
is the poor Jacobin's whole speech and confutation." Haw-
thorne impishly wondered whether "anyone had ever seen
Washington in the nude," and added, "It is inconceivable. He

had no nakedness, but was born with his clothes on, and his hair powdered, and made a stately bow on his first appearance in the world."

The exalted image cracked perceptibly later in the century when Washington's impassioned letters to his friend's wife came to public attention. Yet, the inkling that he was not a paragon made him more warmly appealing than tales of his incredible virtues and his cold, forbidding portraits ever had; and historians with the hope of explaining the superhero began to examine his life realistically.

A prime difficulty in understanding the kind of person he really was lay in the diverse opinions of those who had observed him at close range. Alexander Hamilton, who was more intimately associated with him than any other man, once resigned from General Washington's staff in a pique and wrote, "The Great Man ought for once to repent his ill humour." Yet, after they had composed their differences, Hamilton praised his chief as "cool headed and self-controlled." Gilbert Stuart, who painted several portraits of Washington, observed, "All his features were indicative of the strongest, and sometimes ungovernable passions," but a Dutch clergyman, after visiting him at Mount Vernon in 1788, commented on his "repulsive coldness." Thomas Jefferson praised him as "a wise, a good, and a great man," but described him as "possessing a heart not warm in its affections." To contrast him with "the satanic Jefferson," the Federalist press extolled him to such an absurd degree that John Adams, a Federalist himself, once exploded to a friend, "The history of the Revolution will be one continuous lie! The lesson of the whole will be that Dr. Franklin's electric rod smote the earth and out sprang General Washington. That Franklin electrified him with his rod, and thence forward those two conducted all the policy, negotiations, legislatures and wars." Yet, another time, Adams lauded "the modest and virtuous, the amiable, generous and brave George Washington."

The first attempts by biographers to portray the father-hero as a many-sided figure, with a few human shortcomings, were largely ineffectual. Hero-worshiping Americans were not yet ready to believe that the nation's shining example of patriotism and honor was anything but perfect. And the conception of the flawless Washington persisted as an inspiration to schoolchildren through several awed generations.

In the 1920s, however, popular writers began to emphasize the hero's petty faults in enterprising rather than accurate profiles, with the blemishes largely obscuring his splendor. J.P. Morgan, before the end of the decade, acquired some of Washington's letters and burned them because he said they were "smutty," thus giving credence to the charge that the model of rectitude had a bawdy sense of humor and told obscene anecdotes.

Debunking the long ennobled profile was becoming a national pastime when the Washington Bicentennial of 1932 launched a campaign to reverse the trend. The publication of thirty-nine volumes of Washington's writings, edited by John C. Fitzpatrick, was a monumental contribution, but reams of material expounding the hero's leadership in war and peace overshot the mark. One writer, for example, concluded:

> He was bolder than Alexander, more crafty than Hannibal, wiser than Caesar, more prudent than Gustavus Adolphus, more resourceful than Frederick the Great, more sagacious than Napoleon, and more successful than Scipio; and his star will not pale by the side of theirs.

Such effusions brought negative reactions from a public satiated with the myth but eager to learn more about the flesh-and-blood man. Readers turned to sensational best sellers which, on the basis of fragmentary clues, purported that Washington coveted his neighbor's wife, craved great wealth and unsuccessfully courted two heiresses before he married the richest widow in Virginia, had several illegitimate children, used his slaves immorally, contracted syphilis in early manhood, and died as the result of a cold he caught on an assignation with his overseer's wife on a bitter December day.

With two exceptions, those charges had circulated during Washington's lifetime, and the assignation story stemmed from legends that had sprouted during the Revolution. The theory that as a young man he fell madly in love with his best friend's wife, who lived at Belvoir estate near Mount Vernon, did not develop until almost eighty years after he died.

Even with all the available facts pieced together, the degree of the young Washington's attachment to Mrs. George William Fairfax can only be surmised; but, at least, the indication that he was infatuated with her over a long period fits John Adams' definition of an inaccuracy—"It squints at the truth."

After Mrs. Fairfax's death in England, in 1811, her correspondence from Washington was sent to relatives in America who guarded it from the public until 1877, when two of the letters appeared in the New York *Herald Tribune*. One was his avowal of love, written from Fort Cumberland on September 12, 1758, after he was engaged to Martha Custis. The other, from Raystown, less than four months before he married, reiterated his romantic obsession with Sally Fairfax. Eighty-one additional letters to Mrs. Fairfax were published in 1886, but a full picture of what probably was a one-sided amour will never be available, for none of her correspondence to him was preserved. While he was engaged in the French and Indian War, Washington destroyed everything she wrote to him, as would have any gentlemanly soldier whose life was constantly in danger; and, after his death, Martha Washington burned most of his personal correspondence, which may have contained enlightening recollections from the Fairfaxes after they went to live in England. However, Washington's final letter to Sally, after he had not seen her for a quarter of a century, indicates that time did not dim his devotion to her.

Washington was sixteen when he was brought into the dazzling Fairfax orbit by his half brother Lawrence, son-in-law of Colonel William Fairfax, who, with his family, resided at Belvoir. The English-born colonel was agent and cousin of Thomas, Lord Fairfax of Leeds, inheritor of a royal grant of more than five million acres in Virginia. The nobleman employed young George to chart his Shenandoah Valley lands under the guidance of twenty-four-year-old George William Fairfax, Lawrence Washington's brother-in-law; and the two began a friendship that was to continue until George William died in England almost forty years later.

Washington's career as a surveyor progressed nicely. After his work for Lord Fairfax was completed, he assisted in laying out the new town of Bellhaven (later renamed Alexandria). But he was unhappy, for romance was eluding him. Jane Souther, one of his earliest flames, apparently was indifferent to him. A mysterious Low Land Beauty mentioned in one of his letters as "my former passion" was equally unreceptive. Sentimental rhymes he wrote to two or three other girls brought unsatisfactory results, and he could get nowhere with beautiful Betsy Fauntleroy, daughter of a wealthy planter. The gangling youth, who was shy and slow of speech, had begun to despair that any desirable female would ever be interested in him when George William Fairfax married Sarah (Sally) Cary, in December 1848, the same month in which Washington was appointed surveyor for Culpepper County, Virginia.

A frequent visitor at Belvoir for some time after that, he got a taste of the pleasures and privileges attendant on wealth. The Fairfaxes were accustomed to the finer things of life, and so was George William's bride. Colonel William Cary, her Cambridge-educated father, owned Ceely's, an estate with an opulent mansion overlooking the James River and also maintained town houses in Hampton and Williamsburg. His library was one of the finest in the colonies and he had provided excellent private tutors for his daughters. Sally could converse in French, was well-grounded in the arts, knowledgeable about public affairs, and accomplished in the drawing-room graces of the day—dancing, card-playing and charades.

Sally was two years older than George Washington, and at first he appeared to be attracted to her younger sister Mary, who came to Belvoir for an extended visit. But Mary's charms paled beside those of witty and fascinating Mrs. Fairfax when she began to pay special attention to the impressionable George. She read the classics and played whist and loo with him, taught him to dance, advised him on his wardrobe and helped him to look after it, and induced him to perform with her in amateur theatricals. (Some of his letters to her later recall his enjoyment at playing Cato to her Juba in Addison's tragedy, *Cato*.)

He was stimulated and flattered by her attention and, in time, was completely enchanted with her. The spell was to last at least seven years. But he did not spend all his time hanging around Belvoir during that period; nor did Sally's impact on his emotions prevent his attentions to young ladies eligible for marriage. After a trip to Barbados, where George contracted smallpox and nearly died, he became a district adjutant in Virginia and renewed his courtship of Betsy Fauntleroy. With a fine regard for correctness, he apprised her father by letter of his intention "to wait on Miss Betsy in hopes of revocation of my former cruel sentence and see if I can meet any alteration in my favor." Colonel Fauntleroy lived on the grand scale and could hardly think of Washington, with an unprofitable farm as his only inheritance, as a promising suitor for his daughter. He ignored the letter. George proposed marriage to Betsy, anyway; and she rejected him.

At twenty-two, the new lieutenant colonel of the Virginia militia was in for one of the most depressing periods in his life. With a miscellaneous band of Continentals and the militia, he would engage in several abortive attempts to oust the French and subdue the Indians on the Western frontier. And his eventual rise to the rank of colonel and commander in chief of all the Virginia forces would not offset his disappointment at not achieving his prime ambition, a regular commission in the British army. Meanwhile his life as a soldier was bearable only because he could occasionally get back to civilized surroundings.

After Lawrence Washington died, George leased Mount Vernon (it would come into his possession later), but there, too, he was dejected, lonely and often ill. His mother had moved from Ferry Farm to Fredericksburg, and though he visited her frequently, she was of little comfort to him at any time and was often difficult. His spirits were lifted only at Belvoir. There Sally looked after him when he was indisposed and enlivened his recoveries with a round of theatricals, dances and card-playing. Her captivation of him carried over when he returned to the frontier, and in letters to her he repeatedly recalled their good times together.

The depth of her feelings for him is conjectural. More than likely she was in love with her handsome, understanding husband and merely diverted by Washington. Perhaps she never expected him to take her sallies seriously. Anyway, she enjoyed teasing him, and having at her beck and call the towering young officer who was becoming more attractive every day must have been pleasant. Besides, under her tutelage, he became a superb dancing partner and a passable talker.

At any rate, even if she had returned his affection, divorce and remarriage for her would have been both legally and socially out of the question. Precepts of the Church of England rigidly ruled the mores of Virginia aristocracy, and after Lord Thomas Fairfax died, she was in line to become Lady Fairfax and to inherit extensive holdings in England.

Her husband presumably took in tolerant stride her flirtations with Washington. Fairfax probably did not regard his callow friend as a rival at any time and thought the involvement was merely the natural reaction of a young romantic to a sophisticated, older woman. However, Fairfax's misgivings about his wife's coquetry may have prompted his letter to her from England, where he went to spend a brief time after his father's death. He wrote, "Permit me, Sally, to advise a steady and constant application to those things directed at your welfare which may afford me the greatest satisfaction on my arrival."

Some time before that his half brother Bryan had openly disapproved of Sally's constant badinage of her devoted swain, while Bryan's sister, Sarah Fairfax Carlyle, had written to Washington at camp that fighting the enemy was "a nobler prospect than reflections of hours past that ought to be banished from your thoughts." Furthermore, she had expressed the hope that fortune would bring "someone who may recompense you for all the Tryals past."

When he was twenty-five, Washington came to his senses and determined to free himself of his absorption in his friend's wife by marrying someone with wealth and social status approximating hers. On his way to Boston on military business, he stopped in New York to visit an old acquaintance, Beverly Robinson, and met twenty-six year-old Mary Eliza (Polly) Philipse, Robinson's attractive sister-in-law. She was an enormously rich heiress, with baronial ancestry and impeccable social standing.

Washington lingered in New York almost a week and escorted Polly around the city. Then he returned from Boston and devoted four days to her. Whether or not he proposed marriage is academic. He probably did; but, anyway, his courtship was fruitless, for she was in love with an urbane, highly articulate suitor, Lieutenant Colonel Roger Morris. (Two years later, she married him. Their mansion on Harlem Heights would be General Washington's New York headquarters for a brief period in 1776 while they were Tory fugitives.)

A meeting in April 1758 ended Washington's search for a

wife. At the Virginia home of Major and Mrs. Richard Chamberlayne, he saw a petite and pretty widow, Martha Dandridge Custis, and they took to each other immediately. In all probability, he had met her before—in Williamsburg, when her late husband, Daniel Parke Custis, and Lawrence Washington served together in the House of Burgesses. Perhaps, knowing she was visiting the Chamberlaynes, George purposely stopped off in the course of a trip to Williamsburg to offer his condolences to the widow of seven months.

She was twenty-six, a few months older than he, with two small children; but she had an estate of fifteen thousand acres in and around Williamsburg, a handsome residence in Williamsburg, a country place called The White House in New Kent County, twenty thousand pounds, and more than two hundred slaves. With her wealth and amiability, she could have married any one of a number of men with more distinction than Colonel Washington had at the time. But she must have been impressed with his ardent interest in her, as well as his steady, blue-gray eyes, erect carriage and dignified demeanor. At any rate, the meeting was at a propitious time for both. Her lawyer had just advised her to employ "a trusted steward" to look after her properties; and the resourceful young officer, who had managed to increase his own estate by several thousand acres while pursuing a military career, appeared to be the ideal person to handle her fortune. Furthermore, he had given up hope of obtaining a regular British army commission. He was weary of soldiering and eager to settle down at Mount Vernon, with all the appurtenances of a substantial country gentleman, including a seat in the House of Burgesses. Though he had twice been defeated for election to that, he was determined to try again.

Washington's courtship of Martha Custis proceeded swiftly. Within a few weeks, he had called on her three times at her home, and they were planning to be married as soon as a conventional period had elapsed after her husband's death.

When and how he told Sally is not clear, for he joined the Forbes expedition against Fort Duquesne in June and was at the frontier for several months. In all probability, she first learned of his engagement from her husband, for in his friend's absence Fairfax was supervising improvements at Mount Vernon, with plans to complete them by the following January. Anyway, Washington wrote to her from camp late in August, "I have always considered marriage as the most interesting event in one's life, the foundation of misery or happiness." Sally, in reply, must have teased him about his new love, for back from Fort Cumberland, dated September 12, 1758, came his emotional confession, couched in ambiguous phraseology against the unhappy chance that the message might be read by someone other than Sally:

> Tis true, I profess myself a votary of love. I acknowledge that a lady is in the case, and further confess that this lady is known to you . . . Yes, Madam, as well as she is to one who is too sensible to her charms to deny the Power whose influence he feels and must ever submit to . . . Misconstrue not my meaning; doubt it not, nor expose it. The world has no business to know the object of my love declared in this manner to you, when I want to conceal it . . . But adieu till happier times, if ever I shall see them. I dare believe they are as happy as you say. I wish I were happy also.

Sally's return letter either treated the outpouring lightly or virtually ignored it, for he pressed the point in a message to her from Raystown on September 25:

> Do we still understand the true meaning of each other's letters? I think it must appear so, though I would feign hope the contrary as I cannot speak plainer—but I'll say no more and leave you to guess the rest . . . Adieu, dear

Madam, you possibly will hear something of me or from me before we shall meet.

He and Martha were married the following January, after he had resigned from military service and had been elected to the House of Burgesses. They spent their first months together in Williamsburg and then settled down at Mount Vernon, where life was very much as he had hoped it would be. "I am now I believe fixed in this Seat with an agreeable Consort for Life," he wrote to a kinsman in Britain eight months after his wedding. Meanwhile his association with Sally and George William Fairfax continued. Martha was brought into the friendship, and there was much visiting betweeen Mount Vernon and Belvoir until the Fairfaxes left their estate in Washington's charge and sailed for England in 1773, never to return.

Sally did not become Lady Fairfax; her husband died in 1787 without having attained the family title. His estate in America was worth little after the Revolution; the mansion at Belvoir burned to the ground; and Sally spent her final years in straitened circumstances in Bath, England.

Washington was sixty-six and she was sixty-eight when he wrote his last letter to her, a year before he died, and included this:

> So many important events have occurred, and such changes in men and things have taken place as the compass of a letter would give you but an inadequate idea of. None of which events, nor all of them together have been able to eradicate from my mind the recollection of those happy moments, the happiest of my life, which I have enjoyed in your company.

A postscript from Martha expressed her fondness for Sally and gave some local news. Martha perhaps knew all about

George's romantic fixation on their lovely neighbor at Belvoir in the past and was confident through the years that the continuing friendship posed no more of a threat to her own happiness than did his practice of inviting the most delectable ladies in any company to dance with him.

Her union with George, held intact by mutual respect, need and tenderness, had worked out as satisfactorily as if it had been motivated by compelling passion. And there are no reliable indications that it was ever anything but harmonious, although that was not the way evil whispers had it in the darkest days of the Revolution.

Any suggestion of discord in the marriage would have been hotly disputed by everyone who knew the family at Mount Vernon during the sixteen years before the war. However, that period covered the rise of gossip that the respected squire had a shady episode in his past.

A Captain Thomas Posey owned Rover's Delight, a farm near Mount Vernon and often rode over to drink Madeira wine with Washington while they reminisced about their experiences together in the Forbes campaign of the French and Indian War. The profligate Posey also managed to talk about his troubles in running an unprofitable farm and trying to support his children—Lawrence, Thomas, Price and Milly— and a second wife. He borrowed money from anybody he could, and was always in debt and sometimes in the hands of the sheriff. Washington bailed him out of the guardhouse twice, gave him cash time and again, signed several unsecured notes, and finally took a mortgage on Rover's Delight. When Posey repeatedly failed to make the payments, Washington wrote him stern letters but for some mysterious reason hesitated to foreclose and eventually bought the farm at a bankruptcy sale.

Posey and his family continued to be welcome at Mount Vernon. His daughter Milly was a playmate of Patsy Custis,

Martha's daughter. Washington paid for Milly's dancing lessons, and she moved into Mount Vernon and lived there for several years. Price Posey attached himself to Martha's son, Jacky, and repeatedly fleeced him. Washington advised young Thomas Posey on his career and sent Lawrence Posey through school.

The master of Mount Vernon was always lending money to somebody, but he generally ascertained how it would be used and managed to be repaid. He provided funds for several worthy friends when they needed help to educate their children and then, in due course, collected the debts. But his incredible generosity to a known deadbeat and his dependents puzzled the community and, in time, raised unkindly speculations.

The whispers started when busybodies noted a remarkable resemblance between Lawrence Posey and his benefactor, and before long, neighborhood talk ran as follows: The youngster's age indicated that he was born while eighteen-year-old George Washington was in Barbados, where his half brother Lawrence had taken him because a local girl was about to bear George's child . . . Posey married the mother and brought up the boy as his own and periodically extorted financial assistance from the natural father for silence through the years.

It is unlikely that Washington ever heard the story, and no part of it has ever been verified. But it was publicized as factual in the twentieth century, when a letter from him to Lawrence Posey was discovered, and the barely readable salutation was taken to be "My dear Son." However, a scholar, noting that Washington made the final *n*'s and *r*'s in his writing almost identical, detected a faint dot over the *o* in "Son" and concluded that it was meant to be "Sir." The impersonal context of the letter confirms that theory.

(The Posey story was among several unsubstantiated tales about Washington's illegal parenthood. Rumors that a member of his Cabinet was his son cropped up in his second term as President and were resuscitated decades after his death, along with conjectures that he had still other illegitimate offspring.)

The first organized campaign to destroy confidence in Washington began shortly after Congress unanimously elected him Commander in Chief of the Continental army.

The battles at Bunker Hill and Lexington already had strengthened the resolve of the North, and the appointment of a military leader from the South rallied support from that part of the country. But the war was not universally popular in the colonies. The cities were filled with Tories actively hostile to what they regarded a foolhardy rebellion. Many others in America hoped for acceptable adjustments with the mother country and were receptive to any criticism of the Continental commander. At the same time, the British Ministry realized that a quick subjugation of the rebels was imperative for retaining loyalties to the Crown and forever establishing British authority throughout the colonies. And they recognized one individual as the prime stumbling block—General Washington, who had caught on with a hard core of the rank and file as the personification of independence. If he could not be physically destroyed, he had to be disgraced.

A chance to cast suspicions on his morals opened a month after Washington took command of the Continental army in Cambridge. A letter to him from Benjamin Harrison, a member of Congress, was intercepted by a British patrol a few miles from Philadelphia. General Thomas Gage sent it to the Earl of Dartmouth, royal secretary for the colonies, in London. As released for publication in the London *Daily Advertiser*, the missive contained routine political news of little interest to readers unacquainted with the workings of the Continental Congress. But about the same time, a purported copy of the letter, with the insertion of a salacious paragraph, appeared in two colonial Tory publications, the Massachusetts *Gazette* and the Boston *Weekly Newspaper,* and was reprinted in the September issue of *The Gentleman's Magazine* of London and, concurrently, in the *Caledonian Mercury* of Scotland. The incriminating passage follows:

> As I was in the pleasing task of writing to you, a little Noise occasioned me to turn my head around, and who should appear but pretty little Kate, the Washer-Woman's daughter over the way, clean, trim, and rosy as the Morning. I snatched the sudden, glorious Opportunity, and, but for that cursed Antidote of Love, Sukey, I had fitted her for my General against his Return. We were obliged to part, but not until we had contrived to meet again, and if she keeps the Appointment, I shall relish a week's longer stay. I give you now and then some of the Adventures to amuse you, and to unbend your Mind from the cares of War.

The paragraph has never been authenticated. General Gage declared that Admiral Sir Thomas Graves kept the original letter and sent him a duplicate, which was transmitted to the Earl of Dartmouth. However, a copy including the opprobrious paragraph was found later among Gage's papers; so, presumably, he sent the original letter to London and lent the false copy to Tory newspapers. (The original is believed to be the one so designated today in the Public Records Office in London, wtih the accompanying statement that it was duplicated for five different files of the British government shortly after it was received. A verbatim copy of that letter and facsimiles of the duplicates, now in the Library of Congress, appear to be complete; and they do not contain the portion about "Kate" and "Sukey.")

Publication of the letter created a sensation. To Puritan New Englanders, it was conclusive proof that the intended recipient, a Virginia-born slaveholder, was immoral and therefore unfit to be the Continental commander. Repercussions in Congress shook almost everybody but jovial Ben Harrison, who took the whole thing as too ridiculous to deny. His colleagues, accustomed to his ribald humor, assumed he had written the letter and were annoyed at the intimation that General Washington could be thus amused. John Adams reflected the general opinion of the body when he labeled Harrison "another Sir John Falstaff" and described his language as "disgusting to any man of delicacy and decorum."

Washington presumably ignored the uproar and remained on friendly terms with Harrison, for, shortly afterward, the latter visited the supreme general in Cambridge and stayed three days. "It was a pleasant sojourn," one of Washington's aides noted in his diary, and went on to describe the visitor as "a facetious, good humored, sensible and Spirited Gentleman." Nonetheless, the spirited gentleman's "letter" reinforced subsequent suspicions about the chief commander.

Scandal about General Washington broke out in earnest following an attempt to assassinate him in the summer of 1776. His forces held New York; but British soldiers, 25,000 strong, were entrenched on Staten Island, British warships controlled the harbor, the East River and the Hudson, and British secret agents and Tory spies were everywhere. Washington's life was constantly in danger, and the Elite Guard was doubled at his residence—Mortier's mansion in Lispenard Meadow (later, Richmond Hill).

In June, rumors erupted at Fraunces' Tavern that British agents, operating from the harbor, and Tories, within the city, had conspired to kill the supreme American commander and several members of his staff. Thomas Hickey, a British army deserter who was a member of Washington's Guard, was apprehended and brought to secret trial before a committee of the New York Assembly. His testimony implicated eight members of the Guard and also the Loyalist governor of New York,

William Tryon, and New York Mayor David Matthews. Tryon took refuge on a British warship. Matthews and several other conspirators were dispatched to a Connecticut prison. Hickey was hanged in a field near Bowery Lane on June 28.

In his General Orders for the Day, Washington emphasized the man's inglorious finish in these words:

> The unhappy fate of Thomas Hickey, executed this day for mutiny, sedition and treachery, the General hopes will be warning to every soldier in the army to avoid those crimes, and all others, so disgraceful to the character of a soldier, and pernicious to this country, whose pay he receives and bread he eats—and in order to avoid those crimes the most certain method is to keep out of the temptation of them, and particularly to avoid lewd women, who, by the dying confession of this poor criminal first led him into practices which ended in an untimely and ignominious death.

The authentic record of Hickey's trial was never made public, but the reference to "lewd women" in Washington's memorandum soon provoked a libelous attack on him, with similar imputations. John Bew, publisher of the *Political Magazine of London* and printer for the British Ministry, put out a pamphlet entitled *Minutes of the Trial and Examination of Certain Persons in the Province of New York,* a supposed account of the Hickey trial, discovered after British troops captured the city in the autumn of 1776. It professed "to furnish entertainment to those who wish to know the particulars of this mysterious transaction." The content included confessions of individuals identified as William Cooper, John Clayford and William Savage; they brought in a Mary Gibbons as an accomplice in the assassination plot. According to the text, one of the witnesses described her as "a New Jersey woman of whom General

Washington was very fond," and continued, "He maintained her genteely at a house near Mr. Skinner's at North River—and came there often, late at night."

The testimony further went that Mary Gibbons in the course of her intimacy with Washington stole secret documents from him and passed them on to Clayford, who returned them for replacement after making copies for Governor Tryon; also, that she reported to Clayford her paramour's confidential complaints about the uncooperative Northerners in Congress. She was quoted: "General Washington often said he wished his hands were clear of the dirty New Englanders."

There were just enough facts in the pamphlet to give it a truthful flavor. It included bona fide names of several persons in the New York Assembly; a man named Skinner had a house on the North River; and the time and place of the trial and some of the proceedings could be verified. But no Cooper, Clayford or Savage had testified before the committee, and nobody had ever heard of a Mary Gibbons. Yet, James Rivington, a Tory who often used his New York *Royal Gazette* to espouse the British cause, published the account in full; and it was widely circulated, especially in New England.

Bew and Rivington shortly afterward brought out *The Battle of Brooklyn,* an incongruous farce that had as its denouement General Washington embracing his Tory mistress, with the full approval of a portly Virginian. Benjamin Harrison and Mary Gibbons were not mentioned by name, but the malicious implication was obvious; and the playlet was wildly applauded by the throng of British soldiers and Tories who saw it performed in Brooklyn.

The smear campaign had just begun. The fortunes of war turned against the American forces late in August. General Washington moved his headquarters to the Roger Morris house on Harlem Heights in September and began his retreat to the Delaware the following month. His demoralized troops had scarcely cleared New York when this item appeared in Rivington's *Royal Gazette:*

> Mr. Washington, we hear, is married to a very amiable lady, but it is said that Mrs. Washington, being a warm Loyalist, is separated from her husband since the present troubles, and lives, very much respected, in the city of New York.

Rumors along that line continued until Martha returned from Mount Vernon the following spring, to join her husband at his headquarters in Morristown, New Jersey.

About that time Bew published a booklet, *Letters from General Washington to Several of his Friends in the Year 1776.* The collection was ostensibly found in the portmanteau of a "mulatto fellow, Billy," one of Washington's servants, when he was taken prisoner at Fort Lee, New Jersey, in November of that year. Seven messages were included: one to Martha Washington; one to her son, John Parke (Jacky) Custis; and five to Lund Washington, manager at Mount Vernon.

The letter to Martha was dated June 24, 1776, the time of her husband's supposed involvement with "Mary Gibbons." The salutation "My Dearest Life and Love" was not in keeping with those in Washington's authentic letters to his wife, and the opening paragraph was strange, for it implied that he was disturbed at her annoyance because he had written to her infrequently. The context that followed was particularly damaging; it expressed General Washington's esteem for the British monarch ("I love my king, you know I do; a soldier, a good man, cannot help but love him . . . How peculiarly hard then is our fortune to be so traitorous to so good a King!")

However, intimate references in the letter gave it plausibility. For instance, it urged Martha to submit to smallpox inoculation without delay—in Philadelphia. And, like the messages to Jacky Custis and Lund Washington, it mentioned relatives, management problems at Mount Vernon, and political happenings in Virginia.

The general connotation of all the letters, however, was that General Washington longed for reconciliation with the mother country, thought the war was a mistake, deplored his own role in it and wanted to resign, could not get enough support from Congress to feed and clothe his army, anyway, and was convinced that British authority was better than mob rule. Rivington reprinted the spurious letter to Martha in handbill form and extracts came out in Philadelphia. In Britain the war party was strengthened by its publication in *The London Chronicle* and *The Gentleman's Magazine.*

The Bew–Rivington propaganda coincided with fresh peace proposals—on British terms—when morale in Washington's forces were at a low ebb. His restive soldiers, as well as a number of civilian patriots, were horrified at the prima facie evidence that the supreme commander was fundamentally unsympathetic to the cause of independence. And growing antagonism to him on that score was accelerated by an undercover Tory drive to denigrate him further by rekindling the "Mary Gibbons story" and inferences of the "Harrison letter" as indications of his immorality.

The sensational effect of the propaganda on the Puritan American mind must have surprised the British as much as it delighted them, for they easily tolerated lax morals in their own high command. Shortly after General William Howe replaced General Gage, he acquired as mistress a prominent Boston matron, Mrs. Joshua Logan, who became known as the Sultana of the British Army, and was warmly welcomed with her paramour at both social and official functions. Howe made her husband his Commissary of Prisoners, and the general himself was knighted after his regiments won the Battle of Long Island.

Washington was infuriated by the fabricated letters; he did not publicly deny them, but to a fellow Virginian in Congress, Richard Henry Lee, he confided: "The enemy are governed by no principles that ought to actuate honest men; no wonder then, that forgery should be among their other crimes. I have seen a letter published in a handbill in New York, and extracts from it in a Philadelphia paper, said to be from me to Mrs. Washington, not one word of which did I ever write." He also pointed out that his wife was inoculated in Philadelphia some time before the date on the counterfeit letter, and that his servant Billy (William Lee) was not captured when Fort Lee fell. Later, in private messages to other members of Congress, he further denied that he had written any of the letters and attributed the material to John Randolph, the King's last Attorney General in Virginia. A confirmed Loyalist, Randolph was believed to be an informer for the British Ministry; and, as he had been a guest at Mount Vernon many times before the war, he was well prepared to provide the personal touches that made the letters believable.

Congress as a whole discounted the scandals about the supreme general, but a few members began to distrust his military prowess after his defeat in New York. Then, as a British force moved on Philadelphia, they were receptive to suggestions from some of Washington's officers that he should be replaced by General Horatio Gates, whose army had vanquished Burgoyne's at Saratoga.

The ringleader of what came to be known as the Conway Cabal was General Thomas Conway, an Irish soldier of fortune who had once served in the French army. The chief commander for some time had suspected Conway of disloyalty and had tried to block his promotion to major general. It had gone through, anyway—Congress controlled all promotions above the rank of colonel. Conway took his advancement as an indication of Washington's dwindling influence and forthwith devised the plot to remove him, with the help of Gates, Quarter-master General Thomas Mifflin and several other officers of lesser rank.

By letters—many of them anonymous—to persuadable members of Congress, the conspirators called attention to Washington's amorphous military experience, his tactical errors in the New York campaign, and his stubborn reluctance to accept advice from anybody, except favorites at headquarters who were as incompetent as he. Concurrently, Gates' illustrious background as a British army regular, his victory at Saratoga and his ingratiating personality were cited in glowing terms.

The intrigue was initially successful. Congress appointed Gates chairman of the Board of War, which made him Washington's superior in civilian authority and strengthened him as a rival in the military. Mifflin was placed on the board, and Conway became inspector general of the army. Washington saw the combined power of the three as a threat to his position, but he was powerless to counteract the perfidy until he had definite proof of it. Finally, an anonymous message highly critical of him came to the attention of his loyal friend, Henry Laurens, president of Congress, who promptly forwarded it to supreme headquarters.

Although the letter clearly indicated that it had been inspired by Conway, the prime culprit, Washington ignored him but confronted Gates and Mifflin and demanded explanations for their complicity in the intrigue. Gates abjectly apologized. Mifflin declared he had never doubted his chief's ability but admitted he had disapproved of his superior's tendency to listen to subordinates whose judgments were not always sound.

Washington then strengthened his position by informing his friends in Congress of his reaction to the plot. To Laurens, he complained: "My enemies take ungenerous advantage of me. They know the delicacy of my situation, and that motives of policy deprive me of the defence I might otherwise make against their insidious attacks." His letter to Richard Henry Lee was even more to the point: "I have undergone more than most men are aware to harmonize so many discordant points. But it will be impossible for me to be of further service if such insuperable difficulties are thrown in my way."

Gates was ordered back to the army, and his prestige further declined when his forces were routed at Camden, South Carolina. Mifflin was removed from the board and was succeeded as Quartermaster General by Nathaniel Greene. Conway, after being assigned to an obscure post in upper New York, sent a scorching letter to Congress with his resignation. When it was promptly accepted, he tried to rescind it and offered to stay on in the service in any capacity. While he awaited an answer that never came, General Thomas A. Cadwalader severely wounded him in a duel. Believing he was about to die, Conway wrote a letter of profound apology to Washington and ended it as follows: "May you long enjoy the love, veneration and esteem of all those whose liberties you have asserted by your own virtues."

Even more pernicious than the Conway Cabal was the effort shortly afterward of British-born General Charles Lee, second in command of the Continental army, to undermine Washington's influence with Congress, first by deprecating his military skill and then by assailing his character. An envious, egocentric officer, Lee regarded his military background, with distinguished service abroad and also in the French and Indian War, as much better than that of his commander in chief. And after the latter's forces had to retreat from New York, and Lee's army was victorious at Charleston, South Carolina, he complained to Congress about the supreme general's "fatal indecision" and described his tactics as "damnably inefficient."

The inevitable clash between the two men came in the heat of the Battle of Monmouth Courthouse, New Jersey, on June 28, 1778. Lee, in charge of the American forces, was leading them in full retreat from Clinton's redcoats, when Washington rode into the fray, sharply rebuked Lee and then reversed his orders. The result was a decisive victory for the Americans and a turning point of the war. However, Lee felt that he had been personally, and needlessly, affronted. In letters to Washington he complained about the indignities he had suffered on the battlefield, and in messages to Congress, he insisted that he had been humiliated, in full view of his fighting forces, by "a known incompetent." Worse still, he grumbled to everyone within the sound of his voice that he had been insulted by an evil man, who had been known to treat his slaves cruelly and immorally, "but so secretly that his transgressions were difficult to detect."

Infuriated that anyone would thus slander Washington, young John Laurens, of the supreme headquarters staff, challenged Lee to a duel and wounded him, but not mortally. Meanwhile, even though a few members of Congress seemed to be impressed by Lee's complaints and charges, Washington ordered his arrest and court-martial. He was adjudged guilty of disobedience to, and disrepect of, his superior officer and, also, of making an unnecessary retreat on the battlefield. After being suspended from his command for twelve months, he left the service; but he continued to criticize Washington's military judgment, and, covertly, to vilify him to anyone who would listen.

Through the last four years of the war, most of the scandalous talk about Washington receded, however, and fragmentary gossip of a less serious nature was relatively abortive. Whispers, for instance, that he was unduly attracted to the beguiling spouse of one of his officers followed reports that he spent an entire evening dancing with Kitty Greene, wife of his quartermaster general, at a party the Greenes gave at the encampment in Middlebrook, New Jersey, in March 1779. He had danced with her for most of the evening, but what outsiders did not know was that Martha Washington and Nathaniel

Greene heartily approved. Martha rarely danced. Greene had a permanently stiff knee. The twenty-five-year-old Kitty was enjoying her first party after the birth of her third child (her first was named George Washington; her second, Martha Washington), and the supreme commander was giving her a treat in his favorite diversion. Greene in a letter to Colonel Jeremiah Wadsworth proudly wrote of the party: "His Excellency and Mrs. Greene danced upwards for three hours without once sitting down . . . It was a pretty little frisk." The host's obvious delight in telling many others about the gay evening counteracted the last of the wartime legends that General Washington was a philanderer.

Sporadic personal criticism of him during the final years of the Revolution was generally restricted to vague but recurrent reports that he had a penchant for vulgar talk. One persistent rumor in lower echelons at Valley Forge was that he had tried to bolster the spirits of his soldiers as they crossed the Delaware on that stormy December night in 1776 by telling a yarn that could never be repeated in polite mixed company. No such story has ever been found, nor is there any reliable evidence that Washington's rather heavy-handed humor devolved into bawdy discourse at any time. But some of his postwar letters would be cited by twentieth-century muckrakers as proof that he was not above earthy reflections. For instance, the king of Spain sent him a jackass, which he named Royal Gift. Lafayette arranged for the shipment to Mount Vernon, and Washington later wrote to him:

> The Jack I have already received from Spain in appearance is fine, but his late Royal master, tho' past his grand climacteric, cannote be less moved by female allurements than he is; or when prompted can proceed with more deliberation and majestic solemnity to the matter of procreation.

In similar vein, Washington wrote to a friend who patronized the Mount Vernon stud farm: "Particular attention should be paid to the mares which your servant brought, and when my Jack is in humour, they shall derive all the benefits of his labor, for labor it appears to be."

Before leaving Mount Vernon to assume the highest military post in the Revolution, Washington had confided to Patrick Henry, "From the day I enter upon command of the American armies, I date my fall, and the ruin of my reputation." But although that ruin appeared to be imminent several times during the war, he emerged at the end as the most celebrated figure in America; and the flagrant scandals and petty gossip that had threatened his good name appeared to be forever dissolved in the adulation around him.

He had cherished the hope of once more being "a private citizen of America, on the banks of the Potomac . . . under my own Vine and Fig-tree, free from the bustle of a camp and in the intrigues of a court." That dream was soon dispelled by an avalanche of visitors, portrait painters, gifts and letters from around the world, and by his own program to stabilize his private fortune by improving his five Mount Vernon plantations and developing his Western tracts. But instead of being allowed "to glide gently down the stream of life," as he had wished, he was swept back into public service by election as a Virginia delegate to the Constitutional Convention in Philadelphia. There, by unanimous vote, he became convention president. In the four succeeding months, while the Constitution was being worked out, he occupied the most prestigious position in the body; and in a single speech he impressed his colleagues with his dignity, objectivity and uncommon sense. By the end of the convention, it was a foregone conclusion that he would be President of the fledgling nation.

In the meantime, Washington was bedeviled by incipient gossip that he had been dishonest in a business dealing. It had to do with the Shenandoah Valley tracts he had acquired many years previously but had not seen for the eight and a half years of the Revolution. Squatters had settled on some of the land and neighboring farmers had cultivated a sizable part on the assumption that thus they could establish their ownership. When Washington reclaimed the property after the war, the interlopers hotly disputed his title; but he managed to confirm it and, shortly thereafter, took over full control of the land.

His certain election as President was drawing near when he heard rumors that in the first place he had illegally appropriated the tracts from Lord Fairfax, and, more recently, had evicted the deserving farmers who had as much right to the property as he did. He tried, with no success, to get to the source of the gossip. Then, as it threatened to develop further, he answered it in a newspaper statement which fully explained how the disputed tracts legally came into his possession and ended by challenging the insidious assailants to identify themselves and present proof of their charges. Nobody came forward, and the babble stopped. That was the first and last time Washington openly took steps to stop a brewing scandal.

After he accepted the presidency, he wrote to his old friend Henry Knox that "movements to the Chair of Government will be accompanied by feelings not unlike those of a culprit who is going to the place of execution . . . I am sensible that I am embarking the voice of my Countrymen and a good name of my own on this voyage; and what the returns will be made for them, Heaven alone can foretell." Returns to the country would be immeasurable, for his skill in negotiating the unchartered voyage would be largely responsible for keeping the nation intact and establishing the authority of the new government at home and abroad. Immediate returns to him, personally, would be divided between extravagant praise from the Federalists and unremitting strictures from the Democratic-Republican press, along with a backwash of suspicions about his character.

*   *   *

President Washington had no personal contact with journalists. His Secretary of the Treasury, Alexander Hamilton, did; and he wrote for *The Gazette of the United States,* which was founded in New York in 1789 and edited by James Fenno. Hamilton was in the Cabinet and running things pretty much his way six months before Thomas Jefferson, after serving five years as Minister to France, was appointed Secretary of State. Press criticism of the administration, therefore, was relatively minimal as the new President and his wife and two of her grandchildren settled into the first executive residence ("five windows wide and three stories high") on Cherry Street in New York City.

Before the official calendar got under way, however, peevish complaints of Senator William Maclay of Pennsylvania, leader of the Anti-Federalist opposition in Congress, were faintly echoed by colleagues who agreed with him that Washington's gestures during his Inaugural Address were maladroit, his words unimportant and scarcely audible, and his American worsted suit, with dress sword and silk stockings in the European court tradition, inappropriate to the occasion. Maclay was not to be long on the official scene; the following year he would lose his bid for reelection, but he constantly criticized Washington during his first ten months in office. Specifically, Maclay noted that the President was haughty and impatient in his dealings with the Senate and that his levees and state dinners were ponderous and dull, with great formality, overly abundant food, and a host who "now and then said a sentence or two on some common subject."

The original executive residence was inadequate for extensive entertaining. After a more spacious dwelling—Macomb's Mansion on Broadway—became the President's home, enough guests could be accommodated to dispel the impression that Washington wished to mingle only with small, exclusive groups. However, since the suspicion persisted that he yearned to be a king, Congress debated the propriety of his courtlike levees and his royal manner of bowing stiffly to guests and never shaking hands with anybody. The legislators also argued about his title. John Adams, presiding over the Senate, was all for a pompous designation, and the body finally recommended that it should be, "His Highness, the President of the United States and Protector of their Liberties." But James Madison in the House reminded his colleagues that the Constitution referred to the chief magistrate as "President of the United States." That title became the accepted one; Washington was addressed simply as "Mr. President," and Martha was generally called "Lady Washington," as she had been by many persons since the early days of the Revolution.

Any adverse comment about the President before the capital moved from New York to Philadelphia were mere "fleabites" —his own term for petty criticism—compared to what was said and published about him within the next six years. Lines were already sharply drawn between the Federalists, who favored Hamilton's idea of a strongly centralized government, and the Anti-Federalists (better known as the Democratic-Republicans or simply Republicans), who adhered to Jefferson's conception of a government literally "by the people"—meaning the plain people, with diffused power and maximum freedom of the individual. While basically agreeing with Hamilton, Washington was determined to hold himself above partisanship, and to act as a fair mediator of all policy disagreements within his official family. Besides, he appreciated the value of advice from the two brilliant Cabinet officers with conflicting opinions; for he felt he could gauge from them the temper of the country as a whole and draw objective conclusions before making his own decisions. But he had not reckoned that he would be caught in the crossfire of bitter partisan controversies in the press.

Increasingly annoyed by *The Gazette of the United States,* in which Fenno lavished unstinted praise on Hamilton and espoused the Federalist principles, Jefferson and Madison encouraged in October 1791 the establishment of *The National Gazette,* with Philip Freneau, a Princeton classmate of Madison, as editor. And to balance Fenno's salary as printer for the Treasury and the Senate, Jefferson made Freneau a translating clerk in the State Department at $250 a year.

Freneau had attracted wide attention as a satirist of Tories and then had become famous as the Poet of the Revolution. *The National Gazette* soon identified him as a forceful press spokesman for the Republican party—with Hamilton his initial target. First assailing the Secretary of the Treasury as an unprincipled manipulator, intent on turning the nation into a monarchy, Freneau then lambasted the President as an Anglomonarchical pawn, who held himself aloof from the common people and had no conception of the kind of government they wanted. Hamilton, in turn, in an article for Fenno signed "An American," accused Jefferson of employing Freneau to undermine Washington's administration.

An all-out newspaper war ensued, with vitriolic charges and countercharges, much to the President's distress. He demanded explanations from Hamilton and Jefferson, and each defended his position in writing. Jefferson denied that he had ever influenced Freneau in any way, and stressed Hamilton's malfeasance in using both his high office and Fenno's newspaper to destroy the loyal opposition. Hamilton insisted that the Secretary of State was secretly providing Freneau with material that would lead the nation into anarchy.

Washington regarded a cleavage in the Union as a truly dreadful possibility. He maintained a semblance of peace within his official family by making it clear to both Hamilton and Jefferson that while he respected the opinions and the patriotism of each, all final decisions on policy would be made by him alone. At the same time, he urged that they desist from their battles through the press. Meanwhile, he set an example by adhering strictly to his own official rule of publicly ignoring all criticism.

His decision to retire at the end of his first term did more than anything else to bridge the gap between the conflicting factions. Even his sternest critics realized that he was indispensable to keeping the country from irrevocable division. Both Hamilton and Jefferson strongly urged him to stay in office, as did many others in both parties, and even Freneau was quiescent until after Washington was committed again. He was reelected by a unanimous vote. (John Adams, going in again as Vice President, was galled because his majority was less than in the first election.) In his second term, however, Washington would be subjected to the most volatile press censure in his life, and during his final year in office, an undercurrent of slander would add to his troubles.

The French Revolution deepened the dissension between the political parties shortly after Washington agreed to serve for four more years. The Republicans, generally sympathetic with the overthrow of the French monarchy, insisted that the United States should honor its alliance with the French people to provide aid in time of need. The Federalists argued that such an agreement was made with a government that had been deposed, and after King Louis XVI was guillotined, they held that aid to the French revolutionists would alienate monarchical Britain.

The President's neutrality proclamation of April 23, 1793, was just in time; without it, England's declaration of war on France, Holland and Spain would have drawn the United States into the conflict. However, Freneau in *The National Gazette* blasted the proclamation as evidence of Washington's devotion to crowned heads and followed through by publishing a lampoon portraying Hamilton and other Federalists as forcing the President to enunciate the neutrality measure, with threats to guillotine him if he did not comply.

41

Jefferson's account of a Cabinet meeting, later, described the enraged President as defying "any man on earth to produce a single act of his since he had been in government which was not done by the purest motives . . . that *by God* he had rather be in his grave than in the present situation; that he had rather be on his farm than to be made *Emperor of the World;* and yet they charged him with wanting to be King; while *that rascal Freneau* sent him three of his papers every day . . . that he could see nothing in them but an impudent design to insult him . . ."

The President's wish to have Freneau removed from the State Department's payroll was painfully obvious to the Secretary of State. "But I will not do it," Jefferson wrote in his diary. "His [Freneau's] paper has saved our Constitution, which was galloping fast into monarchy, and has been checked by no one means so powerful as by that paper."

Freneau's abuse continued unabated until he left the State Department of his own volition in October 1793 and then gave up his editorship two months before Secretary Jefferson retired to Monticello. By then, the Republican party had an even more unrestrained press mouthpiece in Benjamin Franklin (Benny) Bache, who edited the *Aurora* and had a personal grudge against the President.

The namesake and grandson of the famous Dr. Franklin believed Washington had helped to block the petition of Richard Bache (Benny's father) to be Postmaster General in 1782, after Benjamin Franklin as envoy to France had effectively implemented aid to the American Revolution. Then, too, Benny's own application for a government job was turned down, and he regarded that as another example of Washington's ingratitude to the late Dr. Franklin.

With vengeance on Washington as his motivation, therefore, Bache, in the *Aurora,* supported the French cause and charged the President with putting on royal airs, possessing "treacherous mazes of passion," and being a "despotic, anemic counterfeit of the English Georges." The assaults intensified when the controversial Jay Treaty of November 1794 linked the United States with Britain against France; and, finally, to accentuate the impression that Washington had been consistently loyal to the British Crown, Bache published the seven false letters which Bew originally brought out during the War of Independence, and embellished them with a preface as to their authenticity "in spirit if not in actual form."

To strengthen further his campaign against the President, Bache published an attack by the British-born Thomas Paine, whose works, *Common Sense* and *The Crisis,* had helped to fan the revolutionary spirit in America. Paine had returned to England in 1787 and had written *The Rights of Man,* a fiery denunciation of monarchy, in which he had lauded Washington as superior to any European crowned head. After the book was suppressed in England and Paine was indicted for treason, he fled to France and there incurred the enmity of Robespierre and was jailed. Frantic with fear that he would be guillotined, he sent impassioned messages, urging Washington to effect his release. The President could not comply; his Neutrality Act prevented his interceding with the French revolutionists even to help his dear friend Lafayette, who was languishing in an Austrian prison. Paine managed to gain his freedom and then vented his wrath on Washington in an open letter, in the *Aurora,* reading in part: "And, as to you, Sir, treacherous in private friendship (for so you have been to me, and that in the day of danger), the world will be puzzled to decide whether you are an apostate or an imposter, whether you have abandoned good principles, or whether you ever had any . . ."

In a subsequent issue of the *Aurora,* Paine harped on Washington's "apathy" and "ungratefulness," and Bache followed with a series of editorials suggesting broadly that the President's shortcomings also extended into his private life.

The Federalist press countered by praising Washington as a quasi-saint and labeling Jefferson "the satanic agent" behind the incessant revilement. Specifically, Jefferson was charged with secretly promoting the attacks on the President by Bache and Paine, as well as by James Thomson Callender, whose newspaper articles were beginning to attract wide attention.

Callender, who had fled to America after being indicted for sedition in his native Scotland, was employed by a Philadelphia newspaper to report proceedings in Congress. He also wrote special articles for the Richmond *Examiner,* and in many of them he excoriated the President. A typical Callender commentary labeled Washington "twice a traitor," and went on, "He authorized the robbery and ruin of his own army and then devastated the country."

The mounting press criticism of the President incited hearsay that angled off from his controversial policies and revived wartime suspicions that he was morally profligate. Vestiges of former charges about his intimacy with slaves and inferences from the "Harrison letter" developed into backyard talk that somebody had seen a letter from Washington to a friend, inviting him to Mount Vernon to enjoy the blandishments of a beautiful octoroon. No such document was ever produced, but the story was repeated in multiple versions until, in time, gossip confused both the sender and the recipient of the invitation. It was said to have been issued by Washington to Lafayette, then to Hamilton, and finally, to Jefferson, while a counteractive rumor had it going from Jefferson to Washington, with Monticello as the base of iniquitous pleasures.

Even more extensively spread was the canard purporting that young Washington on his trip to Barbados had an affair with a married woman and fathered Alexander Hamilton. Knowing that Hamilton was illegitimate, scandalmongers recalled that during the war, General Washington often referred to his favorite lieutenant colonel and private secretary as "my son," and everyone knew that President Washington was ideologically and personally closer to his Secretary of Treasury than to any other man. The discrepancy in Washington's visit to Barbados in 1751 and Hamilton's birth, registered in Nevis (today's St. Croix) in 1757, was easily explained by inventive gossipers. They pointed out that births of illegitimate children were recorded irregularly, if at all, in those days, and suggested that after his mother left her husband and went to live with James Hamilton, a Scot, who claimed to be Alexander's father, she probably falsified her son's natal day for the record. No evidence has ever been found that she was in Barbados at any time, and Washington never visited Nevis; but those facts, if known, were carefully evaded as the story was told again and again, while he was President.

The whispering campaign turned up still other invidious tales about his private life; but in the meantime, he was beset by another problem, which was thoroughly aired in the press. Edmund Randolph, whom Washington appointed Secretary of State after Jefferson resigned, was suspected of soliciting money in return for conspiring with the French against the Jay Treaty. And when a letter from French Minister Fauchet to his government clearly implicated Randolph, the President demanded his resignation. Randolph published a *Vindication*, which was more of a slam at Washington's loyalty to Britain than a defense for his own actions. The Republican press publicized Randolph's accusations and then called for impeachment of the President "for several reasons besides his fealty to Britain." These took in his war record, which was reviewed unfavorably, and also the charges that he had overdrawn his salary by $4,750, the inference clearly being that he had stolen that amount from the government.

His salary had been debated in Congress when he accepted the highest post. Several members were all for complying with his suggestion that he be recompensed, as he had been during the war, with an expense account in lieu of wages. However, several in the body remembered that whereas he would have received only $48,000 if he had accepted the $500 a month that was voted for the Commander in Chief of the Revolution,

45

his expenses for the eight war years came to $447,220.21, according to the smallest estimate. Furthermore, a legislator who had thoroughly scrutinized the account reported that it covered not only living necessities but also such luxuries as a new "chariot" and expensive saddlery and imported wines, as well as 6 percent interest on his own money, which he used during the early years of the war. Finally, taking no chances on unlimited underwriting of Washington's tastes for the finer things of life, Congress fixed his annual pay as President at $25,000.

The salary was woefully insufficient. In order to run his official household, he supplemented his staff of fourteen white servants with seven slaves from Mount Vernon; yet he had to dip into his private means and to borrow money to meet many bills. There is no evidence, however, that he defrauded the government or any individual of a single penny during his entire life. That charge while he was President seems merely to have been part of the ruthless drive to denigrate him.

Vacationing at Mount Vernon during his final summer in office, Washington wrote to Jefferson that he had not thought it possible that while doing his best to establish national unity, he would be accused of being an enemy of one nation and subject to the influence of another and "in such exaggerrated and indecent terms as could scarcely be applied to Nero, a notorious defaulter, or even a common pickpocket."

After his *Farewell Address* was published, several months before he retired, he had a brief reprieve from political censure, but it continued to rankle him—and, most of all, he seemed to resent Bache's republishing of the counterfeit letters. On his last day in office he broke the silence with which he, as President, had publicly met all criticism, and in a lengthy statement addressed to Secretary of State Timothy Pickering he stressed again that the letters, first brought out by Bew and later by Bache, were forged and that none of his correspondence "was found in care of my mulatto servant, Billy, who, it is pretended, was taken prisoner at Fort Lee, 1776." Pickering promptly released the statement to newspapers and it was widely printed—but not in the *Aurora.*

Bache was not yet finished with Washington. As John Adams was inaugurated President, the lead editorial in the *Aurora* proclaimed, "This ought to be a day of JUBILEE . . . The man who is the source of all misfortunes in our country is this day reduced to a level with his fellow citizens, and is no longer possessed to power to multiply evils upon the United States." Even more vehement was Bache's blast the following afternoon:

> If ever a nation has been debauched by a man, the American nation has been debauched by Washington. If ever a nation has been deceived by a man, the American nation has been deceived by Washington. Let his conduct, then, be an example for future ages. Let it serve to be warning that no man be an idol. Let the history of the federal government instruct mankind that the mask of patriotism may be worn to conceal the foulest designs against the liberties of the people.

Washington was heartsick when he retired to Mount Vernon; and his resentment of Bache soon was reflected in his personal correspondence. Two days after he retired, he wrote to Jeremiah Wadsworth, "I shall thank you for the refutation of the impudent forgeries of letters, carrying my signature, which Mr. Bache has taken so much pains to impose on the public as genuine productions. This man has a celebrity in a certain way. His calumnies are exceeded only by his Impudence, and both stand unrivaled." In several subsequent messages to intimates, Washington deplored the spurious correspondence and justified his repudiation of it in the official statement to Secretary Pickering.

One indirect result of the press barrage against the first chief executive would be the passage of the Alien and Sedition Acts after he retired. Bache would be among the first to be indicted, but he would die of yellow fever before he could be brought to trial.

Washington, even after leaving the highest office, was not to enjoy the tranquillity of Mount Vernon for the remainder of his days. Despite all the criticism that had been leveled against him, he was still America's Number One indispensable man, and without consulting him in advance President Adams called him out of retirement to serve again as supreme commander of the army when an undeclared war with France had already begun at sea. Reluctantly, Washington took over once again, with Hamilton his second in command, and began the difficult task of reorganizing and enlarging the fighting forces. And, once again, he was hailed with great fanfare as the Father-Hero of the country when he arrived in Philadelphia in November 1798. He was lavishly feted for four days, and was greeted with ovation after ovation as he appeared with President Adams at the opening of the third session of the Fifth Congress. When open war with France did not eventuate, he resumed the life he loved at Mount Vernon. There he died, seventeen days before the end of a century in which he left his mark on history as no other President has to this day.

Although Washington's official papers were preserved for posterity, two years after he died Martha destroyed a number of letters he had written to her, and in so doing obscured forever the controversy about their relationship which might have been settled by disclosure of the intimate correspondence. (Popular writers in the twentieth century speculated that she burned most of the letters because they showed that she and her husband were often at odds during the Revolution.) As we have seen, Washington disposed of all personal correspondence after he took over as supreme military commander. Martha Washington at that time kept her letters from her

husband in a hidden drawer of a writing desk which was purchased from the presidential mansion by a Mrs. Samuel Powell
after Washington retired. Mrs. Powell found the letters and
sent them to Mount Vernon, and shortly thereafter George
and Martha destroyed most of them. After his death she
burned all the others, with the two exceptions that are extant
today—one written from Fort Duquesne a few months before
their marriage; the other, from Philadelphia just after he was
elected Commander in Chief. While less impassioned than at
least two of his messages to Sally Fairfax, both these letters
express his deep affection for his wife.

There does not seem to be a particle of evidence that Washington was anything but the most faithful of husbands. But
beginning some eighty years after his death and continuing
intermittently since, stories echoing wartime suspicions of his
depraved use of slave women have persisted without a scintilla
of proof. The most nebulous of all the slanders purported that
his death resulted from a chill and consequent cold he suffered
after a rendezvous with his overseer's wife on a December
afternoon. That slur obviously harked back to suspicions
sparked by "the Harrison letter" and fanned by General Lee's
charges during the War of Independence. A supporting factor
was the confusion of the master of Mount Vernon with his
distant kinsman Lund Washington, who managed the estate
for a quarter of a century. Lund's wife could not bear children,
but he fathered a son by a black housekeeper at Mount Vernon
in 1770. Given the surname of Washington, the boy moved
with his mother to a neighboring state, grew up there, married
twice and had several offspring who were widely regarded as
George Washington's descendants, even though a genealogical chart of the Washington family, published before 1850,
clearly shows Lund Washington as the progenitor. Furthermore, the document includes a notation that he freely admitted his unlawful paternity before he retired from the management of Mount Vernon.

Twentieth-century exposés of George Washington's personal life suggested that the almanac in which he kept his diary indicated that he was intimate with his slaves. His custom of listing his female properties with circles, dots, checks and curves around some of the names was interpreted by several writers as possible evidence that he had immorally used the women thus designated. Reliable historians, after careful examination of the pages, concluded, however, that the numerous mysterious markings were Washington's own private stenography for the work records of his slave women.

If all the printed or spoken rumors about Washington's illegitimate children could be substantiated, he would be the most prolific progenitor in our history, or, as one twentieth-century researcher archly put it, "the father of our country in more ways than one." Every generation since his death has included people professing to know his direct descendants, and in some instances individuals have claimed that honor on their own.

A Providence, Rhode Island, court case, *Bowen vs Chase* in 1872 focused attention on the eccentric seventy-eight-year-old plaintiff, George Washington Bowen, who insisted that he was George Washington's son. The trial attracted wide attention because Bowen's late mother, the notorious Eliza Jumel, had designated her niece, Mrs. Nelson Chase, as her sole heir. When Bowen went to court to break the will, the trial brought out the background of his mother, owner of the fabulous Jumel Mansion, formerly known as the Roger Morris Mansion (General Washington's New York headquarters for a brief time).

The daughter of Phebe Kelley, a prostitute, of Providence, Mme. Jumel was the former Betsy Bowen, also known as Eliza Brown, a prostitute. When she gave birth to a son in October 1794, she followed the fashion of the day by naming him after the President of the United States. She never divulged the identity of his father, and shortly after the boy was born she left him in the charge of Reuben and Freelove Ballou, with whom she had been living, and departed Providence, never to return.

In 1833 Eliza, after a stormy marriage to Stephen Jumel ended in his death, created another sensation when she became the wife of Aaron Burr. Innumerable persons recalled gossip that Alexander Hamilton, whom Burr killed in a duel, had once been enchanted with her. At any rate, she wanted the prestige of being the wife of a former Vice President, and Burr needed her money; she handed over six thousand dollars to him on their wedding day. The marriage had lasted only a few months when she instituted a divorce suit on the grounds that her seventy-eight-year-old husband had "recently committed offenses at diverse times with diverse females." When the divorce was granted, she resumed the name Eliza Jumel and willed her entire estate to her niece.

Bowen instituted legal action to obtain the fortune a year after his mother died. The jury ruled against him, and he took his case to the Supreme Court. There the judgment of the lower court was eventually confirmed, but for thirteen years while the case pended, the possibility that George Washington was Bowen's father was the subject of wide speculation. Much was made of the plaintiff's striking resemblance to the first President. Tall, with a broad, high forehead, a prominent but nicely proportioned nose and deep-set eyes, Bowen further accentuated his claim to being the great man's son by affecting Washington's style of dress.

The publicity attendant on the lengthy trial naturally prompted the curious to search official records to find out where and when Washington might have consorted with Betsy Bowen. As President, his only visit to Providence was in August 1790, when she was among the pretty girls whom Abner Dagget hired to wait on the official party at his Golden Ball Inn. But her son was born four years later. Furthermore, so far as could be determined, she had never been out of Providence until after that, and the idea that President Washington could have gone there unobserved at any time was preposterous. Yet Bowen, until he died at the age of ninety, persisted in claiming that Washington was his father, and Bowen's progeny for many years boasted that they were descendants of our first President.

When the debunking of George Washington became popular in the 1920s, the story took on a new angle with the suggestion that Bowen could have been Washington's *grandson!* As supreme commander, General Washington visited Providence in June 1775 and stayed two days. He had a full schedule, but all his moments were not accounted for in any record. Gossips pointed out that he could have met Phebe Kelley and fathered Betsy Bowen at that time. In support of that theory a popular author in the 1920s wrote that gossip in Providence in 1886 was that Betsy was given to claiming that her father was a distinguished man, and that her mother in drunken moments had told her he was Geroge Washington. There, again, documentary evidence repudiated scandal, for Betsy's birth was registered in Providence less that six months after General Washington's first visit there.

Sometimes heard in the nation's capital even today is the legend that the sizable Syphax families of the city descended from George Washington. The story goes that he cohabited with a slave at Mount Vernon and produced a daughter. She married a slave named Syphax and they had several sons and daughters, whose progeny became respected black residents of Washington, D.C., and Virginia.

The *Afro-American* on April 22, 1939, however, shattered that theory in a feature article with the banner, "Washington Custis Head of 16 Syphax Families" and the subtitle, "Chart Shows How the Syphax Families Trace Their Lineage Direct to Martha Washington." The report went that George Washington Parke Custis, Martha's grandson, was the father of Maria Castle by Airy Carter, a slave maid at Mount Vernon, and that Maria married Charles Syphax and bore him ten children, "whose many descendants have contributed largely to the George Washington Custis lineage."

Cited in the article as authorities were Dean E. Delorus Preston, Jr., of Edward Waters College, and Professor Sterling Brown, of Howard University, who had based their premise on hearsay and Custis' will, manumitting all his slaves but leaving a special legacy to Maria Castle (Syphax). "It is stated," wrote Preston, "that Custis recognized Maria as his child and gave her a piece of property in the Arlington estate." (Maria was deeded seventeen acres of the estate, which was a haven for slave fugitives during the Civil War and later became a part of Freedman's Village, maintained by the government.)

"It is stated" might well have been Preston's phrasing for "rumored," but his unequivocal published conclusion was, "Maria Syphax was the daughter of George Washington Parke Custis, and a maid of Martha Washington."

Since 1868, when William Syphax, son of Maria and Charles, became the first black member of the board of trustees for colored schools in the District of Columbia, a number of Syphaxes have distinguished themselves in educational and government fields. Meanwhile their achievements through the years have often been credited to their alleged direct descendancy from George Washington. Other stories purporting that our first President had several other illegitimate children have cropped up in the current century. Conversely, the theory has periodically surfaced that an illness early in his life left him incapable of fatherhood.

George Washington as the fallible man will continue to be the subject of fanciful surmises, primarily because efforts to extricate the human being from the myth have been largely unsuccessful. In any event, nothing seriously derogatory about him has ever been proved, and none of the scandals and criticism that permeated his career has ever minimized his greatness.

From the maelstrom of conflicting reports he comes through as a person who had few shortcomings and no major ones—unless the discreet yearning for his friend's wife can be so regarded. Whether he was endowed with qualities far superior to those of his illustrious contemporaries is irrelevant, for the combination of his attributes made him the one indispensable factor in achieving victory and independence for the nation and, later, in preserving its unity through the most perilous period in our history. Therefore, he dominates the American pantheon as a superhero, who lived long enough to see his grandest dreams realized and his name exalted above all others—despite the slanders.

II

Miscegenation and Mr. Jefferson

A champion of freedom of the press, Thomas Jefferson was the most effective single force in preserving it during a dangerous period in its history. Yet he was persistently libeled during most of his years in public office. One scandal, particularly, which was fostered by the press throughout the country while he was President, has been periodically revived since his death to foment racial tensions. And offscourings of it besmear his personal image in some quarters even today.

Political censure of Jefferson had been intermittently accented by slurs on his character for years before he entered the 1800 campaign for the presidency. He was prepared for a volley of Federalist charges that he was an infidel, a plagiarist, coward, embezzler, drunkard and "Jacobin" (tantamount to being branded a Communist in the Joseph McCarthy era). But he was considerably shaken within six months after he became President when a journalist whom he had befriended as an advocate of Republican principles wrote that Mr. Jefferson had been a known libertine since his bachelor days. Federalist publications across the nation featured the slander in sensational versions; and, in time, the smear spread to conjectures about his conduct with women while he was Minister to France. By the end of his first term as President suspicions had been thoroughly promoted through the press that he tried to seduce the wife of a former college classmate, carried on illicit affairs with at least two matrons in Paris, and fathered several children by an octoroon slave at Monticello.

None of these charges has been fully proved—or refuted— to this day. Jefferson partially confessed to one by way of invalidating others; yet his lame defense, prompted by his natural reluctance to divulge anything about his personal life, left him open to even worse presumptions. Publicly he ignored the most damaging libels, but he complained about them in confidential letters. And shortly after his retirement, he expressed his opinion of the press: "The man who has never looked into a newspaper is better informed than he who reads them; inasmuch as he who knows nothing is nearer to the truth than he whose mind is filled with falsehoods and errors." Two years after he left the presidency, memories of his mistreatment by journalists still rankled; he observed that he had served "traducers in a term of twelve to fourteen years in the terrific station of Rawhead and Bloody Bones." Yet, three years before he died, he wrote to the Marquis de Lafayette, "But the only security for all is in a free press."

Political criticism of Jefferson, which eventually degenerated into slander, began while he was Secretary of State and a constant irritant to Secretary of the Treasury Alexander Hamilton. Jefferson had not angled for Cabinet office; he had expected to resume his duties as Minister to France after a vacation at Monticello in 1789. And he had no intention of founding a political party; earlier that year he had written, "If I could not go to heaven but with a party, I would not go at all." However, the sharp differences between his philosophy of government and that of Hamilton soon became apparent.

Congressmen in the Federalist party constantly criticized the Secretary of State. Connecticut Senator William Samuel Johnson, for example, declared, "Mr. Jefferson is too greatly democratic for us at present; he left us in that way, but we are infinitely changed, and he must alter his principles." But far from doing that, Jefferson made his doctrine the loadstone for his new Republican party, and it soon gathered forceful adherents in Congress and elsewhere.

Jefferson worked quietly, and often covertly, to achieve his political ends, much to the annoyance of Hamilton. The articulate Secretary of Treasury would have preferred to thrash out differences in open debate, but the soft-spoken Secretary of State, who wrote more effectively than he talked, insisted on "a calm interchange of opinions" in Cabinet meetings, and resorted to other methods to thwart Hamilton. As we have seen, Jefferson encouraged the famed "Poet of the Revolution" Philip Freneau to start *The National Gazette.* The eloquent writer forthwith launched strong attacks on Federalist principles, and, later, was even more unrestrained in criticizing Hamilton and the President as "toadies of the British crown."

Washington was furious; he raged about "that rascal, Freneau!" in a Cabinet meeting. But he had the good judgment not to insist on the editor's dismissal from the State Department, despite Hamilton's charges that Jefferson was providing Freneau with much of the inflammatory material that appeared in *The National Gazette.* Jefferson denied by letter to the President that he had "directly or indirectly written, dictated or procured a single sentence or sentiment" for the Republican sheet, and Freneau confirmed that in an affidavit. However, disenchanted with Jefferson after he repudiated French Minister Edmond Genêt for interfering in American politics, Freneau would later produce a file of agitative articles which he said the Secretary of State had either written or suggested for

The National Gazette. That would be Jefferson's first embarrassing experience with a journalist of his own political persuasion —but not his last.

The quick growth of the Republican party was responsible for a concerted effort to destroy Jefferson's reputation. The drive got under way with pointed reminders from his detractors that while he was Minister to France, he had recommended to friends in this country the dissolute French envoy who preceded Genêt—and who shocked respectable Americans by flaunting his affair with the woman who accompanied him to the United States.

Actually, Jefferson was only slightly acquainted with the Marquis François de Moustier, the newly appointed French Minister to the United States, and his sister-in-law, the Marchioness de Brehan, but in letters from Paris to James Madison and John Jay, Jefferson had written that de Moustier was a brilliant diplomat and that the marchioness was the estimable wife of an officer in the French army. She and the new emissary should be shown every possible courtesy, the American Minister suggested.

Madison, one of Jefferson's confidants, and Jay, chief of foreign affairs, warmly welcomed the French diplomat and his traveling companion, and introduced them around as friends of Jefferson. Therefore, despite de Moustier's propensity for wearing earrings and red heeled slippers, he and the marchioness enjoyed an enviable social schedule—until they shared the same hotel rooms on a trip through New England, and gossip drifted down from Boston that they "neglected the most obvious precautions for veiling their intimacy." From then on, reputable citizens had nothing to do with them.

Repercussions reached Minister Jefferson in France. De Moustier complained about the sudden social freeze in America, while Madison and Jay wrote that the indecent connection between the envoy and his sister-in-law had appalled high-principled Americans. Jefferson apologized for having recommended the offensive pair and declared that he was as surprised as anyone else to learn of their adulterous relationship. Concurrently, he wrote placative letters to de Moustier. When they were ignored, Jefferson asked the Marquis de Lafayette to use his influence with the French foreign ministry to arrange a leave of absence for the envoy. While that was being worked out, de Moustier sent his mistress back to France and departed for the Mississippi area, where he stayed until he was recalled. However, he continued to be a problem; in Paris he complained bitterly that he had been discourteously treated in the United States. Jefferson finally wrote, for President Washington's signature, a letter to King Louis XVI assuring him that his emissary had "the entire approbation of our Government while he was in America." A copy, with a medal on a gold chain "as testimony of these sentiments," went to de Moustier.

Such gestures, patently promoted by the American Minister to appease the licentious Frenchman, aroused suspicions that Jefferson's own moral standards had eroded during his years abroad. After he became Secretary of State, that impression was strengthened by vague rumors about his questionable conduct with married women in Paris and with the slave girl who had taken his younger daughter to join him in the French capital.

Gossip to that effect would grow and be fully exploited after he became President, but evil presumptions about his past, coupled with increasing political animosities, began to affect his social prestige shortly after the seat of government moved from New York to Philadelphia. The changing attitude was not immediately apparent; patricians in the new capital city could not ostracize the Secretary of State, an aristocrat by birth and habits, who was world famous for having written the Declaration of Independence. For some time he continued to be a familiar but increasingly unpopular guest at exclusive functions in the city where, as he wrote, "the laws of nature oblige me to move in circles which I know to bear me peculiar hatred." Eventually, he withdrew from the Federalist social round and inaugurated a party schedule to suit himself. He had leased a fine residence, furnished it handsomely, and staffed it with servants from Monticello. His house soon became a popular gathering place for those who were receptive to his political philosophy, and under the direction of Adrien Petit, who had been his steward in Paris, Secretary Jefferson's dinners became famous.

His effective use of the art of dining enhanced his appeal to the masses, for he was living proof that Alexander Hamilton and his affluent following had not cornered the market on cultivated tastes. At the same time, Jefferson's practice of treating his guests to Lucullan feasts drew criticism from Federalist writers and other antagonists, who equated his epicurism with iniquity and insinuated that he was a hypocrite, a ruthless political conniver—and worse.

Under the name of Catullus, in Fenno's newspaper, Hamilton predicted that the Secretary of State's "true character will be revealed when the visor of stoicism is plucked from the brow of the epicure; when the plain garb of simplicity is stripped from the voluptuary; when Caesar *coyly refusing* the proferred diadem, is seen to be Caesar grasping the substance of imperial domination." Representative William L. Smith, a Federalist from South Carolina, subsequently declared that Jefferson's "dissemblances long ago excited the derision of many, who know that under the assumed cloak of humility lurks the most ambitious spirit, and that the externals of pure Democracy afford but a flimsy veil for the internal evidences of aristocratic splendor, sensuality and Epicurianism."

Toward the end of 1792 Jefferson was disgusted with the incessant harangue from his opposition, and particularly with Hamilton's efforts to undercut him. Finally, he offered to resign from the Cabinet, but yielding to President Washington's persuasion, he stayed on for almost a year. Then, after being sharply criticized for endorsing Thomas Paine's *Rights of Man,* which justified the French Revolution and flayed President Washington and Vice President Adams, he retired to Monticello. Working there as a private citizen, he was able to consolidate his party over the next few years; and as its standard bearer, he almost defeated John Adams for the presidency in 1796. Still, having lost to a majority of only three votes, he automatically became Vice President. Then, with his sole responsibility that of presiding over the Senate, he had time to strengthen his party still further.

To that end, he cultivated such firebrands in journalism as Benjamin Franklin Bache, editor of the *Aurora,* his successor, William Duane, and other forceful advocates of Republican principles. As would be expected, their support prompted Federalist charges that the Vice President was manipulating journalist extremists for his own purposes, at government expense. But his critics would have been delighted if they could have foreseen that he would pay heavily for the cooperation he received, for some time at least, from one radical writer.

Scottish-born James Thomson Callender was in his midthirties when he fled from Britain in 1793, after being indicted for sedition. He arrived in America before Jefferson resigned from the Cabinet; but so far as can be determined the two did not meet until after Jefferson became Vice President and Callender was dismissed from *The Philadelphia Gazette* because of his disparaging comments about Federalist legislators.

Despite the journalist's potential usefulness to the Republican cause, it is difficult to understand how he and Jefferson could ever have been on close terms. Jefferson was increasingly untidy as time went on, but he had a healthy respect for cleanliness. Callender was ushered out of Congress Hall because "his clothes were filthy and lice covered," according to William Cobbett, in the pro-Federalist *Porcupine's Gazette.* Bache, in the *Aurora,* described him as "a lousy Scotch candidate for Botany Bay" and "a dirty little toper, with shaved head and greasy jacket, nankeen pantaloons and woolen stockings." However, Callender's presumably initial contact with Jefferson appeared to be at an opportune time for both; the journalist's recently finished *History of the United States for 1796* boosted the Republican party, praised the Vice President, and brought to public attention a disgraceful episode in Alexander Hamilton's past.

The year designated on the "history" was misleading as to Hamilton. He had retired from the Cabinet in 1795 and was engaged in practicing law in New York when the part about him was published in advance of the full work. The chapter disclosed that a secret Congressional committee in 1792 investigated charges that the Secretary of the Treasury had increased his personal fortune by speculating on the basis of confidential government information. The account further revealed that although Hamilton categorically denied the major accusation, he confessed to the legislators that a sordid sexual affair had subjected him to blackmail while he was on the government payroll.

To the amazement of both friends and foes, Hamilton published a detailed defense of himself. Explaining that the investigation was the indirect result of his "amorous connection" with a Mrs. James Reynolds in the summer of 1791, he stated that the intrigue was promoted by Mr. Reynolds' "privy and connivance, if not brought on by a combination of husband and wife with a design to extract money from me." Hamilton divulged also that from time to time he paid Reynolds substantial amounts to keep him from telling Mrs. Hamilton about the affair, but he emphasized that he never was party to the unethical speculations that aroused Congressional suspicions and finally landed Reynolds in jail.

Ecstatic at having goaded the formidable Federalist into public admission that he was a common adulterer, Callender wrote to the Vice President that Hamilton's apologia was "worth all that fifty of the best pens in America could have said against him . . . My sales have repaid all my hopes." Jefferson expressed his own elation to an intimate friend: "I understand that finding the strait between Scylla and Charybdis too narrow for his [Hamilton's] steerage, he preferred running plump on one of them. In truth, it seems to work very hard for him; and his willingness to plead guilty seems rather to have strengthened than weakened the suspicion that he was guilty of speculations."

The time was not far distant when the bold Scotsman, with even more embarrassing results, would enflame suspicions about Jefferson's character. Meanwhile the two saw little of each other. The Vice President was preoccupied in trying to forestall passage of the Alien and Sedition Acts, which had been framed to silence all journalists whose writings could be construed by the President as "against the government." With James Madison, Jefferson canvassed Congress, stressing that official curbs would violate the free flow of information, which had been guaranteed by the First Amendment. "Were it left to me to decide whether we should have a government without newspapers or newspapers without government, I should not hesitate to prefer the latter," Jefferson declared at the height of the controversy. But constraints on the press had been favored by many since the days when rambunctious editors castigated President Washington; and the XYZ Affair, in Adams' administration, followed by the undeclared war with France, convinced the majority in Congress that national security depended on silencing extremist writers and banishing other enemies of the government. In 1798 the Alien bill was passed, empowering the President to expel all suspected foreigners. The Sedition Act also went into effect, making it punishable by fine and imprisonment "to speak or write about the President or Congress with intent to defame or bring them into contempt or disrepute."

Callender was unable to find employment while the laws

were pending, and when they were enacted, he knew that he was in for even more serious trouble. However, he expected the Vice President to keep him out of jail, and to give him financial help in the interim. He took refuge at Raspberry Plain, the Virginia plantation of Senator Mason, and bombarded his distinguished friend with appeals for money. Jefferson, through Mason, finally instructed his agent in Richmond to send fifty dollars but to keep his own name "out of sight."

Callender's next move was to Richmond, where he wangled a minor position on the Richmond *Examiner* and worked on his book, *The Prospect Before Us.* The moment he had proofs of the first section, he rushed them off to Jefferson with a request for his comments. The Vice President promptly replied, "Such papers cannot fail to produce the best effects," and ordered several copies of the forthcoming book. The postscript of his letter reflected his own touchy situation: "You will know from whom this comes without a signature, the omission of which has been rendered almost habitual with me by the curiosity of the post office." Having openly argued that the Alien and Sedition Acts were "so palpably in the teeth of the Constitution as to show they mean to pay no respect to it," the Vice President suspected that his correspondence might at any moment be opened by Federalist postal clerks, searching for evidence that could bring him to trial for sedition.

The repressive acts were doomed to eventual failure. They confused legitimate criticism of the government with treason and on that basis soon had strong legislative opposition in the states, thanks to the groundwork of Jefferson and Madison. However, the laws were so ruthlessly administered for a time that the latter half of John Adams' administration was known as the Federalist Reign of Terror. More than twenty Republican editors were indicted, and most of them were convicted and jailed. Foreign-born agents and writers left the country in droves to avoid arrest. Even members of Congress were under sharp surveillance. Representative Matthew Lyon, of Vermont, was fined a thousand dollars and sent to jail for four months after castigating President Adams in the *Vermont Journal*. The mounting resentment of the laws was shown, however, when Lyon's constituents paid his fine by popular subscription and reelected him to Congress while he was still behind bars.

Callender's precarious plight had been aggravated in the meantime by the untimely publication of his book with a section—which Jefferson vowed he had not previously read—branding George Washington "a traitor, a robber, and a perjurer" and describing President Adams as "not only a repulsive pedant, a gross hypocrite, and an unprincipled oppressor, but in private life, one of the most egregious fools upon the continent."

Indicted for sedition and brought to trial before the arch-Federalist Judge Samuel Chase, Callender was committed to prison for nine months, fined $200, and ordered to post a bond of $1,200 for good behavior over a period of two years. The harsh sentence shocked the country; nevertheless, the journalist was rushed off to the jail in Richmond, where he seethed and wrote importunate letters to the Vice President. The latter by that time was absorbed with problems of his own. He had decided to run for the presidency, and the charge that he was "an unprincipled conniver, who hired radical writers to do his dirty work" was Sunday School talk compared with other imputations that already were being aired about him.

No national campaign in our history has been more vicious than the one in 1800. Mudslinging smeared all four candidates: John Adams and Charles Cotesworth Pinckney, the Federalists; and Thomas Jefferson and Aaron Burr, the Republicans. Alexander Hamilton, who had never liked Adams, supported Pinckney against the "senile and inefficient" Federalist incumbent, while the Republicans drummed on Adams' "Toryism" and "devotion to monarchies." Abigail Adams complained, "I have heard so many lies and falsehoods propagated to answer electioneering purposes that I am disgusted with the world." But to the surprise of many, her husband took the onslaught philosophically and was even amused by some of it. For example, on hearing that he had sent General Thomas Pinckney, brother of the other Federalist candidate, to England to procure four mistresses—two for himself and two for Pinckney—Adams wryly observed, "I do declare if this be true, General Pinckney has kept them all for himself and cheated me out of my two."

Every personal criticism that had ever been used against Jefferson was brought out again, and others were added. The old charge that he was a "Jacobin" came up repeatedly. Also, he was called a plagiarist (on revived rumors that he had copied the Declaration of Independence from a treatise by John Locke), a slanderer of George Washington, and a "white livered coward" for having fled from British troops invading Virginia in 1781, when he was governor. Newer allegations were that he was profane, habitually drunk (on his own French wines), and in the words of one critic, "guilty of other moral lapses too indecent to mention." However, the most detrimental canard of all was that he was an infidel, intent on destroying Christian orthodoxy.

Exploding first in New England, where Federalists controlled the clergy and the press, the gossip that he did not believe in God had nationwide repercussions. Many people remembered that he had been largely responsible for the Virginia legislature's original Freedom of Religion bill, stipulating that "no man shall be compelled to frequent or support any religious worship." The Reverend John M. Mason identified "national regard or disregard of religion" as the main issue of the campaign, and warned that anyone voting for Jefferson "would do more to destroy the gospel of Jesus than a whole fraternity of infidels." *The New England Palladium* predicted, "Should the infidel Jefferson be elected to the presidency, the seal of death is that moment set on our holy religion, our churches will be prostrated, and some infamous prostitute, under the title of goddess of reason, will preside in the sanctuaries now devoted to the worship of the Most High." Even more derogatory were the Reverend Cotton Mather Smith's allegations that "the ungodly Jefferson" amassed wealth with funds embezzled from a widow when he administered her estate, and that he was also guilty of "gross immorality on other accounts."

Alarmed Republicans urged Jefferson to demand evidence or retractions from the Reverend Smith, but although the beset candidate privately assured a perturbed Connecticut supporter that he had never defrauded a widow—indeed, that he had never handled a widow's estate—he avoided being drawn into controversy with churchmen. "From the clergy I expect no mercy," he wrote. "They crucified the Saviour. Minister and merchants love nobody . . . In every country and every age the priest has been hostile to liberty."

Jefferson's refusal to proclaim his spiritual faith worked against him at the polls, for many in his own party interpreted his silence as confirmation that he actually was an infidel—and voted for Aaron Burr. As a result, the two Republican candidates got 73 electoral votes each (Adams got 65), and the tie had to be resolved in the House of Representatives.

Apprehensions about Jefferson's religion persisted even after he won the thirty-sixth Congressional ballot, on February 17, 1801. On learning the news, pious women in Massachusetts secreted their Bibles in water coolers and lowered them into wells to guard against seizure by the new "infidel President." Such precautions would have been averted if Jefferson, as a candidate, had clarified his religious belief, for it was conventional in most respects. He was a member of the Episcopal Church and he frequently attended devotional service, although he refrained from taking communion (as did George Washington). Furthermore, he contributed generously to the building of churches and the livelihood of indigent preachers; and he was an avid reader of the Bible. His interest in the New Testament, particularly, would flourish during his presidency. He would compile a selection of the maxims of Christ from texts of the Evangelists, later to be supplemented by his own French, Greek and Latin translations. Finally, three years before he died, he would define his religious faith as follows: "To the genuine precepts of Jesus Himself, I am a Christian in the only sense in which He wished any one would be; sincerely attached to His doctrines in preference to all others; ascribing to Him every *human* excellence and believing He never claimed any other."

Had he made such a statement during his 1800 campaign, he might not have silenced the orthodox clergy—with its resolute belief in the divinity of Christ—but he would have convinced many other people that he was not an infidel. Also, he would have averted later suspicions that his immoralities tied in with his total lack of spiritual faith.

In the highest office, he insisted on being addressed and referred to as "Mr. Jefferson," instead of "Mr. President" and "the President of the United States," and he did away with entrenched social procedures. At the same time, he called for fewer immediate changes in government than his critics had gloomily predicted. However, he demanded—and got— prompt repeal of the Judiciary Act, which had enabled lame-duck President Adams to pack sixteen new circuit courts with Federalist judges a few hours before he left office. But he could not remove Adams' prize lifetime appointee, Chief Justice John Marshall, Jefferson's cousin but also his powerful political enemy. The Chief Justice would oppose the President forcefully and frequently over the next eight years; and Marshall's venerative, five-volume biography of George Washington, published from 1804 to 1807, would depict his hero's first Secretary of State as so disloyal that Jefferson would label the work "Federalist propaganda." However, he might well have been relieved that the biography did not touch on any of the scandals that began to plague him shortly after he was inaugurated.

The first malicious gossip about the new President began after he had invited Secretary of State and Mrs. Madison to reside in the executive mansion until they could lease a suitable house in the fledgling capital city and she had presided as hostess at several presidential dinners. Such an arrangement was proper, for Jefferson was a widower, as was Vice President Burr, while Mrs. Madison's husband was the ranking Cabinet officer. However, back-fence busybodies conjectured that Dolley's enviable social ascendancy was due to the President's indecorous devotion to her. Overnight, gossip erupted that the two were having an affair, virtually under the nose of Dolley's unsuspecting husband. This talk bothered the fifty-eight-year-old President enough for him to write to an influential fellow Virginian, St. George Tucker: "I thought my age and ordinary demeanor would have prevented any suggestions in that form, from the possibility of their obtaining belief." With characteristic optimism, he added, "I believe all persons concerned are too conscious of their innocence to feel the burden."

The Alien and Sedition Acts expired under their own terms at the end of the Adams administration, and the President lost no time in effecting the release of those who had been jailed. But he let himself in for trouble when he ordered remittance of the unexpired part of Callender's sentence, for the Scotsman assumed that Jefferson would also take care of the unpaid fine. The President asked his Attorney General, Levi Lincoln, to handle the matter, but David Mead Randolph, the federal marshal at Richmond, refused to accept Lincoln's opinion that the fine should be suspended. Meanwhile Callender managed to borrow enough money to defray the penalty; then, a free man once more, he wrote urgent letters to Jefferson, demanding repayment, either from him or the government. While the President vacillated the journalist wrote Secretary Madison that it had been seven weeks since he had "a written message from Mr. Jefferson with the solemn assurance that he 'would not lose one moment' in remitting my fine . . . I now begin to know what Ingratitude is."

Callender shortly afterward denounced the President to Virginia's Governor James Monroe and then wept bitterly as he begged for coach fare to the capital city. Whether or not Monroe complied is not clear; anyway, Callender was in Washington the following week—and infuriated because the President was too busy to see him. He vented his indignation on Secretary Madison, grumbled about his impoverishment, and finally mentioned that he had "come across a piece of history that Mr. Jefferson's enemies would love to possess." He would never have to divulge it, he said in effect, if the President would do something for him—such as, make him postmaster at Richmond.

Madison promptly transmitted the veiled threat to Jefferson, but the latter, labeling the brazen writer "totally unfit" for the job he wanted, flatly refused to make the appointment. However, hoping to help the disgruntled man in another way, he suggested to Madison and Monroe that Callender's fine might well be refunded by private contributions. Then, setting an example, Jefferson arranged to pay fifty dollars, a fourth of the total amount, out of his own pocket, and listed the sum in his personal account book as *Charity.*

Young Meriwether Lewis, the President's aide who was sent to deliver the gift, had a stormy reception. Callender in a fury accepted the contribution "not as charity but a due . . . in fact hush money." Then, just before dismissing Lewis, he growled something about having information that he could and would make use of "in a certain case."

Conveying Lewis's report of the encounter to Monroe, Jefferson wrote, "Such a misconstruction of my charities puts an end to them forever . . . He [Callender] knows nothing of me which I am not able to declare to the world myself. I gave him from time to time such aids as I could afford, merely as a man of genius suffering under persecution, and not as a writer in our politics. It is a long time since I wished he had ceased writing in them."

Callender, by then fully aware that he could expect no further favors from the President, determined to disgrace him. After obtaining editorship of the *Richmond Recorder*, an insignificant Federalist weekly, the journalist searched the countryside for every vestige of scandal that had been whispered about Jefferson. Within a few weeks, he had dug up enough dirt for a sensational smear.

The series began on the political level, with intimations that Callender's censure of Washington and Adams had been instigated by Jefferson, and that the latter had also provided material for the exposé of Hamilton. But the full force of the calumny was projected later, with two shocking stories that Callender pieced together from fragmentary rumors and published for the first time.

One account purported to divulge the actual reason for the long-time enmity between Jefferson and former Senator John Walker, a rigid Federalist. Mutual acquaintances had generally assumed that the two prominent Virginians, who had been close friends from boyhood, parted company in 1790, when Secretary Jefferson supported his fellow Republican, James Monroe, for Walker's Senate seat. Callender alleged, however, that Walker's hatred started when he learned about Jefferson's attempts to seduce Mrs. Walker, both before and after Jefferson's own marriage.

Callender's second charge was that Sally Hemings, a slave at Monticello, had been Jefferson's mistress for years. "By this wench Sally, our President has had several children," Callender wrote, adding that he had "been told" that "the comely octoroon" and her master were parents "of more than five

71

children, and Tom, the eldest, is said to bear a striking, though sable, resemblance to the President himself. . . . There is not an individual in the neighborhood of Charlottesville who does not believe the story, and not a few who know it . . . The African Venus is said to officiate as a housekeeper at Monticello."

The libels spread throughout the country; for other newspapers reprinted them, and Callender himself produced pamphlets with exaggerated versions and circulated them widely. Jefferson could do nothing to stop the onslaught, for having championed freedom of the press when it victimized Washington and Adams, he could not openly denounce published attacks on his own reputation. But he confided his distress to Monroe: "I am really mortified at the base ingratitude of Callender. It presents human nature in hideous form." And he sent clippings of the derogatory articles to Attorney General Lincoln with this note: "I had no conception there were persons enough whose stomachs could bear such aliments as the enclosed papers contain . . . To punish, however, is impracticable . . . until the body of the people, from whom juries are taken, get their minds to rights, and even then I doubt its expediency."

For more than a year, pro-Federalist publications played up the miscegenation slander in a variety of ways. *The Port Folio* of Philadelphia, for example, published a series of scathing satires worked up by the editor, Joseph Dennie, who despised Jefferson and often had ridiculed him as The Mammoth of Democracy. Dennie's first follow-up of Callender's libels was in verse, "Supposed to have been written by the Sage of Monticello, to be sung to the tune of Yankee Doodle," with these words:

> Of all the damsels on the green
> On mountain, or in valley,
> A lass so luscious ne'er was seen

As Monticellian Sally

> *Chorus:* Yankee Doodle, who's the noodle?
> What wife was half so handy?
> To breed a flock of slaves for stock
> A black amour's the dandy . . .

When press'd by load of state affairs,
I seek to sport and dally,
The sweetest solace of my cares
Is in the lap of Sally.

> *Chorus:* Yankee Doodle, etc.

What though she by her glands secretes?
Must I stand, Shill-I-shall-I?
Tuck'd up between a pair of sheets
There's no perfume like Sally.

> *Chorus:* Yankee Doodle, etc.

Shortly after that appeared, the *Columbian Centinel* of Boston featured an article, later reprinted in Philadelphia, describing Jefferson's daughters as weeping uncontrollably after being ordered to address the pretty Negress in their household as Mother. Among innumerable lampoons coming out toward the end of 1802 were these verses, which appeared in the Boston *Gazette* and later in the Richmond *Recorder:*

In glaring red, and chalky white,
    Let others beauty see;
Me no such tawdry sins delight—
    No, *black's* the hue for me!

Thick pouting lips! How sweet their grace!
    When passion fires to kiss them!
Wide spreading over half the face,
    Impossible to miss them.

73

Oh! Sally! hearken to my vows!
Yield up thy sooty charms—
My best belov'd! My more than spouse
Oh! take me to thy arms.

About the same time, Callender editorialized in his newspaper:

Put the case that every white man in Virginia has done as much as Thomas Jefferson has done toward the utter destruction of its happiness, that eight thousand whites had each of them been the father of five mulatto children. Thus you have FOUR HUNDRED THOUSAND MULATTOES in addition to the present swarm. The country would no longer be habitable, till after a civil war, and a series of massacres. We all know with absolute certainty that the continent has as many white people as could eat the whole race before breakfast.

Such spleen, pandering to rising racial sensitivities, obviously aimed to degrade Jefferson with influential people in both the North and the South. However, the calumny had begun to lose its effect by July 1803, when Callender, a heavy drinker for years, plunged or accidentally fell into the James River and drowned in water three feet deep. By that time, readers who had relished his spicy disclosures for some time were satiated. Besides, national pride in Jefferson's accomplishments had submerged much of the concern about his private sins. He had negotiated the "second American revolution" smoothly enough, pleasing his own party and upsetting the established order far less than the Federalists had predicted. The country under his leadership had peace, prosperity and, through the Louisiana Purchase, a boundary extending to the Rocky Mountains. His prospects for reelection in 1804 were excellent, indeed.

In May of that year an association that had been disrupted by Callender's writings was temporarily resumed. Abigail Adams, for the first time since her husband left office, wrote to Jefferson after the death of his twenty-six-year-old daughter Polly (Mrs. John Eppes). Eager to reestablish the friendship, he replied that Polly had been devoted to Abigail ever since the child visited her in London while he was Minister to France. Then he expressed regret that "circumstances should have arisen, which seemed to draw a line between us," and continued, "I can say with truth that one act of Mr. Adams' life, and only one, ever gave me a moment's displeasure. I did consider his last appointments to office as personally unkind, but after brooding over it for some little time and not always resisting the expression of it, I forgave it cordially . . ."

Mrs. Adams was not so forgiving. Her tart response to Jefferson, whom she had described years earlier as "one of the choice ones of the earth," was that he got exactly what he deserved for hiring "human refuse like Callender to attack President Adams." And when Jefferson tried to convince her that Callender had never been in his employ or under his direction, she gave abrupt notice that she had "closed the correspondence."

Despite the excitement that the libels of Jefferson had generated previously, they were scarcely mentioned in the 1804 campaign. He was reelected by a majority of 162 to 14 electoral votes, carrying all participating states except Connecticut and Delaware. But his sweeping victory did not erase his resentment of journalists who had attacked his character during his first term. In his second Inaugural Address he declared, "The artillery of the press has been leveled against us, charged with whatever its licentiousness could devise or dare," and went on, "The abuses of an institution so important to freedom are deeply to be regretted." Later, he wrote to Massachusetts Governor James Sullivan, "I certainly have known and still know, characters eminently qualified for the most exalted trusts who could not bear up against the brutal hackings and hewings of those heroes of Billingsgate." He cited George Washington ("the great character of our country") as one whose services would have been lost "if he had been assailed with the degree of abandoned licentiousness under those of which the Federal bands have shown themselves capable. He would have thrown up the helm in a burst of indignation."

Jefferson himself must have been tempted to throw up the helm many times during his second term. For although it began on a high wave of acclaim, his prestige declined as his problems of keeping the Union intact—and the country from being drawn into the war between France and Britain—were compounded by renewed assaults on his character.

In the vanguard of the odious revival was Joseph Dennie, who delighted in reminding readers of his *Port Folio* that the President had a mulatto mistress, and who attracted wide attention by featuring verse on that theme by Thomas Moore, the young Irish poet. Moore had arrived in Washington with the British Minister and Mrs. Anthony Merry, and he soon shared their dislike of Mr. Jefferson. The latter had initially displeased the punctilious envoy by receiving his credentials unceremoniously, and in dress Merry later described as "indicative of utter slovenliness and indifference to appearance." Shortly afterward, the British diplomat and his wife were vexed at having to find seats for themselves at a presidential dinner, while Mr. Jefferson escorted Mrs. Madison to the table and placed her in the seat of honor, on his right. Finally, when Merry perceived that the President was more cordial to a group of American Indians than to foreign emissaries at an official reception, he left in a huff, vowing he would never again set foot in the executive mansion. After that, Mrs. Merry complained that the President was "a man of no respect for proprieties" while her husband cultivated anti-Jeffersonians in

New England and, eventually, almost persuaded his government to underwrite Aaron Burr's plot to set up a separate government in the western United States.

Thomas Moore, meanwhile, wrote to London friends that the British Minister and Mrs. Merry had been treated "with the most pointed incivility by the present democratic President, Mr. Jefferson." Then Moore became a boon companion of Dennie, and an occasional contributor to *The Port Folio*.

Moore's lines about Jefferson and his Negro mistress, featured in the magazine and widely quoted, were preceded by the editor's paraphrase of Horace, as follows:

> Dear Thomas, deem it no disgrace with slaves to mend thy breed,
> Nor let the wench's smutty face deter thee from thy deed.

Moore's contribution continued:

> The patriot, fresh from Freedom's council come,
> Now pleas'd, retires to lash his slaves at home,
> Or woo, some black Aspasia's charms,
> And dream of Freedom in his bondmaid's arms!

Among others who called wide attention to the slander, in verse, was thirteen-year-old William Cullen Bryant. His lines, published in Boston, read:

> Go wretch! Resign the presidential chair,
> Disclose thy secret measures, foul or fair;
> Go, search with curious eyes the horned frogs,
> Mid the wild waste of Louisianian bogs;
> Or, where the Ohio rolls his turbid stream,
> Dig for huge bones, thy glory and thy theme,

Go, scan, Philophist, thy Sally's charms,
And sink supinely in her sable arms;
But quit to abler hands the helm of state.

The Sally Hemings story started with her mother, Betty, the daughter of John Hemings, an English sea captain, and a full-blooded African slave of John Wayles (later, Jefferson's father-in-law). According to published memoirs, Betty was Wayles' mistress after his wife died, and within the next fourteen years she bore several children, including Sally, James and John, who were given her father's surname.

Historians, holding that Betty produced twelve offspring by four men, have pointed out the lack of conclusive evidence that Sally was Wayles' daughter, but the relationship, which made her Mrs. Thomas Jefferson's half sister, might have been the reason that Sally, two of her brothers and their mother enjoyed preferred treatment at Monticello, after moving there as part of Martha Jefferson's inheritance from her late father. Betty and Sally lived in the manor house; they looked after Mrs. Jefferson during her last illness and were in her bedroom when she died. After Jefferson became Minister to France, he summoned James Hemings to Paris to master the art of French cookery, while John Hemings became a proficient carpenter at Monticello. Later, when an older servant became ill just before she was to take little Polly Jefferson abroad to join her father, fourteen-year-old Sally Hemings went with the child, by way of London, where they stayed with John and Abigail Adams for two weeks before going on to Paris.

Although suspicions about Jefferson and his slave had come up while he was Secretary of State, his political enemies at that time were neither as numerous nor as vicious as they were after he became President. However, for several years there had been whispers that his "Black Sal" became his mistress while he was Minister to France, that she was pregnant when she returned to America with him and his daughters, and that her first child by him died shortly after he took Cabinet office. Such rumors could not be corroborated, then or later. Immediately after the ship bearing Jefferson and his party back to America docked, Sally was whisked off to Virginia, where she stayed for the remainder of her life and was inaccessible to anyone except intimates. A reliable record shows, however, that she bore four children, from 1798 to 1806, and traducers of Jefferson have been quick to note that even though he served as Vice President and then as President during those years, he was at Monticello nine months prior to each birth.

Perhaps the prime reason the miscegenation scandal persisted was that Jefferson never denied it, except in a general way. Conversely, he admitted, in two official letters that as a young bachelor he tried to make love to the wife of his boyhood friend, John Walker. The confession was brought about by the intermeddling of Henry (Light Horse Harry) Lee, the Virginian whose sobriquet dated to his brilliant command of the irregular cavalry and infantry under General Washington. Lee would also go down in history as governor of Virginia, a member of Congress, and the father of the famous Robert E. Lee; but while Jefferson was chief executive Lee was an out-of-power Federalist, deeply in debt and obsessed by the conviction that the President, whom he heartily disliked, was somehow responsible for the creditors who had been hounding him for months and might send him to debtors' prison. Whether he was the first person to tell Callender that Jefferson had tried to seduce Mrs. John Walker cannot be proved, but there is evidence enough that Harry Lee had much to do with using that scandal to force the President to the most humiliating admission of his lifetime.

The troublemaker's opportunity arose in January 1805, after the *New England Palladium* precipitated a bitter debate in the Massachusetts legislature by publishing a "Miscellany" of grievances against the President, including charges that he not only had "taken to his bosom a sable damsel" but also had "assaulted the domestic happiness of Mr. Walker." Minns and Younger produced the *Palladium,* and also handled printing for the legislature, and angered Republicans in that body demanded that the official account be withdrawn at once. Federalist Representative John Hulbert defended the printers on grounds that they had merely reissued accusations made by Callender—and never denied by the President—and then proceeded to review the scandals in lurid detail. A Republican legislator called Hulbert "a libeler of Callender's stripe," and the ensuing debate, involving incensed lawmakers on both sides for hours, was duly reported in the *Columbian Centinel.* Within a month, Jefferson's enemies were harping on "the common reports," which his friends tried to discredit as "the Callender-Hulbert libels."

At that point, Harry Lee easily persuaded Jack Walker that the slander of his wife could be eradicated only by public disclosures of the truth which would not only clear her good name, but also further embarrass the President. As a result, Walker's dictated testimony, as it may be read today in Lee's handwriting, referred to "Mr. J." as "a friend of my heart and one of my bridemen" [in the Walker-Moore wedding, in 1764] and asserted that "Mr. J." tried to convince Betsey Walker "of the innocence of promiscuous love" during her husband's protracted absence from home on business in 1768; that "Mr. J." made overtures to her several times over the next three years; and that some months after he married, he again approached her "in an indecent manner"—and again was repulsed. "And all this time I believed him to be my best friend and so felt and acted toward him," Walker declared. He went on to state that he did not learn of his friend's perfidy until years later, when he started to name "Mr. J." executor of his will and Betsey, wondering "how I could place such trust in him," divulged the story that she long had concealed "because of her fear of its consequences which might be fatal to me."

Further egged on by Lee, Walker dispatched a copy of his

statement to the President with a demand for "satisfaction," even though he was well aware that resort to swords or pistols was out of the question. The affair of honor in which Aaron Burr killed Alexander Hamilton had turned public opinion against dueling; and, long before that, it was common knowledge that Jefferson, like Washington, never used that method of settling differences. Anyway, when the President ignored Walker's challenge, Lee volunteered to urge him in person to do something at once to placate the humiliated husband. Exactly what happened in the subsequent interview was never divulged, but Jefferson must have appeared eager to make amends, for Lee later wrote to him: "I repeated to Walker my conviction of your sincere desire to do everything which truth and honor would warrant to give peace to his mind and oblivion to the cause of his disquietude."

Lee had already sent copies of Walker's testimony to Federalist editors, and several had printed it, along with the suggestion that an affirmation or denial of guilt was past due from the President. But despite the renewed press assault on him, Jefferson appeared to be as tolerant of antagonistic journalists—and as intent on preserving freedom of expression—as he was earlier; when Baron Alexander von Humboldt, the eminent German scientist, saw a copy of the *Richmond Recorder* on the President's desk and asked, "Why is this libelous journal not suppressed—or its editor at least fired and imprisoned?" Jefferson had gently replied, "Put that paper in your pocket, Baron, and should you hear the reality of our liberty—the freedom of the press—questioned, show this paper and tell where you found it."

Yet, finally realizing that the furor about his reported indignities toward Mrs. Walker had to be quelled in some way, Jefferson partially confessed his guilt in an official letter to Attorney General Lincoln, and sent a duplicate to Secretary of the Navy Robert Smith, with this note:

The inclosed copy of a letter to Mr. Lincoln will fully explain its own object, that I need say nothing in that way. I communicate this to particular friends because I wish to stand with them on the grounds of truth, neither better nor worse than they make me. You will perceive that while I plead guilty to one of the charges, that while young and single I offered love to a handsome lady, I acknowledge its incorrectness. It is the only one in truth of all those allegations against me.

Lincoln and Smith circulated the messages to other officials, and the general public soon learned that the President had admitted his deplorable conduct toward "a handsome lady" in his bachelor days. Virtually everyone in Virginia knew that the lady was Betsey Walker; and many speculated that she might have been more receptive to the young Jefferson than her husband believed, and that the President was overly gallant in exonerating her. Contrary rumors were that he was conscience-stricken about his behavior of more than thirty years before, and that he had sought Walker's forgiveness in a confidential letter. (No such communication has ever come to light, but after Jefferson retired it was said that once, when he learned that Jack and Betsey were ill, he sent them pears and apples from Monticello, and Walker graciously acknowledged the gift.)

The agitation about Jefferson's attempted defilement of Mrs. Walker subsided quickly, but in the meantime, scandalmongers probed his history for evidence that he was dissolute in other connections in his younger days. They must have been disappointed to learn that in most respects the tall, freckled-faced, sandy-haired student was more exemplary than the majority of his classmates at William and Mary College. He did not swear or gamble or use tobacco. He was a good scholar and had already begun to evince the versatility that one day would inspire a biographer to describe him as "a man who could calculate an eclipse, survey an estate, tie an artery, plan an edifice, try a case, break a horse, dance a minuet, and play a violin." And he was romantic. For three years, beginning when he was twenty, he fancied himself in love with his idealized "Belinda" (Rebecca Burwell), but he was shy and sensitive and had mastered none of the nuances of successful courtship when he decided to ask her to marry him. He confided his intention in a letter to a friend, and added, "If she consents, I shall be happy; if she does not, I must endeavor to be as much as possible." Concurrently, he told another intimate, "If Belinda will not accept of my service, it will never be offered to another."

She did not accept—if, indeed, he ever actually got up enough courage to propose marriage. She became the wife of his college classmate, Jacquelin Ambler, and Jefferson determined that he would forgo romance forever, and would concentrate on building up his law practice and his estate. Never again, he vowed, would he be openly attentive to any maiden; and he was not emotionally involved with any matron except, perhaps, Betsey Walker, until 1770, when he began his courtship of Martha Wayles Skelton, the twenty-one-year-old widow of Bathurst Skelton, who had been his fellow student at William and Mary.

There are few available facts about the fragile, auburnhaired young woman who became Mrs. Thomas Jefferson. Servants were to remember her as "pretty" and "sweet-faced," while friends described her as "intelligent" and "talented." She and her small son were residing with her father at The Forest, his plantation on the James River, when Jefferson became seriously interested in her. She could accompany her violin-playing suitor on her harpsichord; she shared his interest in literature, art and architecture and his enjoyment of horseback riding; but as the romance progressed, and Jefferson's intent to marry her became obvious, her father for some obscure reason was displeased.

John Wayles, born in England and educated there for the law, had amassed a fortune in lands and slaves after coming to America. Perhaps he hoped his daughter would marry a man with higher social position and more money than Jefferson had at the time. Yet, the young man had a better than average heritage, a good education and excellent prospects. His mother, the former Jane Randolph, was related to the prominent Randolphs of Virginia; his father, Peter Jefferson, also had Randolph blood intermingled with less distinguished but still respectable strains. And twenty-nine-year-old Tom Jefferson had substantially increased his inherited estate, was engaged in a profitable law practice, and held a seat in the House of Burgesses. Furthermore, he had completed plans for a mansion in the Andrea Palladio tradition, to crown the 865-foot peak at Monticello (Italian for "little mountain"), his plantation near Charlottesville.

Wayles finally gave his consent to the marriage. It took place at The Forest on New Year's Day, 1772. Jefferson and his bride spent their honeymoon in the one-room brick cottage that he had built at Monticello in his cynical bachelor days, when he named the site The Hermitage.

Martha's son died within a year after her second marriage, and over the next nine years she bore Jefferson five daughters and a son. Three children died in infancy; three daughters were to survive their mother, but only two would live to maturity. Jefferson's years as a husband were the most rewarding in some respects, the most agonizing in others, in his entire life. He wrote the Declaration of Independence, served with distinction in the state legislature, and then was elected governor of Virginia during the War of Independence. But disgrace threatened him while he served as governor, for he was officially accused of cowardice because, just before the invading British troops moved on Monticello, he had sent his family to safety and then followed on horseback. The Virginia Assembly later exonerated him, but the traumatic experience left him with a distaste for public service, and although he could have been reelected governor, he declined to run again.

He retired to Monticello, expecting to devote the remainder of his life to his family and an unspectacular career as a country squire. But his prospects for happiness faded as his wife's health steadily deteriorated. She died at Monticello in September 1782, after extracting from her thirty-nine-year-old husband the promise that their daughters would never have a stepmother.

Despondent for almost two years, Jefferson destroyed all their personal correspondence and other mementos, which might have given future generations more than a shadowy conception of the woman he so deeply loved. Meanwhile he accepted appointment to assist Benjamin Franklin, Minister to France, and John Adams in working out commercial treaties abroad.

Shortly after arriving in Paris with his twelve-year-old daughter, Martha, Jefferson was plunged into a dazzling world with the wise and witty though ailing Benjamin Franklin as his sponsor. A year later, after having succeeded Franklin as Minister, he was very much at home in the city's brilliant salons.

For once in his life the celebrated Virginian dressed in the height of style. With the advice of the finest tailor in Paris he had an elaborate wardrobe—knee breeches, knee and shoe buckles, silk stockings, ruffled shirts and embroidered waistcoats in the Versailles fashion. His resplendent attire was set off with a sword and a huge topaz ring for special occasions, such as the reception at which he presented his credentials as the new American Minister to Their Majesties, King Louis XVI and Queen Marie Antoinette. His appearance drew favorable attention, and so did his conduct. Everyone within earshot was impressed when the Count de Vergennes, the French Premier, asked, *"C'est vous, Monsieur, qui remplacez le Docteur Franklin?"* and Jefferson softly replied, "No one can replace him, sir. I am only his successor."

Jefferson was mentally stimulated by his contacts in Paris, but he was appalled by the eroticism that permeated the fashionable circles in which he moved. He observed that even the nobility did not have "the kind of happiness which is enjoyed in America by every class and people . . . Intrigues of love occupy the younger and those of ambition the older . . . Conjugal love having no existence among them, happiness is utterly unknown." And to a fellow Virginian who asked his advice about sending his son to college abroad, he wrote:

> Why send an American youth to Europe for an education? He forms friendships which will never be useful to him . . . He is led by the strongest of all human passions into a spirit of intrigue, destructive to his health, and in both cases, learns to consider fidelity to the marriage bed an ungentlemanly practice . . . It appears, then, that an American coming to Europe for his education loses in his knowledge, in his health, in his habits, and in his happiness.

Minister Jefferson had leased a spacious house, L'Hôtel de Langeac on the Champs Elysées, furnished it tastefully, staffed it with eight servants, and employed as his steward Adrien Petit, a famous French chef. James Hemings was transported from Monticello to work under Petit in the kitchen. Little Martha (Patsy) Jefferson lived in a Paris convent. Colonel David Humphreys, secretary of the legation, resided with Jefferson, as did his personal secretary, twenty-five-year-old William Short. Meanwhile, both Jefferson and Humphreys worried considerably about Short's attachment to the beautiful but unhappily married Duchesse d'Anville.

Although he negotiated a crowded social calendar, Jefferson continued to be depressed. He had not recovered from the grief that engulfed him when his wife died; and his sorrow had been accentuated, several months after he reached Paris, by the death of his youngest daughter, Lucy Elizabeth, whom he had left with relatives in Virginia. He asked his sister-in-law, Mrs. Elizabeth Eppes, to send his other daughter, six-year-old Maria (Polly), to Paris as soon as possible. Some months would pass before she arrived, accompanied by the young slave, Sally Hemings. In the meantime, the novelty of cultivating new acquaintances and entertaining friends from America had begun to pall on Jefferson to such a degree that he retired periodically to rest and meditate in the Carthusian monastery where he maintained quarters. But nothing seemed to help his flagging spirit. "I am burning my candle of life without present pleasure or future object," he wrote as his despondency deepened. "I take all the fault on myself, for it is impossible to be among people who wish more to make one happy." However, through the American painter John Trumbull he soon would meet a young woman who would dispel his dejection—and captivate him.

The forty-three-year-old Jefferson's ideal of womanhood would not appeal to twentieth-century feminists, but twenty-seven-year-old Maria Hadfield Cosway conformed to it in every way. She had delicate features, violet-blue eyes and blond hair; and, in his words, "qualities and accomplishments belonging to her sex, which might form a chapter apart from her; such as music, modesty, beauty and that softness of disposition which is the ornament of her sex and the charm of ours."

The basic facts of her background were these: she was born of English parents, in Florence, Italy, and was educated in a convent; she spoke six languages, painted landscapes, played the harp and the pianoforte, composed music and had an excellent singing voice. A few years before she met Jefferson she married Richard Cosway, an eccentric but celebrated miniaturist. Cosway was seventeen years older than his wife, and vain, even though he was physically unattractive. He was known around the Royal Academy in London as Monkey Face and The Tiny Cosmetic, and also as The Macaroni Miniature

Painter, because he affected the foppish "macaroni" style of dress—a mulberry silk coat, embroidered in a strawberry design, set off with a powdered wig surmounted by a tiny tricorne hat. But he was rich as well as famous, while Maria Hadfield was virtually penniless. On their wedding day, he settled 2,800 pounds on her; and within a short time, she made Schomberg House, their residence in Pall Mall, a rendezvous for fashionable Londoners.

"Everybody well known found their way to the Cosways' receptions," went a contemporary account. The Duchess of Devonshire and Horace Walpole were among regular guests of the Cosways; and the handsome but notoriously profligate Prince of Wales, Richard's patron, was there often enough to arouse suspicions that he had lascivious designs on the lovely hostess.

The success of the parties at Schomberg House eventually aroused envy and drew sharp criticism. After a typical soiree, at which paintings of both the husband and the wife were displayed, Peter Pindar, a popular satirist, wrote:

> What vanity was in your skulls
> To make you act so like two fools,
> To expose your daubs, tho's made with wonderous pains out?
> Could Raphael's angry ghost arise
> And on the figures cast his eyes,
> He'd catch a pistol up and blow his brains out.
>
> Muse, in this criticism I fear
> Thou really hast been too severe;
> Cosway paints miniatures with truth and spirit
> And Mrs. Cosway boasts a fund of merit.

Shortly after these verses appeared in a London publication, Cosway took Maria to Paris for an extended vacation. But within a week, he was persuaded to paint miniatures of the Duchesse d'Orléans and her children and also of the Duchesse de Polignac. He began to work at once, leaving Maria to find her own amusement.

That was no problem, after she met the American Minister. As soon as he learned she had never before been in Paris, Jefferson arranged to conduct her to the landmarks of the city and to the châteaux and gardens of the surrounding countryside. At first, the two were accompanied by John Trumbull or William Short or, on rare occasions, Cosway. But Trumbull soon left for London; Short dropped out to spend all his spare moments with the delectable Duchesse d'Anville; and Cosway became preoccupied with his commissions. From then on, almost every morning for weeks, Jefferson called for Maria at an early hour and they rode off in his carriage to visit scenes that he thought she might enjoy. Sometimes they attended the theater and concerts; often they spent hours at art and science exhibitions; now and then, he dispensed with his carriage, so they could walk and talk, hours on end.

Whether or not Jefferson was deeply in love with Maria, or she with him, is doubtful. But, certainly, she fascinated him and lifted his spirits immeasurably. He was distressed when her visit to Paris neared its end. (Cosway had finished his commissions and had gone on to Antwerp, where she would join him before they returned to London.)

By that time, whatever the degree of Jefferson's affection might have been, he was well aware of the insurmountable barriers to anything more lasting than a warm friendship with the delightful woman. Even if she had been free to marry, he was constricted by his promise to his dying wife; and Maria's devout Catholic faith forbade divorce, even if she had been so inclined. At any rate, with her departure imminent, Jefferson broke all his other engagements, hoping to spend every possible moment with her. But that happy prospect was also thwarted while they were taking a last long walk together, and he fell and fractured his right wrist. In agony for days afterward, he could not escort her anywhere, and when, at her insistence, he managed to take her for a carriage ride on her final full day in Paris, the jostling carriage caused him such intense pain that after a sleepless night, he sent a message that he could not see her off as he had planned, since he would have to forgo her "charming company for that of the surgeon."

In a note by return courier she expressed her deep disappointment, mentioned her husband's promise to bring her back to Paris the following April, and added, "I . . . shall long for next spring." Jefferson promptly forgot all about his lame wrist; within an hour he was on his way to lunch with Maria at Port St.-Denis before she boarded the afternoon coach for Antwerp.

Her departure had a profound effect on Jefferson, for a few hours later he wrote with his left hand an astounding, eighteen-page letter to her. He observed that after "the last sad office" of seeing her off, he walked "more dead than alive" to his own conveyance; then, after returning to his house, he sat before the fire "solitary and sad" to take down a dialogue between his HEART and his HEAD, which he wanted her to read.

The missive contained enough references to Richard Cosway to give the impression that it was meant for both husband and wife, but the integral message was patently for Maria. The HEART recalled memorable trips to "the Pont de Neuilly, the hills of St. Germain, the chateaux, the gardens, the statues of Marley . . ." The HEAD observed: "You wrack our whole system when you are parted from those you love, complaining that such a situation is worse than death." The HEART prophesied that "the talented friends" would return to Paris and might also visit America some day—"especially the lady, who paints landscapes so inimitably," and observed that "if the lady should ever become a sorrowing widow, a devoted friend will be waiting for her in America." The discourse rambled on in similar vein, for pages, before Jefferson promised that future dispatches would be briefer. Finally, he urged Maria to make her letters "brim full of affection," so that he "might read them like a lover, who when writing the words *je t'aime* wishes the whole alphabet had entered into their composition."

After that outburst, he must have been disappointed at her brief, fairly impersonal reply, in Italian; but he wrote back that her letter showed she still thought of him ("little, indeed, but better a little than none"); and he sent her copy of a love song from a popular opera. The ensuing correspondence, which included twenty-five letters while Jefferson was abroad, would continue intermittently until a few years before he died. However, when Maria returned to Paris, as she had planned, his ardor had cooled considerably; and although her husband did not accompany her—and she stayed four months—she and Jefferson were rarely alone together. She chided him from time to time about no longer arranging trips to amuse her, until he countered that with her "clouds of company," they could not "unpremeditatedly mount into my phaeton and hie away" to places they had enjoyed together in the past.

Jefferson was in full control of his emotions before Maria left Paris. He would write to her regularly for some time, addressing her as "Dearest friend," and he would be solicitious about her for the remainder of his life; but his main absorptions during his remaining years abroad included travel—he visited the south of France, Germany and Italy—and the companionship of his daughters. Soon after arriving in Paris, Polly was enrolled in the convent school with her sister, but both girls spent much time with their father at L'Hôtel de Langeac (where Sally Hemings served as a maid).

He had rewarding male associations, as well as a coterie of attractive women friends. Among the latter was the lively and flirtatious Mrs. John Baker Church, the former Angelica Schuyler, of New York, a subject of gossip on both sides of the Atlantic. Shortly after she met Jefferson, Mrs. Church and her rich husband returned to America for a brief stay. Within a month, her open familiarity with her brother-in-law Alexander Hamilton, and her constant reference to him as her *petit fripon* (little rascal), aroused surmises that she was his mistress. His pregnant wife Eliza appeared to be oblivious to the reputed relationship, and the talk recessed when the Churches went back to Paris. There Angelica promptly resumed her friendship with the American Minister and they spent much time together. They had close ties. Her daughter Kitty was a convent classmate of Polly Jefferson; Angelica was an intimate of one of Jefferson's most stimulating acquaintances, Madame de Corny, wife of a French veteran of the American Revolution; and having been a confidante of Maria Cosway in London before the latter met Jefferson, Angelica served as an intermediary between the two. For example, when he learned that Maria's marriage was increasingly unhappy, and that she was planning an extended trip to Italy, alone, he asked Angelica to suggest that she go to America instead, "for the way will ever be wrong which will lead us apart." He had already decided to vacation at Monticello, and following his request to Angelica, he wrote to Maria, asking her to accompany him and his daughters—for a visit. In reply, she declined, but thanked him "for the flattering compliment" and promised, "I shall certainly be with you in spirit."

Jefferson had not seen Maria in more than a year and a half, and he would never see her again, but just before he sailed from France in October 1789 he sent her this note: "Adieu, my very dear friend. Be our affections unchangeable, and if our little history is to last beyond the grave, be the longest chapter that which shall record their purity, warmth and duration."

Maria bore Cosway a daughter shortly after Jefferson became Secretary of State, but marital problems continued to beset her. The self-centered artist had a flagrant affair with Mary Moser, the noted English painter, to whom he had long been attracted, and Maria, depressed and in failing health, left him and their infant and went to France and then to Italy. She stayed away from London for three years while talebearers babbled that she had deserted her child to travel with a succession of lovers—Luigi Marchesi, the noted singer; Vincent Lunardi, secretary to a Neapolitan envoy; and Jan L. Dussek, the Bohemian pianist and composer. (It was later established that she had spent much of the time recuperating in a convent.)

Serious illnesses of both Cosway and their daughter eventually brought Maria back to London to take care of them. He recovered; the child died within a year. Mary Moser had married, and Cosway was eager to resume his union with his wife. Maria agreed, and for the remainder of his life she looked after him devotedly while his health steadily deteriorated and he was increasingly beset by morbid hallucinations.

During Maria's deeply troubled times, President Jefferson kept up with her through mutual friends, and he knew that she was at her ailing husband's bedside while distortions and untruths about her were used in the whispering campaign in America. But he could do nothing to stop either that gossip or the revival of broad hints that he had also committed adultery with Angelica Church and, perhaps, several other matrons during his five years in Paris.

Nevertheless, Jefferson's magnificent achievements counteracted the slanders to such an extent that had he chosen to run for a third presidential term, he would have won. He still was the uncontested head of his party; he still had the confidence of the majority; and the Federalist party was shattered. He was able to choose his successor, James Madison, and to have much influence toward bringing about his victory—122 electoral votes against his opponent's 47.

"Never did a prisoner released from his chains feel such relief as I shall on shaking off the shackles of power," the sixty-six-year-old Jefferson wrote to Pierre du Pont, shortly before the 1809 inauguration. Four days after that event, he mounted his horse and rode out of Washington, D. C., never to return.

No new gossip directly implicated Jefferson after he resumed his life at Monticello, but scandals involving some of his relatives reinforced quondam suspicions that the moral aberrations of which he had been suspected were due to consanguinity. For many years Virginians had theorized that the blood relationship of Jefferson's parents was responsible for the mental deficiencies of two of their offspring. Their daughter Elizabeth was deranged; at thirty, she wandered away from home and was found dead in the woods. Their son Randolph, youngest in the family, was described in the memoirs of Isaac, a Monticello slave, as "a mighty simple man; used to come out among the black people, play the fiddle and dance half the night; hadn't much more sense than Isaac." Thomas Jefferson, very much concerned about his brother, Randolph, counseled him through the years and helped him support a sizable family at Snowden Plantation, a few miles from Monticello. (In the Rare Book Collection of the Library of Congress today, twenty-eight letters, exchanged from 1807 to 1815, show a deep bond of affection between the brilliant man and his retarded brother.)

Less than three years after he retired from the presidency, a monstrous crime committed by two of Jefferson's nephews indicated that there may have been moral, as well as mental, abnormality in the inbred family line. Lilburn and Isham Lewis, sons of Jefferson's sister Lucy—who had married her cousin, Charles Lewis—owned and operated a plantation in Kentucky. The young men were habitually intoxicated, and they had been suspected of extreme cruelty to their slaves even before one of their runaway blacks was caught and returned. To make an example of him, the brothers assembled all their other slaves in the plantation meathouse and, before their eyes, stabbed the seventeen-year-old youth to death, dismembered his body, and threw the pieces, one by one, into a burning stove. After the horrified witnesses talked, neighbors found the bones of the slain man, and a white lynching mob was stopped only by hasty indictments that brought the murderers to trial in Kentucky. The brothers announced just before the verdict that they had a signed pact to slay each other if they were adjudged guilty, but they changed their minds when the judge sentenced them to life imprisonment. Lilburn later accidentally killed himself; Isham escaped from jail, was apprehended and sentenced to hang, but got away successfully the second time. Rumors ran that he finally joined the army under an assumed name, and was mortally wounded in the Battle of New Orleans.

There is no reference to the Lewises' crime in Jefferson's correspondence or other papers, nor is his reaction mentioned in contemporary accounts. Anyway, it was not the first sensational offense to evoke dark inferences about cognation in his lineage. Some five years after he retired from the presidency, his eccentric relative John Randolph of Roanoke resuscitated a family scandal that had brought on a court trial while Jefferson was Secretary of State. Specifically, Randolph in 1814 publicly accused his cousin Anne Cary (Nancy) Randolph of having killed his brother and their illegitimate child twelve years before, and of having had intercourse with a slave before she married rich but elderly and peg-legged Gouverneur Morris so she could "sink her harpy fangs into an infirm old man!"

Nancy countercharged that John Randolph was "a bold-faced liar!" Recriminations flew back and forth until every detail of the old court trial had been thoroughly rehashed. Entangled with Randolph intermarriages, the principals were difficult for even their contemporaries to keep straight, but the main figures and their connections were as follows: Nancy was a cousin and also a sister-in-law of Jefferson's daughter Martha, who was married to her own cousin Thomas Mann Randolph, Jr.; Nancy's sister Judith was the wife of their cousin

Richard Randolph, which made him, also, Nancy's brother-in-law. The initial scandal broke when Nancy was suspected of being Richard's mistress and, with him, was tried in 1792 on the charge that they had slain their child at birth. The main witness against Nancy was her aunt, Mrs. Carter Page, whose mother was a Randolph. Martha Jefferson Randolph testified for Nancy, and another relative, John Marshall (later to be Chief Justice), was a counsel for her defense.

After Nancy and Richard were acquitted, Secretary Jefferson complimented his daughter on her conduct as a witness, and urged her to show more affection than ever to her vilified sister-in-law (and cousin). Presumably, Martha Randolph followed her father's advice; however, she did not rise to Nancy's defense later, when Richard was poisoned and suspicions were divided as to whether Nancy or his wife had administered the lethal dose. Although the two women were not brought to trial, they quarreled violently, and Judith openly accused Nancy of fornication with a slave.

When John Randolph recalled all of this complicated tale in his castigation of Cousin Nancy in 1814, there was no reaction from Monticello, for Jefferson in retirement had reasons enough to disssociate himself from his squabbling relatives. Talkative and temperamental John Randolph of Roanoke, long in the House of Representatives, had sometimes been an unpredictable problem to Jefferson as President, even though both were Republicans. Furthermore, Jefferson heartily disliked Nancy's husband, Gouverneur Morris, who had succeeded him as Minister to France but, later, had become one of his implacable Federalist foes in the Senate. Besides, by that time the Sage of Monticello was inured to calumny. Certainly, he had survived his own share of it; in his words, he had been "a fair mark for every man's dirt."

A prodigious correspondent throughout his adult life, Jefferson wrote 1,667 letters during the first year after he retired from the presidency. Intermittently corresponding with Maria Cosway, he learned that after her husband died in his eightieth year, she used much of the fortune he left her to start a seminary for devout young women in Lyons, France, and a similar school in Lodi, Italy. "Who could imagine that I would take up this line?" she asked in a letter to her old friend when she was fifty-six. "It has afforded me a satisfaction unfelt before," she went on. "I long to see you." His last note to her recalled their happy days in Paris and indicated once more that their relationship had been above reproach. The closing line was this: "The religion you so sincerely profess tells us that we shall meet again, and we have all so lived as to be assured that it will be in happiness." (Maria was highly honored, later. Emperor Francis II of the Two Sicilies created her a baroness of his realm; and her school at Lodi became a religious center after she died there, in 1838, at the age of seventy-nine.)

Much of Jefferson's correspondence in his final years pertained to slavery and showed that his basic convictions about it were much the same as those expressed in his *Notes on Virginia* (1781–82). He still deplored the system. He still was searching for a practicable way that it could be ended. He still believed that Negroes should not only be freed but also trained to support themselves and then colonized outside the United States. And less than six months before he died he reiterated his "aversion to the mixture of colour" in America. In view of that, Jefferson enthusiasts cannot believe that the Sage of Monticello procreated at least four children by a black mistress. Yet, just as the slander was cut to order to degrade President Jefferson, so it has been used since his death, successively serving the Abolitionists, traducers of the South during the Reconstruction and, finally, twentieth-century integrationists.

From the 1830s to the 1860s, Abolitionists made much of "miscegenation and Mr. Jefferson"—not so much to tarnish his name as to excoriate slavery. In the vanguard of the crusaders, Angelina R. Grimké, the eloquent Quaker from South Carolina, wrote a letter to *The Liberator* in June 1837, declaring, "The best blood in Virginia flows in the veins of slaves. Yes, even the blood of Jefferson!"

Not long afterward, Alexander Ross, a Kentuckian and reputedly a close friend of Abraham Lincoln, stated publicly that after Jefferson's death, two of his daughters "by an octoroon slave" were sold on the block in New Orleans. "Both those unfortunate children by the author of the Declaration of Independence were quite white, their eyes blue, and their hair long, soft and auburn in color," he declared. "Both were highly accomplished. The youngest daughter escaped from her master and committed suicide by drowning herself."

Ross presumably was "the Southern gentleman" whom Dr. Levi Gaylord quoted in the Abolitionist publication, *Friend of Man,* in 1838: "I saw for myself THE DAUGHTERS OF THOMAS JEFFERSON sold in New Orleans for one thousand dollars." After that was reprinted in *The Emancipator,* the theme was featured in a poem, "Jefferson's Daughters," in an Edinburgh, Scotland, journal. Subsequently, verses along the same line appeared in William Wells Brown's anti-slavery song book, as follows:

> Can the blood, that, at Lexington, poured o'er the plains
> When the sons warred with tyrants their rights to uphold . . .
> Can the tide of Niagara wipe out the stain?
> No! Jefferson's child has been bartered for gold!
>
> The daughter of Jefferson sold for a slave!
> The child of a freeman for dollars and francs,
> The roar of applause, when your orators rave,
> Is lost in the sound of her chain, as it clanks.

Brown also wrote a popular epic, "Clotel; or, The President's Daughter," describing a slave auction, at which Jefferson's mistress and one of their daughters were sold to the highest bidder. While that slander was widely circulated throughout America, Frederick Douglass, the famed Negro journalist and orator, asserted on a lecture tour of England that a granddaughter of Thomas Jefferson was among the liberated slaves who colonized Liberia.

The third President's reputed intimacy with his beautiful octoroon had been discussed so widely in this country by 1860 that few persons were surprised when it cropped up in that year's presidential campaign. Hoping to divert Abraham Lincoln's slim support in the South to the advantage of his opponent, Stephen A. Douglas, backers of the latter spread the story that Lincoln had described the Great Southerner, Thomas Jefferson, as "a slaveholder who brought his own children under the hammer and made money of his debaucheries." Lincoln promptly labeled the statement "a base forgery."

The disparagement of Jefferson's image was offset to some extent in the 1860s by the published reminiscences of a long-time overseer at Monticello, and also by a servant who was born there. Both recalled a merciful master who despised slavery and was unfailingly kind to his Negro dependents (he never referred to them as "slaves").

At sixty-five, Captain Edmund Bacon, who had superintended Monticello for twenty years, dictated his *Memoirs,* which came out in 1862. "Mr. Jefferson was always kind and indulgent toward servants," Bacon remembered. "He could not bear to have a servant whipped, no odds how much he deserved it . . . He did not like slavery . . . I have heard him prophesy that we should have just such trouble with it as we are having now." Bacon revealed also that while most of Jefferson's servants were emancipated under the terms of his will, "he freed one some years before he died, and there was a good deal of talk about that. She was nearly as white as anybody and very beautiful. People said he freed her because she was his own daughter. She was not his daughter; she was ＿＿'s daughter. I know that. I have seen him come out of her mother's room many mornings when I went up to Monticello early."

Bacon was referring to Sally Hemings' daughter, Harriet, whom Jefferson manumitted four years before he died. The man the former overseer professed to have seen "many a morning" was believed by many to be Peter Carr, a son of Jefferson's widowed sister, Martha, and her late husband, Dabney Carr. Peter virtually grew up at Monticello, and he was said to be excessively fond of "Dusky Sally" Hemings, who was three years younger than he. According to local gossip in connection with Callender's libel of President Jefferson, Sally had been Carr's mistress for some time, but Jefferson took the blame in order to protect his thirty-two-year-old nephew, who by then was married and had several legitimate children.

Bacon later filled in the blank in his memoirs by obliquely identifying the white fornicator as "a nephew of Jefferson Carr." However, Ellen Randolph Coolidge, Thomas Jefferson's granddaughter, later noted that the "general impression" within the family was that Peter Carr's brother, Samuel, was the father of Sally's children. Mrs. Coolidge described him as "the most notorious, good natured Turk that ever was master of a black seraglio kept at other men's expense."

Isaac Jefferson's *Memoirs of a Monticello Slave,* dictated to Charles Campbell in the 1840s and published a generation later, covers more than forty years at Monticello, and gives some intimate glimpses of familiar figures there. The old slave, who identified himself as "the son of Great George and Ursula," like many others of his time, took his master's surname. He affectionately remembered that Jefferson was always kind to his "servants," who in turn loved and respected him. Isaac further recalled, "Folks said these Hemings'es was old Mr.

Wayles' children," and he referred to Betty Hemings as "a bright mulatto woman" with several children, including Sally, who was "mighty near white . . . very handsome, long black hair down back." Isaac did not connect Sally with Jefferson in any way, however, and his only reference to her offspring was this: "Sally had a son named Madison who learned to be a great fiddler."

Madison Hemings also turned out to be a resourceful chronicler. Reconstruction tensions had triggered a volley of stories about hybridism in the South when he proclaimed in the Pike County (Ohio) *Republican,* on March 13, 1873, that he was the son of Thomas Jefferson and Sally Hemings. He wrote that his mother, a daughter of Betty Hemings and John Wayles, was born in 1773 and later that year was moved with her mother, brothers and sisters to Monticello. After taking Jefferson's daughter to Europe, Sally, during her eighteen months in Paris, "became Mr. Jefferson's concubine, and when he was called home she was *enceinte* by him." She did not wish to return to America ("She was just beginning to understand the French language well, and in France she was free . . ."), but she agreed to accompany her master back to Monticello after he promised that any children she might bear would be freed at the age of twenty-one. Soon after returning to Virginia, she gave birth to a child ("of whom Thomas Jefferson was the father"), but the infant lived only a short time. "She gave birth to four others," Madison went on, "and Jefferson was the father of all of them. Their names were Beverly, Harriet, Madison (myself) and Eston . . . We all became free, agreeable to the treaty entered into by our parents before we were born."

Madison further wrote that after being liberated he left Virginia, married the daughter of a slave and a white master, supported a large family as a carpenter in Ohio, and was a respected member of the community. He reported also that his sisters married whites and lived as whites, in Washington, D. C., while his brother Eston settled with his Negro wife in Wisconsin.

Some of the statements in Madison's article have been authenticated. The names of Sally's four children as he listed them are the same as those mentioned with her in Jefferson's *Farm Book.* It was widely known, of course, that Sally took Polly Jefferson to Paris; also, that Sally and her children were either freed by their master or through his will.

However, James Parton, whose life of Jefferson appeared within a year after the Hemings article came out, declared that "the respectable Madison . . . has been misinformed." Parton supported his contention by recalling that Henry Stephens Randall, author of the first definitive biography of Jefferson (1858), told him that the father of Sally's progeny was "a near relative of Jefferson, who need not be named." Parton further asserted that a pocket memorandum of the President's day-to-day activities in 1804 showed that he was not at Monticello when Madison was conceived. But if he correctly noted that he was born in January 1805, then Parton was in error, for that was nine months after President Jefferson was at his home, during the last illness and through the death and burial of his daughter Polly (Mrs. John Wayles Eppes). The chronology proves nothing, of course, for there were other white, and many black males around his slave quarters at the time.

Although the image of Thomas Jefferson has been abased and aggrandized by turns over the past hundred and fifty years, it rose to new heights during the New Deal, when the conception of him as a statesman of unparalleled brilliance was promoted by the Democratic party to counteract the image of Abraham Lincoln as the renowned Republican symbol. Jefferson's prestige reached a peak, in fact, during the 1943 Jefferson Bicentennial, when the Memorial to him was dedicated in Washington, D. C. John Russell Pope's adaptation of Jefferson's design at the University of Virginia Rotunda, to house the heroic bronze figure, evoked bitter criticism when it was begun in 1939. But even though architects, city planners and others disapproved of its neoclassic lines and the Tidal Basin site, the general public was pleased with the beauty and significance of the finished product, and admiration for the great President whom it honors swept the country.

The emphasis on Thomas Jefferson as the idealist, the protector of individual freedom, and the literal democrat submerged for a time all reminders of his suspected moral derelictions. But, more recently, the miscegenation scandal has been reactivated with a vengeance.

An article entitled "Thomas Jefferson's Negro Grandchildren" in the November 19, 1954, issue of *Ebony* magazine alleges Jefferson's "fatherhood of at least five children, and perhaps more, by several comely slave concubines." The report names Sally's children by him, in the order of their birth, as Burwell Hemings, Joseph Fossett, John, Madison and Eston Hemings. Why Joseph's surname differed from that of his brothers is not explained in the article, but it proceeds as follows: Joseph married Edith, Jefferson's cook at Monticello, and they had seven children. Their eldest son, Peter, born in 1816, lived in the manor house and was taught to read and write "by the master's white daughters." After Peter was freed, the account goes on, he migrated to Cincinnati, prospered as a caterer, then entered the ministry and became a recognized Baptist leader throughout Ohio. One of his granddaughters, Mrs. Bessie Curtis, of Cincinnati, is featured in the account, recalling that a fire in the 1920s destroyed the family Bible, which had "Thomas Jefferson" tooled in gold on the cover, and inside, "in his beautiful handwriting," the names of Joseph and Peter Fossett. The caption on one of her photographs reads: "She heard about her distinguished ancestor when a child," and it quotes her: "We never talked about it outside of family and close friends." Another section pertains to Mrs. Dora Wilburn, a retired nurse and widow in Chicago, who stated that her grandmother was Anna Elizabeth Isaacs, born at Monticello and believed to be a daughter of Jefferson and a slave other than Sally Hemings. A picture of Mrs. Wilburn, holding a copy of the famous Rembrandt Peale portrait of Jefferson, appears with the story, and she is quoted: "My grandmother rocking in her favorite chair, used to tell me about him all the time. She called him 'Grandpa.' " Others, described as "black descendants of Thomas Jefferson" are pictured: Frederick Hamilton, Sr., a Cincinnati lawyer, "a great grandson of Joseph Fossett, son of Jefferson and Sally Hemings"; William Monroe Trotter, a militant newspaper editor in Boston before his death in 1934; and his sister Maude Trotter Steward, whose photograph has this underline: "Mrs. Steward, who heard of the family connection when she was small, says, 'I know it's a fact.' "

There is not a shred of evidence that Joseph Fossett was Jefferson's son. Nor is there the slightest indication, anywhere else, that Sally Hemings had children named Burwell and John. Her children, as listed with her in Jefferson's *Farm Book*, were:

Hemings, Sally	1773
Beverley	1798
Harriet	1801
Madison	1805
Eston	1808

These names and birth years correspond with those used by Madison Hemings, but he did not mention Burwell or John Hemings or Jospeh Fossett. There was a Joseph Fossett at Monticello, however. A trained blacksmith, he ran away some years before his master died, and was living in Washington, D. C., when he was freed by Jefferson's will. But if Peter was born in 1816, he was not taught to read and write by "the master's white daughters," for after 1804 Jefferson had only one living daughter.

The *Ebony* article was widely circulated, but with scholars quickly disproving its main premise, it was not taken seriously by discerning readers. Much more damaging to popular conceptions of the third President was Pearl Graham's "Thomas Jefferson and Sally Hemings," in the *Journal of Negro History* (April 1961), which incriminated him with arbitrary inferences and distorted facts.

On the basis of names and birth years (1798 to 1806) in the *Farm Book*, Mrs. Graham wrote, "Sally Hemings was Jefferson's concubine for at least ten years and probably twice that time." The statement clearly implies that the fourteen-year-old girl became his mistress shortly after she arrived in Paris, and that she had her first child there. That would have been the son, Tom, whom Callender in 1802 publicized as "about 14." The boy would have been born free, Mrs. Graham reasoned, by way of explaining why he was not mentioned in the *Farm Book*, along with his slave siblings. The writer further mentioned that the odd markings around the names in the record probably indicated that Sally's children, who were born at Monticello, were Jefferson's. (Conversely, most authorities interpret the small strokes and circles as his secret shorthand for work schedules, very much in the manner of George Washington's private stenography, which had prompted surmises of miscegenation at Mount Vernon many years previously.)

Mrs. Graham's article tells the old story—that Sally, a daughter of John Wayles and Betty Hemings, was the half sister of Mrs. Thomas Jefferson, and that Sally and Betty lived in the manor house at Monticello and were with their mistress when she died. Jefferson later gave each of the two faithful servants a gift, Mrs. Graham's report continues; Sally's was a small bell, which was treasured by her descendants for many years before it was presented "by a great granddaughter of Sally Hemings and Thomas Jefferson to the library of Howard University in Washington, D. C."

Another of their great granddaughters, wrote Mrs. Graham,

was Mrs. Anna Kenny Ezell, a White House seamstress during Theodore Roosevelt's administration. Whether or not T.R. was aware of Mrs. Ezell's lineage, he was contemptuous of Jefferson, according to the writer, who went on to state that Archibald Roosevelt told her he could not recall ever having heard his father comment on the third President's morals, but added, "You are quite right in assuming that my father had no good opinion of him . . . My father considered him a physical coward . . . He also felt that Mr. Jefferson had a habit of stating all sorts of principles he never lived up to."

Mrs. Graham's polemic concludes with this blanket indictment of Jefferson:

> He advocated emancipation but insisted that freed blacks be colonized outside the borders of the United States . . . He preached against miscegenation but he practiced it . . . He preached against the urgent necessity of removing all freed blacks from white-occupied land but besought Virginia to permit his emancipated sons to remain in the state.

Jefferson's own writings express his lifelong aversion to slavery, his conviction that emancipation was imperative, and his opinion that the aftermath could best be handled by preparing freed individuals to support themselves in surroundings remote from those in which they had been slaves. With national liberation far in the future, however, he guarded against the possibility that his own manumitted servants (not "sons") would ever become government dependents by requesting the Virginia legislature to allow them to remain in the state, with employment always available to them on the University of Virginia campus.

Mrs. Graham's charge that he practiced miscegenation is based solely on circumstantial evidence. But since the presumption that he seduced a teen-age black and produced children by her cannot be disproved, it has subsisted through the years on racial hatreds.

Concurrently, persons devoted to the idealized Jefferson have cited as proof that he was not immoral his own words: "I have never done a single act or been concerned in any trans-action which I feared to have fully laid open, or which could do me any harm, if truly stated." More realistic proponents, conceding that his private life might not have been spotless, have maintained that in the context of his time, a slave mistress was the normal solution for Jefferson, a national figure, who was a widower at thirty-nine, barred from remarriage by his promise to his dying wife. Perhaps the most sensible view of all was expressed many years ago by William Eelroy Curtis in *The True Thomas Jefferson* (1901):

> He was probably no more immoral than Franklin, Washington, Hamilton, and other men of his time. He was neither St. Anthony *or* a Don Juan. Judged by the standards of his generation his vices were those of a gentleman and as such did not deprive him of the respect and confidence in his community.

III

Attacks on the Saddest of All

The next outstanding nineteenth-century Presidents to be subjected to slander were as different in most respects as two men could possibly be. Yet contentious Andrew Jackson and conciliatory Abraham Lincoln had several notable qualites in common. Both were rugged men from humble beginnings; both were successful lawyers, with service in the United States Congress (Jackson had been appointed twice to the Senate); and both were born leaders who would go down in history as truly great. Furthermore, they were the saddest of all our Presidents, and scandalous abuse of both was tied to their marriages—but in entirely different ways.

Elected to the highest office thirty-two years before Lincoln, the sixty-one-year-old General Jackson was a pitiable figure when he took up residence at the National Hotel shortly before his inauguration on March 4, 1829. A British guest at the hotel later recalled that the President-elect "was in deep mourning" and that "he wore his gray hair carelessly but not ungracefully arranged, and in spite of his harsh, gaunt features looked like a gentleman and soldier."

He had been America's preeminent military figure ever since his forces defeated the British in the Battle of New Orleans. And he was physically impressive; six feet tall, with strong features and a dignified bearing. On that particular morning, however, his eyes were glazed with grief as he walked the few blocks from his hotel to the Capitol to take his oath of office. The ten-inch black band encircling his left sleeve reminded all who saw him that his beloved wife, Rachel, had died less than three months before. He was convinced that she was the victim of the calumny that had permeated his recent political campaign. Bitter memories of her suffering assailed him that morning and would govern many of his actions in the next eight years.

His sadness on his own inaugural day contrasted sharply with his indignation four years earlier, when John Quincy Adams, who had defeated him, was the President-elect. Running against Adams, William H. Crawford and Henry Clay, Jackson had received more electoral votes than any of his opponents, but not a majority, and when the contest had to be decided in the House of Representatives, Clay released his votes to Adams, making him the victor.

Ever ready to fight his country's foe or to settle private differences in a duel, impetuous General Jackson had barely managed to restrain himself from physical violence when he heard that President Adams had made Clay his Secretary of State; the defeated Democrat scoffed, "So you see the Judas of the West has closed his contract and will receive the thirty pieces of silver!"

Four years later, he entered the 1828 campaign with a well-organized political machine and a catchy slogan: "Old Hickory, the Nation's Hero and the People's Friend." Again, he battled John Quincy Adams, and again Jackson's enemies were well aware that he had an Achilles heel—his extreme sensitivity about his illegal first marriage to Rachel Donelson Robards.

Adams' party, the National Republicans, had discovered early in the campaign that ordinary epithets—"liar" and "drunkard"—did not work against Jackson. He was equally impervious to such labels as "quarrelsome roughneck" and "gambler" and "Negro slave trader" and "murderer." They had been used before with little effect, for virtually every voter in the country already knew that General Jackson had a hot temper; that he bet on horse races and cockfights (as a youth, in his native South Carolina, he was lucky enough at dice to get an education on his winnings and to establish a law practice in Tennessee); that he bought and sold slaves in connection with running his plantations; and that he had killed a man in a duel. He would do the same thing again, he reiterated in 1828, if anybody dared to impugn his honor.

The charge that really ignited the campaign and burned him where he was vulnerable was that he was "an adulterer." That hurt, for it reflected on the character of the good woman to whom he had been married for thirty-seven years. And it was technically true.

The inception of the unhappy chronicle was in 1785, when Rachel Donelson, of a respectable pioneer family, and Captain Lewis Robards, son of well-to-do parents, married and went to live with his mother in Mercer County, Kentucky. Lewis was spoiled and unaccountably jealous of his eighteen-year-old bride and he made her and everyone around them miserable.

It was customary on the frontier for unattached men to lodge with families as added protection from marauding Indians, and young Peyton Short, a lawyer who stayed briefly at the Robards' house, was the first whom Lewis accused of making love to Rachel. Lewis' mother defended the young woman and Short took an oath that there had been nothing unseemly between them. Nevertheless, Lewis ordered him to leave and then instructed Rachel's brother to send for her at once, as she would no longer be permitted to live under the Robards' roof. Rachel returned to her mother's house, ten miles from Nashville, where John Overton, a frontier lawyer, and Andrew Jackson, new prosecuting attorney for the Western District of North Carolina (later Tennessee) were boarders at the time.

Lewis Robards was contrite in due course; he begged his wife to return to him. She did, and for the next two years they divided their time between Mrs. Donelson's house and Robards' river farm in a neighboring county. But their sojourns with Rachel's mother were increasingly unpleasant because Lewis' ungovernable jealously had begun to focus on Jackson. Finally Jackson moved to another house, but first he reproved Lewis for his ugly suspicions and suggested that, if necessary, their differences would be settled in the manner of gentlemen, with swords or pistols on a field of honor. Lewis refused to duel, and the confrontation ended—for the time being.

Despite Lewis' persistent nagging, the Robards union lasted for several more months, until Rachel could stand it no longer. In desperation she left her husband's house accompanied by Jackson, who had been dispatched by the Donelsons to take her to the home of her brother-in-law and sister, Mr. and Mrs. Robert Hays, about fifty miles from Nashville.

A record of the Court of Sessions, Harrodsburg, Mercer County, Kentucky, of July 1870 reads: "Rachel Robards did elope from her husband, said Lewis, with another man." However, within a month the husband was again on his knees before Rachel, pleading for a reconciliation. Her adamant refusal this time meant only one thing to him: she and Jackson were in love. Shortly afterward, he accused Jackson of breaking up his home, but he recoiled when the indignant attorney threatened to cut off the accusant's ears if such a charge was ever repeated, and added that he was "tempted to do it, anyway." Thoroughly shaken, Lewis had a peace warrant served on Jackson and then departed for Kentucky, vowing that he would return to get his wife—by force, if necessary. Rachel soon precluded that possibility by joining a small party of travelers on the 2,000-mile wilderness trading route to Natchez, Mississippi.

Lewis forthwith asked the General Assembly at Richmond for a divorce on grounds of desertion. The petition was rejected, but a bill, passed twelve days before Kentucky ceased to be a part of Virginia, granted him the right to sue later, in Kentucky.

He had made a great stir about his intent to divorce Rachel, but he said nothing about the denial of his petition. So, when a confused account of the court action reached Tennessee, everybody there took it to mean that the marriage was dissolved. Jackson joined Rachel in Natchez, and they were married in the spring of 1791. Two years later Robards appeared in the Court of Quarter Sessions at Harrodsburg and exercised his right to sue because his wife was living openly with another man. The divorce was promptly granted.

Jackson's negligence in not having confirmed reports of the court action was the costliest mistake of his life. He would pay for it through years of agony, accented by quarrels, fist fights and at least two duels to defend his wife's honor; and aspersions on her morals as well as his would invariably come up in his political campaigns. Meanwhile the moment he learned his union with Rachel was illegal, he arranged to wed her a second time. The two exchanged vows on January 27, 1794, a little less than two years after their first wedding ceremony.

Gossip about the "Robards-Jackson mixup" subsided quickly in Tennessee, where facts of the case were widely known and understood. Jackson became the state's most famous soldier and Rachel was acclaimed for her philanthropies and her devotion to her husband and their adopted son, Andrew Jackson, Jr. And under her warm aegis, The Hermitage, the mansion her husband built for her near Nashville, became a second home for young relatives, including Andrew Jackson Donelson and his wife, Emily, Rachel's niece.

In Jackson's first race for the presidency, his "marriage to a bigamist" was occasionally brought up, but emphasis on it was slight, indeed, compared to that in 1828, when it became a predominant campaign issue. Adams and Clay had powerful friends in the press who would stop at nothing to denigrate Jackson, and his history of constantly quarreling to defend his wife's reputation served as excellent material. *The Raleigh Register*, for example, summarized Jackson's background as a "disgusting detail of squabblings and pistolings, dirkings and brickbattings and other actions reconciliable neither to regulations nor morals." Clay's confidant, Charles Hammond, in the Cincinnati *Gazette* editorialized on Jackson's unconventional marriage and then published a campaign pamphlet with a garbled version of the story that led up to this question: "Ought a convicted adultress and her paramour husband be placed in the highest office of this free and Christian land?" Peter Force, another close friend of Clay, took up the theme, with more innuendos, in his *National Journal,* and Republican editors throughout the country followed suit.

The attacks on Jackson gave his friend Duff Green, who ran the *United States Telegraph,* an excuse to bring out facts about the marriage that had never been printed in full. From a special committee of Tennesseans who had known Andrew and Rachel Jackson for many years, Green had quietly obtained a volume of details and impressions about the romance and marriage, and his ten-column resumé in an extra edition of his newspapers was a forceful exoneration of the Jacksons.

Green must have prepared the article without consulting his candidate in advance, however, for some apprehension about the general's reaction was shown in Green's note to him immediately after it was published. The editor asked that Mrs. Jackson be tendered "the congratulations of a sincere friend on

the satisfactory and conclusive vindication of her innocence,"
and went on, "I am aware of the delicacy of the subject and under
other circumstances would be the last to intrude such remarks
upon your notice but I have not been without my share of difficulty in the matter." Green also hinted that if the opposition
persisted in perpetrating calumnies, it might be necessary to
retaliate by raising questions about Mrs. Adams' morals.

Jackson replied, "Female character never should be introduced or touched by my friends, unless a continuation of attack should continue to be made against Mrs. J. and then only
by way of *just retaliation* upon the *known guilty*. I never war
against females, and it is only the base and cowardly that do."
He did not object, however, when some of his friends spread
the story that while serving as President Madison's Minister to
Russia, Adams "made use of a beautiful girl to seduce the
passions of Czar Alexander and sway him to political purposes." Nobody actually believed priggish John Quincy
Adams had ever resorted to sexual chicanery—even for patri-
otic reasons—but the charge illustrated the kind of recriminations that accented the increasingly virulent campaign.

Jackson in the meantime personally solicited affidavits as to
Rachel's purity from persons who had known her since child-
hood, and dispersed them with his own comments. A typical
note was attached to a sworn statement he sent to Major William B. Lewis:

> I am more anxious on this subject than perhaps I should
> be, but the Rascality of the attempt to blacken the charac-
> ter of an ancient and Virtuous female who through life has
> maintained a good reputation and who has associated
> with the best circles of society in which she has been
> placed, and this for the basest purpose, by a coalition at
> the head of which I am sure Mr. Clay is, raises in my mind
> such feeling of indignation that I can scarcely control, but

the day of retribution as respects Mr. Clay and his tool Colonel Hammond, must arrive should I be spared.

Jackson was convinced that an unholy alliance of Clay's intimates in Congress and the opposition press was under way to demolish him with a ceaseless and unconscionable whispering campaign. He complained to General Richard K. Call:

> The whole object of the coalition is to calumniate me; . . . forgeries and pamphlets of the most base calumnies are circulated by the franking privilege of Members of Congress, and Mr. Clay; even Mrs. J. is not spared, and my pious mother, nearly fifty years in the tomb, and who, from her cradle to her death, had not a speck upon her character, has been dragged forth by Hammond and held to public scorn as a prostitute who intermarried with a Negro, and my eldest brother sold as a slave in Carolina. This, Hammond does not publish in his vile press, but keeps the statement purporting to be sworn to, a forgery, and spreads it secretly.

During the final weeks of the campaign, Republican censure focused almost exclusively on the "adulterous past" of the Democratic candidate and his wife. A typical diatribe, seven days before the election, appeared in the Raleigh *Register* as a personal warning from the editor:

> I make a solemn appeal to the reflective part of the community, and beg them to think and ponder well before they place their tickets in the box, how can they justify it to themselves and posterity to place such a woman as Mrs. Jackson! at the head of the female society of the United States.

At The Hermitage, Rachel was unaware of the extent of the slander. Relatives and servants, under orders from her husband, managed to keep anti-Jackson newspapers from her, but some of the libels got through to her, for she wrote to a relative, "The enemy's of the Genl have dipt their arrows in wormwood and gall and sped them at me . . . Theay have Disquieted one in a way theay had no rite to do."

As the campaign closed she was exhausted after months of receiving a steady flow of visitors, including countless strangers who traveled long distances to satisfy their curiosity about her. Many were favorably impressed. One caller, for example, wrote that after having heard "industriously circulated a thousand slanders of her awkwardness, ignorance and indecorum," he was "pleasantly surprised to find her most striking characteristics to be an unaffected simplicity of manners, with great goodness of heart." In Washington, D. C., however, haughty hostesses wondered over their teacups what capital society would come to if "that Jackson woman" became First Lady of the land.

However, Jackson, as a symbol of new hope for the common man, had wide appeal. Furthermore, his military eminence as well as his experience in Congress carried weight, and so did his commanding personality. Therefore, the outcome of the election was a foregone conclusion several days before he won by a landslide, and to make Adams' defeat even more humiliating, his Vice President, John C. Calhoun, was reelected.

Within a short time, however, Jackson was the most miserable of devoted husbands. Rachel had collapsed with a heart attack from which there was no hope of recovery. And as she lay dying at The Hermitage, and he heard fragments of the incident that brought on her illness, heartbreaking memories engulfed him.

He knew she had never wanted to be First Lady, that she had said, "I had rather be a doorkeeper in the house of God than to live in that palace in Washington." He recalled that her two visits to the capital city had been anything but happy for her, for the women she met had ignored her, or had eyed her curiously (probably wondering whether she actually smoked a pipe, as some people said). She could hardly wait to return to The Hermitage.

Yet, he also remembered that immediately after his election she appeared to be passably resigned to prospects of living in the White House. She made plans: Andrew and Emily Donelson and their small son would reside there too, since he would be the new President's private secretary; and Rachel ordered for herself the finest materials available in Nashville for a fashionable wardrobe. Jackson was agonized when he learned that while she was having one of her new dresses fitted, she overheard whispers from an adjoining room to the effect that everybody in Washington thought she and Old Hickory had lived together in sin and that her presence in the White House would scandalize society. He was convinced that the heartless remark and other campaign gossip were responsible for her death.

She was buried on the day after Christmas, 1828, in the gown she had planned to wear to the Inaugural Ball. At her funeral Jackson grimly observed: "In the presence of this dear saint I can and do forgive all my enemies. But those vile wretches who have slandered her must look to God for mercy." Weeks later, he wrote her epitaph: "A being so gentle and virtuous, slander might wound but could not dishonor."

A noticeable reversal of Washington opinions about Mrs. Jackson was reflected shortly after she died by Margaret Bayard Smith, the popular social chronicler, as follows:

> Oh what gloom is cast over the triumph of General Jackson by the death of a wife fondly and excessively loved; of a wife, who, it is said, could control the violence of his temper, soothe the exacerbations of feelings always keenly and excessively irritable, who healed by her kind-

ness the wounds inflicted by his violence, and by her universal charity and benevolence conciliated public opinion.

In death, Mrs. Jackson was even forgiven her pipe-smoking habit. Hypercritical capital matrons who had previously deplored it quietly mentioned that many frontier women were addicted to tobacco, and that drawing it through a pipe was preferable, certainly, to the filthy custom of dipping snuff.

On New Year's Day, 1929, Margaret Bayard Smith surprised many Washingtonians with this published item:

> Tonight General Eaton, the bosom friend and almost adopted son of General Jackson, is to be married to a lady whose reputation her previous connection with him both before and after her husband's death has totally destroyed . . . She has never been admitted to good society, is very handsome, and of not an inspiring character and violent temper. She is, it is said, irresistible and carries whatever point she sets her mind on. The General's personal and political friends are very much disturbed about it . . . Dr. Simm and the Colonel Bomford's families are asked. The ladies will not go to the wedding and if they can help it will not let their husbands go.

Busybodies got the full import of Mrs. Smith's ambiguous rhetoric: Senator John Henry Eaton, of Tennessee, a Jackson intimate, was about to marry Margaret (Peggy) O'Neale Timberlake, who was believed to have been his mistress for some time. Mrs. Smith's paragraph would have titillated gossips even more had they known that the President-elect promoted the wedding.

Eaton's first wife had been a ward of Rachel and Andrew Jackson. She died five years before Eaton and Jackson entered the Senate and took lodgings at Franklin House, popularly known as O'Neale's Tavern and operated by William O'Neale.

Living there at the time was his vivacious daughter, Mrs. John Timberlake, wife of a ship's purser who had to spend much time at sea. She later would be called "a former barmaid," but she never was that. She merely welcomed her father's paying guests when she was pleased to do so, and cultivated those who caught her fancy.

A brunette beauty in her early thirties, with a flair for lively talk and an interest in politics, she was much better company and better educated than most of her socially prominent contemporaries. She had attended Mrs. Hayward's seminary in Georgetown, finished at Mr. Kirke's school in Washington, was a star pupil at Mr. Gennaro's dancing academy in Alexandria, Virginia, and studied music in New York.

Within a short time after she met Eaton, their interest in each other was obvious. She stopped flirting with other men; the senator wangled some choice assignments for her seafaring spouse and also financially assisted her father by purchasing his inn, holding it until there was a buyer, and establishing O'Neale and his family in another boardinghouse. The senator moved there, too, and used the house as his Washington headquarters while he directed Jackson's successful campaign for the presidency.

Eaton's affair with Mrs. Timberlake had been bruited around Washington for some time when her husband was found dead in a Mediterranean port. According to the official record, he expired of a pulmonary disease; capital gossip ran that he committed suicide after learning of his wife's affair with the senator.

The scandal doubly distressed Eaton, for the President-elect had promised him a Cabinet post; furthermore, he felt responsible for Mrs. Timberlake's reputation. He wrote to Jackson for advice and Old Hickory promptly answered that Eaton should either marry Mrs. Timberlake at once or move out of her father's boardinghouse.

After the quiet wedding on New Year's evening, the probability that a woman of loose morals would be a Cabinet hostess caused a furor. Margaret Bayard Smith wrote: "Public opinion will not allow General Eaton holding a place which would bring his wife into society." Concurrently, a Philadelphia minister warned the President-elect: "For your own sake, for your administration, for the credit of the government and country, you should not countenance a woman like this." Similar exhortations reached Jackson from many areas. His response was a formal announcement from The Hermitage that Eaton would be in his Cabinet.

When sad and embittered Old Hickory arrived in Washington for his inauguration in March 1829, he was prepared to give no quarter to anyone who had abused his dead wife or to anyone else who tried to scandalize his friends. He would not speak to Henry Clay (in Jackson's opinion "the basest, meanest scoundrel that ever disgraced the image of God"), and he did not make the traditional courtesy call on the retiring President. Instead, through an intermediary, Jackson informed Adams he wished to receive visitors at the executive mansion on Inauguration Day. Adams replied that the mansion would be vacated at once, and he and his wife moved that afternoon to a house they had temporarily leased on Meridian Hill. Like his father in 1801, John Quincy Adams did not attend any of his successor's inaugural events; he was not invited.

Jackson's first Cabinet appointment—despite Vice President Calhoun's strenuous objection—was that of John Eaton as Secretary of War. A capsule preview of the strange happenings that were to shake Washington and affect national politics over the next two years was evident at the Inaugural Ball. The new President did not attend; Andrew and Emily Donelson and her cousin, Mary Estin, represented him. But the two young women, along with Mrs. Calhoun and others in the official circle, were noticeably cool to the Eatons.

A few days later the Reverend Ezra Ely, of Philadelphia,

wrote to the President that the Secretary of War and his bride had been intimate while she was still married to Timberlake, and that she had also been illicitly involved with other males. Jackson hotly replied he would "entertain no rumors or suspicions" about Eaton ("a man of moral worth") or his wife. However, he added, if the Reverend Ely had "facts and proofs sustained by reputable witnesses in the light of day," he should produce them. Ely by return mail expressed the faint hope that "Margaret's repentance would justify the President's faith in her," and got a stinging answer. "Repentance presupposes the existence of a crime," Jackson wrote. "Where is the witness who has thus far come forth in substantiation of these slanderous charges?"

Ely could produce no witnesses, but he managed to rally support from a Washington clergyman, who called on the President to affirm that Mrs. Eaton was, as he put it, "a disgrace to virtuous womanhood." Similar testimonies reached Jackson later, and he was in a frenzy by the time he received another letter from Ely asserting that while Timberlake had been at sea for ten months, his wife had a miscarriage. Ely identified the source as the Reverend John N. Campbell, pastor of the Second Presbyterian Church, of Washington, D. C. Campbell, in turn, said a physician had given him the information and had fixed the date in the autumn of 1821.

Equating the attacks on Peggy's character with those that had victimized Rachel, the President determined to get at the root of the slander and to eradicate it for all time. After ordering an examination of marine records for 1821, he was able to confront Campbell with proof that Timberlake *was* in Washington in the spring of that year. The discomfited cleric spluttered that he had made a mistake in the year, that the miscarriage was in 1882. Jackson scolded Campbell for his inaccuracy and his "lack of common Christian charity" and ended the interview by resigning from Campbell's church, where he had held a membership for several years.

The President then convened his Cabinet—and asked Ely and Campbell to be present—"to examine evidence having to do with the private lives of Secretary and Mrs. Eaton." Major William B. Lewis, brother of Eaton's first wife, read a sheaf of affidavits attesting the impeccable character of John and Margaret Eaton.

The President ordered Ely to come forward with any evidence he might have to the contrary. The minister said he had no proof that Secretary Eaton had ever been guilty of misconduct. "Nor Mrs. Eaton, either?" Jackson asked ominously. Ely weakly said he had no opinion on that, whereupon the President thundered, "She is chaste as a virgin!" Campbell started to object, but Jackson demanded that he "*give* evidence—not discuss it!" The flustered preacher tried to counter; he would prove his points in court, if necessary, he said. But the President abruptly adjourned the meeting, after stern warning that he expected everyone, from then on, to treat the Eatons courteously.

However, he had reckoned without regard for the distaff furor already sweeping Washington. Cabinet wives followed Mrs. Calhoun's example and steered clear of Margaret Eaton; diplomatic hostesses also pointedly avoided her. The President was irritated enough when he heard the Vice President's wife and the Cabinet ladies were ostracizing his friend, but when he was told that the wife of the Dutch Minister Bangeman Huygens left a dinner when she learned Mrs. Eaton was expected, the effect of Old Hickory's angered expletive "By the Eternal!" struck terror through the diplomatic corps. Furthermore, even though Mme. Huygens denied she had ever been rude to Mrs. Eaton, the Dutch Minister and his wife were soon on their way home, by the President's request. He ordered a protocol change, stipulating for the first time that Cabinet members would take precedence over the foreign envoys.

John Quincy Adams, who had been elected to Congress, kept up with what was going on in the executive branch and recorded his impressions in a diary that is as pungent as a gossip column. He must have had a spy in the White House, for he commented on many happenings that were witnessed only by those in the highest official circle. Adams wrote, for example, on July 24, 1831, that the President "was like a roaring lion" about Mme. Huygens, who "had joined in the conspiracy against Mrs. Eaton," and that he had "resolved that he would send Huygens home, to teach him and his master that a wife of a member of the Cabinet should not be treated so." The diarist added, "The private morals of the country are deeply outraged by the appointment of Eaton . . . But what else could be expected from a President of the United States himself an adjudicated adulterer!"

The "Eaton Malaria" spread, even to the White House inner circle. Emily Donelson, Jackson's official hostess, was almost as infected as Mrs. Calhoun and the Cabinet ladies. At the President's insistence Emily returned one call of Secretary and Mrs. Eaton, but using the excuse that she had a three-year-old son to look after and was expecting another child within a few months, she avoided exchanging further visits with them. But she did manage to repay visits of other Cabinet members and their wives and also those of Vice President and Mrs. Calhoun.

While Mrs. Eaton complained to the President, her husband wrote to the twenty-one-year-old Mrs. Donalson:

> You are young and uninformed of the ways of the world, and therefore I speak to you . . . I have understood that a certain family have gratuitously stepped forward to become councellors, to tell you what to do and what not to do; and in secret to whisper slanders about me and my wife . . . You yourself may become the victim of those meddling gossips.

The letter closed with a reference to "your excellent aunt," a subtle reminder of Rachel Jackson's tragic experiences. Emily's response disclaimed "councellors" and went on, "Having drawn my attention to the slanders got up for political purposes to tarnish the reputation of my beloved Aunt you will suffer me to say that the most conclusive proof of her innocence was the respect in which she was universally held by her neighbors."

When the President and Andrew Donelson called on the Eatons the following week, Mrs. Eaton was visibly annoyed because the official White House hostess did not accompany them. And when Emily avoided her on a presidential excursion to Norfolk a few days later, the annoyed woman spoke to Donelson about his wife's discourtesy and broadly hinted that if it continued the President would order her back to Tennessee.

United States Treasurer David Campbell overheard the conversation and later described Mrs. Donelson as "a very amiable little woman, while Her Ladyship [Mrs. Eaton] is *decidedly* the greatest fool I ever saw in a genteel situation." Anyway, when the Donelsons left for Tennessee shortly thereafter, gossip buzzed that their abrupt departure was on presidential order.

Mrs. Eaton then enjoyed a brief period of triumph. Foreign emissaries and their wives, remembering Mme. Huygens' experience, fawned on her at White House functions. British Minister Charles Richard Vaughan, bachelor dean of the diplomatic corps, was notably attentive to her, as were Secretary of State Van Buren, a widower, who had everything to gain by ingratiating himself with the President, and Postmaster General William T. Berry, who had joined the Cabinet later than others in the official family.

Mrs. Eaton's White House ascendancy incited a renewed wave of resentment against both her and the President. The same individuals who contemptuously labeled her "the Unofficial First Lady" and "Bellona, Goddess of War" derided him as King Andrew because his iron will would brook no interference, and also because the White House under his "rule" had been redecorated "like a palace, to please that Eaton woman."

Although Jackson finally broke with Vice President Calhoun over weightier issues, the schism was accentuated by Mrs. Calhoun's snobbish conduct toward Mrs. Eaton. The rift widened when the Vice President's friends in the Cabinet—Secretary of the Treasury S. D. Ingham, Secretary of the Navy John Branch, and Attorney General John M. Berrien and their wives—gave large receptions to which the War Secretary and his wife were not invited. The President summoned the three men to his office and read them a terse statement, clearly indicating that if they persisted in mistreating Mrs. Eaton they had better withdraw from the Cabinet before they were fired.

Jackson then began to weed out pro-Calhoun individuals in his select group of unofficial advisers—his Kitchen Cabinet (so called because the chosen few often exited from the White House through the kitchen door to escape notice of curious persons around the entrance). Duff Green, editor of the *Telegraph*, was the first to be ousted, and after Francis P. Blair, editor of the new *Globe*, succeeded him, Green charged in his newspaper that Secretary Van Buren had promoted the replacement, that he wanted to undermine Calhoun's influence in order to get the vice presidential post for himself.

A consummate politician from Kinderhook, New York, Martin Van Buren had been a flesh-thorn to Calhoun and his crowd for some time, and their enmity grew as he strengthened his hand with the President. Even before that, Calhoun's friends in the press had called Van Buren "an opportunist" and "a corseted, aristocratic dandy" and occasionally had subtly recalled the old rumor—that he was the illegitimate son of Aaron Burr.

That story had started while Van Buren was a young lawyer

in the office of William P. Van Ness (Burr's second in the duel that ended Alexander Hamilton's life). Burr's extraordinary interest in a man twenty-six years his junior prompted many to speculate that Van Buren was his son and the latter's suave personality and flair for political intrigue seemed to bear out that theory. John Quincy Adams noted in his diary "much resemblance of character, manners, and even person between the two men."

In at least one respect, however, the two were perceptively dissimilar. Burr was a womanizer; Van Buren was never emotionally involved with another woman after his wife died at the birth of their fourth son, sixteen years before he entered the Cabinet. His strategic friendship with Mrs. Eaton was merely a road to political advancement, and he traveled it cleverly. While Vice President and Mrs. Calhoun continued to avoid her, the Secretary of State escorted her and her husband to diplomatic receptions, attended their parties, and honored her at dinner. Also, he managed to persuade other officials and their wives to be courteous to her. John Quincy Adams wryly noted in his diary: "Calhoun leads the moral party, Van Buren the frail sisterhood."

Solidly entrenched with the President in the late summer of 1831, Van Buren quietly suggested that a new Cabinet might bring an end to the Eaton imbroglio. Shortly thereafter, he and the Secretary of War submitted their resignations and induced Ingham, Berrien and Branch to do the same. Mrs. Eaton had toppled the balance of power in the United States government.

The President appointed Van Buren his Minister to Great Britain, while Eaton and his wife prepared to leave for Tennessee. Hoping to be reappointed to the Senate, Eaton sought to counteract the scandal about his wife by circulating a pamphlet entitled "A Candid Appeal to the American Public." Similar to one he had written in defense of Rachel Jackson in the 1828 campaign, it began as follows:

In civilized society, a man's house is his castle, and the circle of his family a sanctuary never to be violated. He who drags before the public its helpless inmates, and subjects them to rude assaults, deserves to be considered worse than a barbarian. Against those who commit such a sacrilege, and shun honorable accountability, the public will justify an appeal.

When Eaton was not reappointed to the Senate, the President made him governor of Florida and, later, sent him as Minister to Spain. There Peggy became a great favorite of the Queen of Spain, and the Eatons' daughter eventually married a duke.

Van Buren's unanticipated setback shortly after he left the Cabinet also turned out to be a blessing. He was on his way to London when Senate friends of Calhoun and Clay blocked his diplomatic appointment; but he capitalized on the martyr role, charmed the British, and returned to the United States as a dedicated public servant who had been victimized by loyalty to his President. At Jackson's invitation, the first national political convention in the country nominated Van Buren for the vice presidency, the post that Calhoun had held through two administrations.

Old Hickory's place at the head of the Democratic ticket was already assured, for regardless of the dissension in Washington during much of his first term, he was highly esteemed throughout the country. He defeated his old enemy Henry Clay by a tremendous margin.

The President's sadness gradually subsided during the second term of the "Jackson Revolution," when Emily Donelson returned as White House hostess, and her youngsters and visiting relatives enlivened his hours of relaxation. His hard-won success in increasing the power of the highest office and in bringing about unparalleled monetary reforms was widely appreciated, and his prestige continued to rise. He was one of our few Presidents to leave office more popular than when first elected. Yet, nothing could erase his bitter memories of the censure of Rachel and of character assaults that had caused so much needless contention in his first term. At the final meeting of his Kitchen Cabinet, in Francis P. Blair's house across from the executive mansion, he was asked whether he had any regrets about his eight years in the White House, and he replied that he had two: he wished he had hanged Calhoun—or shot Clay.

With only a small sum in cash and a debt of ten thousand dollars, Old Hickory retired to The Hermitage, which would be his base of operations while he wielded enormous influence in the Democratic party for the next ten years.

Four years before he died, John and Margaret Eaton returned to the United States; and a few months later Eaton died, leaving his widow a small fortune. But the woman who had disrupted the balance of power in the Jackson administration was not destined for a serene existence—ever. At sixty-one, she married Antonio Buchignani, a dancing teacher, after deeding all her holdings to him. He eloped to Italy with her granddaughter in less than a year, and in dire straits the deserted woman worked as a dressmaker in New York for some time. She spent her last years in Washington, and when she died, in 1879, President and Mrs. Hayes sent flowers to her funeral, many notables attended, and an obituary recalled her as "beautiful to see, interesting to hear, and always a perfect lady." A few years previously she had written:

> This I do affirm, that I have been spotlessly faithful to each of my three husbands, and if all were there on the other side of the grave, I could look each of them in the face and say, Margaret was frivolous, wayward, passionate, but so far as you were concerned she was faithful unto death.

Whatever her shortcomings might have been, she was grateful to the President, who had championed her to the fullest extent of his power. Not long before she died she was asked what she thought of Andrew Jackson as a man. "A *man!*" she exclaimed. "He was a *god!*"

Jackson's immeasurable political influence during the last decade of his life, and for many years thereafter, was indicated in four presidential elections before the Civil War. He selected his successor, Martin Van Buren, and was the single most important factor in the nomination and election of James K. Polk. Franklin Pierce, the first New Englander after John Quincy Adams to reach the presidency, and James Buchanan, who had been Jackson's Minister to Russia, also went to the White House on the strength of being staunch Jacksonian Democrats.

There was little left for Van Buren's enemies to bring up against him in the 1836 campaign. His connection with the Eaton affair had been exhaustively exposed and people were tired of talking about it. Gossip about his illegitimacy had also lost its force. Scandalmongers therefore concentrated on his running mate, Richard M. Johnson, of Kentucky. Old Hickory had personally selected him, but even with that prestigious backing, Johnson barely won, for he was said to have a Negro mistress, Julia Chinn, who had borne him two sons. He did not receive a majority; his victory had to come through Congress. And throughout his term there was much gossip about his first slave mistress, who escaped from him and married an Indian, and about Mrs. Chinn, who presided over his dinners and referred to him as "My dear Colonel."

Johnson was not renominated in 1840. Van Buren was, but he lost the election to the Whig candidate, William Henry Harrison. Four years later, the Democrats chose James K. Polk, Jackson's protégé, to oppose Henry Clay.

Polk could thank Old Hickory for the opposition's inability

to attack his character. Twenty-three years before he ran for the presidency, incessant whispers that he was a "woman chaser" threatened his promising career. Jackson advised him "to marry a good woman and settle down," and within six months he wed nineteen-year-old Sarah Childress, a strict Calvinist. From then on, there was no more gossip about him.

Seven years after Jackson died, Franklin Pierce, a loyal Jacksonian of New Hampshire, won the presidency, despite Whig charges that he was a drunkard and a coward in the Mexican War. He was not a coward; he had been prostrated by heat on the battlefield. But he did have a drinking problem and a mentally unstable wife. At the end of his term he was not renominated, but the Jacksonians remained in power with James Buchanan, who had been Polk's Secretary of State and Pierce's Minister at the Court of St. James's.

A Pennsylvanian, born in a log cabin while Washington was President, Buchanan amassed wealth in private law practice and served in the Pennsylvania House of Representatives before he was elected to the United States Congress. Subsequent posts in diplomacy, the Senate and the Cabinet whetted his ambition for the highest office, and ignoring formidable opposition and persistent charges that he was a "vacillating opportunist," he contended for the presidential nomination three times before he got it.

In his 1856 campaign against James C. Fremont for the Republicans and former President Millard Fillmore for the Know-Nothings, familiar criticisms of Buchanan were bolstered by rumors that he had kept a mistress for many years. Patently stemming from conjectures as to why the rich, sixty-five-year-old Democratic candidate had never married, the slander was short-lived. Everyone who knew anything about his personal life could vouch for his stainless character, and many attributed his long bachelorhood to a tragedy thirty-seven years before he became the presidential nominee. He was a lawyer in Lancaster, Pennsylvania, when he became engaged to Anne Coleman, a beautiful heiress. A lovers' quarrel disrupted their wedding plans and she committed suicide. The grief-stricken Buchanan wrote to her father, asking permission to join the family in the funeral procession. The letter returned unopened and friends believed heartbreak at that time prompted the young man to resolve that he would never marry.

The Democratic candidate's two visits to Polk's widow in Tennessee started gossip, however, that he hoped to bring her back to the White House. Her husband had been dead seven years, and Washingtonians recalled that Buchanan had been especially attentive to her while he served in Polk's Cabinet. But the ascetic Sarah Polk did not fit in with Buchanan's idea of a socially brilliant administration. Just after his inauguration he installed as White House hostess his niece and ward, twenty-two-year-old Harriet Lane, who had been with him in London. She was attractive, fashionable and keenly conscious of the nuances of protocol and the importance of entertaining with an elegant flair. The executive mansion soon took on the atmosphere of a European court.

President Buchanan, meanwhile, was harassed by Washington widows, who surrounded him at White House receptions and openly vied with each other to charm him. At the same time, hopeful females with no prospects of meeting him socially wrote affectionate notes, begging permission to call on him at his office. Attorney General Jeremiah Black reported that countless letters came in from women who were utter strangers, asking how and when they could see the President alone, and one widow repeatedly requested Black to make arrangements for her to marry Buchanan as soon as possible.

Social climbers finally gave up on the White House bachelor and cultivated Miss Lane. She had complete charge of his invitation lists, anyway, and the parties she managed were increasingly resplendent. President Buchanan at the end of his single term, which had been beset by threats of secession, could look back on his administration as a social triumph at least. And he was still a bachelor.

Harriet Lane's brilliant tenure as White House hostess had something to do with the personal sadness of Buchanan's successor, Abraham Lincoln. As he struggled to preserve the Union through the Civil War, Mrs. Lincoln dreamed of presiding over a succession of social functions approximating if not surpassing those that had accented the Buchanan administration. Her frustration intensified her physical disorders (migraine and recurring chills and fever), and coupled with grief over the death of the Lincolns' son Willie, eventually affected her mind. Meanwhile, her unhappiness prompted suspicions that it might have been brought on by her husband's unfaithfulness.

At any time other than the catastrophic one in which her husband was elected President, Mary Todd Lincoln might have been a popular First Lady. She was born to wealth in Kentucky; she had attended exclusive schools; and she was politically astute and attractive. As a young lady she was quite a belle, especially during her frequent sojourns with her brother-in-law and sister, Mr. and Mrs. Ninian Wirt Edwards, in Springfield, Illinois. Their home was an exclusive social center, in which spirited Mary Todd was courted by several prominent young men before she fell in love with Abraham Lincoln. Later, she had enjoyed a taste of social life in Washington while her husband served for one term in the House of Representatives and they lived in Mrs. Ann G. Sprigg's boarding-house, which catered to a select clientele. Even then, she dreamed of the day when her Abe would win the highest office. She said to one of his intimate friends, "He is to be President of the United States some day; if I had not thought so I never would have married him, for you can see that he is not pretty.

But look at him! Doesn't he look as if he might make a magnificent President?"

Excessive ambition was one of her dominating qualities. Even more painful to those around her were her ungovernable temper, her jealousy and her extravagance. Yet, she was tender-hearted, deeply religious and, at her best, a stimulating talker with a lively sense of humor. Furthermore, she loved her husband deeply and she was an affectionate mother.

Lincoln appreciated her attributes, excused her tantrums and puzzled everybody by his infinite patience with her. But, in the presidency, he was absorbed much of the time with difficult generals and Cabinet members as he struggled to work out military strategy and to improvise foreign and domestic policies. Besides, there was nothing he could do to ingratiate his wife with the socially entrenched people whom she wanted to impress.

Everything seemed to work against her. Capital snobs looked askance at her expensive clothes. Uninvited nonentities thronged White House functions while distinguished persons were conspicuously missing. And when she tried to limit one reception to five hundred and fifty *invited* guests, the result was disaster. The country had been at war for ten months, and even though the New York *Herald* unexpectedly praised her for "trying to weed out the Presidential Mansion of the long-haired, white coated, tobacco-chewing and expectorant abolitionist politicians," hundreds who had not been invited criticized the President for giving any kind of party while Union soldiers were dying on the battlefield. Meanwhile, a Philadelphia newspaper ridiculed Mrs. Lincoln's elaborate reception in an article entitled "The Queen Must Dance." There were no more White House parties for some time. Eight-year-old William Wallace (Willie) Lincoln died of pneumonia within a month, and the cloud of gloom that settled over the executive mansion was not lifted for more than two years.

Even while she was overwhelmed with grief, Mary Lincoln got little sympathy. Southerners, already antagonistic to her because she had received Abolitionists at the White House, seized on any excuse to criticize her. Typical of their attitude was a South Carolinian's published comment: "Mrs. Lincoln at least had the privilege of seeing her son die, instead of having to send him out to be killed on the battlefield." Northerners were ever mindful that she was from a slaveholding family and that she had a brother, three half brothers and three brothers-in-law in Confederate uniform. Many believed she was a Confederate spy.

Concurrently, Lincoln was berated by extremists in his own party, who were enraged by his leniency toward the South. They labeled him "poor white trash" and "the baboon" and "the Kentucky mule." William Lloyd Garrison publicly impugned his integrity, and the New York *Herald* carried on: "President Lincoln is a joke incarnated. His election was a sorry joke . . . His title "Honest" is a satirical joke . . ."

Lincoln took the mounting criticism in philosophic stride and occasionally managed to alleviate his melancholy with a pertinent anecdote. A master tale teller, he was able even in his darkest hours to relieve tensions with amusing stories, which seemed to put everything in bearable perspective.

The men who worked with him in the White House loved him and felt sorry for him and tried to help him. But their devotion to the chief they affectionately called The Tycoon did not extend to Mrs. Lincoln, particularly after she emerged from her mourning shell and resumed her officious behavior. As before, she constantly irritated the President's secretaries, John Hay and John G. Nicolay. Hay privately called her the hell-cat and complained that she dismissed the White House steward and others on the domestic staff in order to juggle the budget to meet some of her exorbitant clothing bills. But both Hay and Nicolay shared the President's distress at rumors that she was a spy, for they realized, as he did, that she was being victimized by calculated sabotage.

It was the First Lady's inordinate jealousy of her husband, however, that aroused suspicions about his morals. Since the President's social conduct toward women was exemplary—he was merely courteous to them—his wife's apparent mistrust of him, and of any female who had more than a passing word with him, piqued the curiosity of meddlers and led to conjectures that something in the Lincolns' marriage was not as it should be—something, perhaps, which was mysteriously rooted in the past. Meanwhile, impressions that the First Lady was unduly concerned about her own status were corroborated by a series of White House episodes; and as they were noised about Washington, inferences were quickly drawn that Lincoln himself might be responsible for her obvious unhappiness.

Early in the administration her enforced revision of protocol was attributed to her displeasure when any other woman walked beside her husband at White House functions. Established official procedure had long stipulated that the President was to lead reception promenades with the wife of the ranking guest, while the First Lady followed with the woman's husband. The convention vexed Mrs. Lincoln. She complied with it for a time and then gave warning she would endure it no longer. She was quoted: "As Mrs. President I should go on the President's arm. No other woman should precede Mrs. Abraham Lincoln, the wife of the President of the United States." After that, Lincoln was either accompanied by another man, or by her.

Her resentment of beauteous and brilliant Mrs. William Sprague, daughter of Secretary of the Treasury William P. Chase, was said to have started because she thought Mrs. Sprague ignored her and was aggressively attentive to the President at an official party. Subsequently she tried to exclude Mrs. Sprague and her husband, the senator from Rhode Island, from a Cabinet dinner to which relatives of the honor guests were normally invited. Nicolay noted that their names were not on the invitation list and questioned Mrs. Lincoln. He reported later, "There arose such a rampage as the House hasn't seen in a year." In any case, he took the matter to the President, and the senator and his wife attended the dinner. Nicolay further noted that "having compelled her S. Majesty to invite the Spragues, I was taboo." Mrs. Lincoln had decided to bar him from the dinner, but perhaps at Lincoln's insistence, the secretary attended. A guest at the event later observed, "Mrs. President seethed all evening."

Backstairs White House gossip buzzed that Mrs. Lincoln constantly warned her husband about females who might try to monopolize him at social events. A report went that before one reception she cautioned him "not to be flirtatious with silly women," and he reacted with a chuckle and then asked her for a list of the ladies he *could* talk to—and how long.

Whispered reports from Springfield floated to Washington and added to suspicions about happenings in the past. The former Mary Todd's brother-in-law, Ninian Edwards, was said to have objected strenuously to her marrying Abe Lincoln ("a mighty rough fellow," in Edwards' opinion) and once had persuaded her to break the engagement. Converse impressions were that Lincoln called off the wedding once because he fell in love with another girl and that Miss Todd managed to disrupt that romance and married him "for spite." Lincoln's former Springfield law partner William H. (Billy) Herndon reputedly said that the Lincolns' marriage was "unhappy from the beginning, for reasons not to be discussed." (He would discuss them at great length later, much to Mrs. Lincoln's distress.) Others intimated that Mary Todd's relatives opposed her engagement to Lincoln because they thought his parents were never married. (He was not illegitimate; his mother, Nancy Hanks, was.) Still other rumors purported that Lincoln in his younger years "was quite a ladies' man," and that "his wife had always been jealous of him, probably with good cause."

Invidious inferences were drawn from the letter Lincoln wrote shortly after his presidential nomination to eleven-year-old Grace Bedell, of Westfield, New York. It was a reply to her note, suggesting that he grow a beard "because all the ladies like whiskers and they would tease their husbands to vote for you and you would be President." If he did not have time to reply, she added, he might ask his little girl to write, instead. He answered:

My dear little Miss.
　　Your very agreeable letter of the 15th received—
　　I regret the necessity of saying I have no daughter. I have three sons, one seventeen, one nine, and one seven years of age. They, with their mother, constitute my whole family.
　　As to whiskers, having never worn any, do you think people would call it a silly affection if I were to begin now?
　　　　　　　　Your very sincere well wishes—
　　　　　　　　　　　A. Lincoln

Scandalmongers interpreted the peculiar wording of the second sentence (*I regret the necessity of saying I have no daughter*) to mean that he had one whom he could not acknowledge. That theory, bolstered by assumptions that Mrs. Lincoln knew about her husband's illegitimate child, quickly developed into veiled explanations for the First Lady's emotional insecurity.

The traducement had extensive Washington circulation during the President's reelection campaign. And but for his untimely death, it might have come out in the open later, for Mrs. Lincoln's jealous outbursts within a month after her husband's second inauguration invited further unpleasant gossip.

The war was nearing its end when President and Mrs. Lincoln and an official party boarded the *River Queen,* for City Point, Virginia. The official schedule included a review of a part of the Army of the James, commanded by General Edward O. C. Ord, and dinner in honor of the President, with General and Mrs. Ulysses S. Grant as hosts at army headquarters. Mrs. Lincoln was upset even before the boat made its first stop. General Adam Badeau had remarked that they would see General Charles Griffin's delightful wife in the course of the trip, as she had been with her husband at the front for some time —by special permission of the President. The idea that Mrs. Griffin might personally have obtained the favor visibly disturbed the First Lady. Her nerves were still on edge the following day, when the party proceeded to the field inspection. Most of the men were on horseback, well ahead of Mrs. Lincoln and Mrs. Grant, who rode in an "ambulance," a half-open conveyance, with General Badeau. Things were amiable enough on the surface until a young officer reined his horse alongside the vehicle and said, "The President is very gallant, Mrs. Lincoln. He insists on riding by the side of Mrs. Ord." News that the commanding general's stunning wife was leading the procession with the President enraged Mrs. Lincoln. She tried to leap from the carriage. General Badeau had difficulty in restraining her, and when Mrs. Grant tried to calm her she retorted, "And I suppose *you* think *you'll* get to the White House yourself, don't you?" The overwrought woman was still seething when the carriage reached its destination. She greeted Mrs. Ord with such a torrent of abuse that the berated woman retired in tears. For the remainder of the day, Mrs. Lincoln intermittently rebuked the President. Each time, he softly addressed her as "Mother," and tried to soothe her. Finally he took her to quarters where she could not be observed by others.

That evening, when she and the President entertained General and Mrs. Grant on the boat, Mrs. Lincoln demanded that

General Ord be relieved of his command at once, and when General Grant objected she lambasted him. Again, Lincoln tried to placate her, and after he had persuaded her to retire, he explained to his guests that a recurrence of migraine was responsible for her outbursts of temper. When Grant and several other officers boarded the boat the next morning, Lincoln greeted them without his wife; she was "not well," he said. Within a few hours she was on her way back to Washington with a special escort. She had regained her composure two days later, when she rejoined the presidential party for its return to Washington on the weekend of Lee's surrender at Appomattox Courthouse.

As a peace celebration, and also to repay General and Mrs. Grant for their hospitality at army headquarters, Mrs. Lincoln invited them to attend the theater with her and the President on Good Friday evening, April 14. The prospective guests perhaps did not wish to be further embarrassed by the erratic First Lady; anyway, a few hours before the curtain went up at Ford's Theatre, Mrs. Grant sent word that she and the general had to get back to their children before nightfall. Mrs. Lincoln then invited Miss Clara Harris, a senator's daughter, and her fiancé, Major Henry R. Rathbone, to accompany her and the President and to sit with them in the box—where he was fatally wounded.

While the nation grieved for the martyred President, evil insinuations about his character abruptly ceased. And in Washington, particularly, mourning for the Great Emancipator, "the man of sorrow," mingled with memories of the loving kindness he had consistently shown toward his ailing and erratic wife.

Seventeen months after the assassination, William Herndon, Lincoln's law partner for sixteen years, stated in a public lecture in Springfield that his friend's "one and only great romance was with Ann Rutledge." According to Herndon's story, young Abe fell in love with the eighteen-year-old girl while he lived in New Salem, Illinois, and stayed at Rutledge Tavern, run by her father. She was engaged at the time to a John McNamar, who had left the town some months previously; and as she became more and more attracted to Lincoln her conflicting emotions and distress brought on brain fever, from which she died seven years before he married. He was virtually insane for months after Ann's death, the lecture went on, and he never fully recovered from his grief. In Herndon's words, "His heart was buried in her grave."

Rumors that Lincoln had proposed marriage to several girls before he became engaged to Mary Todd had spread around Springfield for years, and some of the talk had mentioned "a New Salem girl," but Herndon was the first person to identify her publicly as Ann Rutledge. His disclosure was reported in the press and the story swept the country.

Mrs. Lincoln, making her home in Chicago at the time, was stunned. She vowed she had never heard of Ann Rutledge, and she urged Judge David Davis, Lincoln's close friend for many years, to get in touch at once with Herndon "to direct his *wandering* mind." Davis did nothing about Herndon, but he must have tried to mollify Mrs. Lincoln by suggesting that every young man has a little romance in his early life, for she replied by letter:

> As you justly remark, each & every one has had a little romance in their early days—but as my husband was *truth itself,* and as he always assured me, he cared for no one but myself . . . I shall assuredly remain firm in my conviction that Ann Rutledge is a myth—for in all his confidential communications, such a romantic name was never breathed . . . Nor did his life or his joyous laugh, lead one to suppose his heart, was in any unfortunate woman's grave—but in the proper place with his loved wife & children.

Mrs. Lincoln's son Robert asked Herndon to refrain from repeating the story, while members of the Rutledge family professed to know nothing about Ann's romance with Abe. Many in New Salem remembered that the lovely girl's death had deeply shocked and disturbed her friends, including twenty-six-year-old Lincoln, but they also recalled that within a year he was courting Mary Owens, daughter of a rich Kentucky landowner, who frequently visited her sister in New Salem. Despite widely expressed doubts, Herndon insisted that his account was accurate; but many people continued to believe that he had exaggerated Abe's love for Ann Rutledge in order to embarrass Mrs. Lincoln.

Herndon had cause to dislike her. She had not disguised her distaste for her husband's junior law partner during their years in Springfield. He drank heavily and was not acceptable to local aristocrats; she would have nothing to do with him. Not once during his long association with Lincoln was he invited to dine in his partner's home.

Several years after Herndon first revealed the story of Ann Rutledge, Ward Hill Lamon, another one-time law associate of Lincoln, repeated it, with embellishments, in his *Life of Lincoln*. Neither the material nor the writing was Lamon's. He had purchased all the letters, interviews, impressions and records Herndon had collected up to two years before the biography was published and had employed Chauncey Black, a journalist, to write the biography.

In addition to playing up Lincoln's romance with Ann Rutledge, Lamon's book related a number of incidents purporting that the Lincoln-Todd union was a disaster from the beginning —indeed, that Lincoln never really loved Mary Todd and had many misgivings about marrying her.

Mrs. Lincoln's agonized reaction to the book was shown in a letter to Judge Davis, referring to the "base character of the author" and "the sensational falsehoods & calumnies, wherewith he may . . . enrich *his* coffers." Then, again, she asked her late husband's old friend to set the record straight; again, he refrained from doing so.

She had been dead for seven years when Herndon's *Life of Lincoln*, in collaboration with Jesse W. Weik, a young journalist, further fixed in the public mind the romance with Ann Rutledge and a mass of allegations about the Lincolns' loveless marriage. Particularly surprising to residents of Springfield was the strange episode Herndon described as taking place on the day Lincoln had mentioned in a letter as "the fatal day of Jan'y. '41."

According to Herndon's book, Mary and Abe had planned to be married on New Year's afternoon, 1841. Everything was in readiness for the quiet ceremony at the Edwards' home: the parlor was banked with flowers, the supper was ready, and Mary and the preacher stood waiting at the appointed hour—but the prospective bridegroom did not appear. The Edwardses and Mary naturally thought Lincoln had lost his mind, and she promptly called off the engagement. Herndon did not explain how it was resumed, but he portrayed his friend as a reluctant bridegroom, eleven months after the first ceremony failed to materialize, and, quoted the best man: "Lincoln looked and acted as if he was going to the slaughter." That was a fitting prelude for Herndon's subsequent contention that Lincoln's "lost love" and his tempestuous marriage were largely responsible for his recurrent melancholy.

The controversial biography came out more than four decades after the marriage, but still living in Springfield were individuals who had known the Lincolns, and most of them gave the book a cool reception. Several vowed they had never heard about the non-wedding day, while members of the Edwards family would not even discuss the book. A few other Springfield residents recalled that Mary Todd had many suitors, including "Little Giant" Stephen A. Douglas, before she accepted Lincoln's proposal; that Ninian Edwards and his wife were lukewarm about the marriage, presumably because of Lincoln's humble background; and that the disheartened Abe became convinced he was not good enough for Mary Todd and began courting Matilda Edwards, Ninian's cousin. As to the marriage, however, old-timers remembered that it was as blissful as most others, except for Mrs. Lincoln's constant complaints about her husband's protracted absences from home while he traveled the legal circuit. At any rate, the dominant impression in Springfield was that Herndon had given a misleading interpretation to virtually everything pertaining to Mrs. Lincoln, and that his Ann Rutledge story was a complete fabrication.

In other areas the biography was generally accepted as factual because the co-author had been closely associated with the subject over a long period. Lincoln biographers for years thereafter drew heavily on Herndon's account. Edgar Lee Masters immortalized Ann Rutledge in his *Spoon River Anthology*, and other writers made much of Lincoln's "lost love" and his turbulent marriage until authorities found that many of Herndon's episodes could not be substantiated. Today, the romance with Ann Rutledge is regarded as fictitious, as are a number of the engagement and marital sequences in the book.

Yet, since it is not credible that Herndon perpetrated the Rutledge story and unpleasant incidents about the marriage solely because he hated Mrs. Lincoln, researchers in more recent years have been increasingly puzzled about his actual motivation.

Herndon idolized his old law partner; he wrote that Lincoln was "the best, the kindest, tenderest, noblest, loveliest since Christ!" Why, then, did he portray Lincoln as dishonest in that he married a woman he did not love? And why did the inventive biographer consistently depreciate the mother of Lincoln's sons? Herndon called his hero "the most secretive man I ever knew," but during their many years' partnership, he must have known more about Lincoln's personal life than most of his other friends and associates. Was Herndon privy to a hidden chapter which, if ever revealed, might destroy Lincoln's image? Did he deliberately produce falsehoods as protective coloring for something more damaging that might someday be exposed?

Skepticism about Lincoln's character drifted through both his presidential campaigns. In 1860, particularly, Herndon and others around Lincoln struggled to promote the idea that the Republican nominee was indeed Honest Abe, and that his only imperfection was his periodic despondency, due to heredity or excessive hardships in youth or, perhaps, thwarted love some years before he met Mary Todd.

Carl Sandburg's exhaustive biography of Lincoln suggests disconcerting impressions about the Republican presidential candidate in the summer of 1860:

> There was about him something spreading and elusive and mysterious . . . something out-of-the ordinary . . . in Springfield and elsewhere, whispers floated of circumstances so misty and strange that political friends wished they could be cleared up and made respectable.

If Herndon's portrayal of Lincoln's personal life was an effort to offset possible posthumous scandal about him, so, perhaps, was Ward Hill Lamon's account, the first book to feature Ann Rutledge, along with distressing incidents in the Lincolns' marriage. Lamon had no reason to dislike Mrs. Lincoln. He had often been a guest in her Springfield home while he was Lincoln's law associate in Danville, Illinois. Later she suggested Lamon's appointment as marshal of the District of Columbia, and he spent much time at the White House. Mrs. Lincoln regarded him as a loyal friend; yet his book was unkind to her. Why? She was also devoted to Lincoln's intimate, Judge David Davis; she promoted his appointment to the Supreme Court, and he was her legal adviser after her husband's death. She was distressed when he did not publicly deny Herndon's first story about Ann Rutledge and Lamon's later account, but she continued to be friendly with Davis—until he approved her sanity trial, which put her behind bars for two years.

The subtle but persistent efforts of Herndon and Lamon and, to a lesser degree, Davis, to perpetuate legends which could explain Lincoln's melancholy bring up the question: Were these three close friends of Lincoln subconsciously joined in a compassionate conspiracy to justify something irregular in his personal life, some dark secret that might later come to light and debase his fame for all time? Recent research has uncovered some indications that they were.

In the 1960s, while ascertaining the importance of a signed lithograph of Lincoln that had been in possession of her family for almost a century, a popular author in New York came across a number of clues that seem to point to conclusive evidence that Lincoln had an illegitimate child. A maze of strange associations and concurrent episodes in his life during his Springfield years were uncovered in the course of the investigation. His prolonged absences from home—about which his wife constantly complained—took on special significance as the researcher traced certain of his mysterious sojourns and activities through the 1850s and, also, some of the pressures that were brought to bear on President Lincoln by persons who could have known something unsavory about his past. Finally, on the basis of a mass of obscure documents, confidential letters, old photographs and contemporary comments, the writer concluded that Lincoln was the father of a girl born in Hazelwood, Illinois, in 1855 or 1856.

The child's history from birth through the years in which she was reared by three successive sets of foster parents—all of whom had connections with Lincoln—will throw new light on our sixteenth President if the girl's relationship with him can be substantiated. Certainly, evidence that he had a child whom he loved but could not acknowledge would explain the curtain of myths that Herndon, Lamon and Davis tried to draw around his personal history, and, also, his wife's jealousy and her insistence in a letter to Davis after Lincoln's death that "he cared for no one but myself."

In any case, the fame of the Great Emancipator, our saddest and most appealing President, could not be reduced by anything that might be brought out today about his private life. Yet, if his political opposition in 1860 could have learned he had a daughter out of wedlock, he would never have been President.

Thirty-two years later, the Democratic nominee for the highest office openly admitted he had an illegitimate son—and went on to the White House.

IV

"Ma! Ma! Where's My Pa?"

Chester Alan Arthur, Grover Cleveland and William McKinley were the last three Presidents in the nineteenth century to be persistently slandered. Yet, only in Arthur's case was the calumny politically damaging enough to gratify his foes; and even with him the character assaults would have been negligible in effect if they had not been subtly orchestrated with other criticism.

When President Garfield died on September 19, 1881, eleven weeks after he was felled by an assassin's bullet, there was wide apprehension across the country about the man who would succeed him in the White House. The general public knew virtually nothing about Vice President Arthur, except that he had never before held an elective office and that President Hayes in 1878 had dismissed him from the collectorship of the Port of New York, a post to which he had been appointed by President Grant. Delegates to the 1880 Republican national convention were well aware, however, that Arthur was nominated to the second place on the ticket as a sop to the powerful New York Senator Roscoe Conkling who, with other Stalwarts in the party, had hoped to return Grant to the highest office. The other faction, the Half Breeds, after having victoriously promoted Garfield to lead the ticket, grudgingly voted for Arthur, Conkling's friend, for the vice presidential nomination.

Hostility to Arthur sharpened after Charles J. Guiteau, a thwarted office seeker, shot Garfield and triumphantly shouted, "I am a Stalwart and Arthur is President now!" The widely publicized follow-up quoted a distressed man, "Chet Arthur! President of the United States! Good God!" He expressed the feeling of many other perturbed people across the nation.

When Arthur took his presidential oath in his house in New York, his good friend Elihu Root observed:

> Surely no more lonely and pathetic figure was ever seen assuming the powers of government. He had no people behind him, for Garfield, not he, was the people's choice; he had no party behind him, for the dominant faction of the party hated his name—were enraged by his advancement, and distrusted his motives. He had not even his own faction behind him, for he already knew that discharge of his duties would not accord with the ardent desires of their partnership, and that disappointment and estrangement lay before him there . . .

Arthur already was anathema to Democrats because he was a Republican, and antipathy from the Half Breeds in his own party intensified when he replaced James G. Blaine, Garfield's Secretary of State, with Frederick T. Frelinghuysen, who had been senator from New Jersey. Pointed disapproval of the new President had surfaced earlier, when he refused to live in the dilapidated White House and said he would pay for redecoration out of his own pocket if Congress would not provide sufficient funds. The appropriation was granted, and he lived for fifteen months in a Nevada senator's residence on Capitol Hill while Louis Comfort Tiffany refurbished the executive mansion. Whether the President's detractors liked it or not—and they professed they did not—officialdom and the elite in residential Washington were in for a resplendent social schedule that would surpass even that of the Buchanan administration.

The program started immediately after the handsome fifty-two-year-old widower and his ten-year-old daughter, Nell—his son, Alan, was at Princeton—moved into the White House and he designated his widowed sister, Mrs. John McElroy, as his official hostess. She presided at elaborate teas for ladies two or three times a month and gave suppers for special friends after the frequent White House receptions. The President entertained at least fifty dinner guests at a time and plied them with epicurean repasts in fourteen courses, with from six to eight imported wines. After attending one such event, Mrs. Blaine caustically observed, "The dinner was extremely elegant, hardly a trace of the old White House taint anywhere, the flowers, the damask, the silver, the attendants, all showing the latest style and an abandon in expense and taste." The President's fondness for luxury was noted further by jaundiced eyes when he rode forth in his magnificent green landau. Drawn by splendid bays, the conveyance was emblazoned with his family coat of arms above the initials "C. A."

His fashionable attire, which set off his six feet height and his mustache and whiskers, also drew adverse comment from those who equated fastidious taste with shallowness. Mrs. Blaine reported that immediately after Garfield died, the incoming President ordered twenty-five suits from the best tailor in New York for White House functions. She went on: "All his ambition seem to center in the social aspect of the situation. Flowers and wine and food, and slow pacing with a lady on his

arm, and a quotation from Thackeray or Dickens, or an old Joe
Miller told with an uninterfered-with particularity—for who
would interrupt or refuse to laugh at a President's joke?—
these make up his book of life, whose leaves are certainly not
for the healing of the nation."

To Mrs. Blaine and her friends the President's grandiose
aptitudes and studied conduct seemed unbecoming in a Baptist minister's son who had been reared in humble parsonages
and was a minor schoolteacher before he became a political
hack and then the controversial customs officer at the Port of
New York. Arthur's critics consistently failed to mention that
he was a Phi Beta Kappa graduate of Union College, where he
had developed an absorbing interest in literature; that his late
wife was the daughter of a naval hero, Commander William
Lewis Herndon, member of a distinguished Virginia family;
that Arthur was quartermaster of New York during the Civil
War; and that for twenty-five years before he was appointed to
the customs post he conducted a profitable law practice in the
city.

From the beginning of his administration the President was
pursued by husband-hunting spinsters and widows. Rumors
flowed constantly that he was on the verge of marriage, and at
one time gossip identified Frances Willard, the temperance
advocate, as his prospective bride. But when no engagement
announcement was forthcoming, and the President showed a
marked lack of interest in a succession of predatory females,
Washington talk started that he had a mistress.

His secretive personal calendar gave some credence to the
gossip. Aside from the White House functions, he kept his
evenings free for his own amusement, and being a self-con-
fessed "night person," he frequently entertained intimates at
late suppers, which went on until 2 or 3 A.M. His concealment
of guest lists from his staff—and, so it was said, even from Mrs.
McElroy—gave rise to rumors that the parties revolved around
his paramour. But imaginative scandalmongers could not

agree on who she was, and her identity has not been established to this day. Some whispers had it that she was the daughter of a Supreme Court Justice; others, that she might be the daughter of his Secretary of State; still others, that she could be a New York widow who had followed him to Washington. A report from a White House maid that he placed a bouquet, every day, before a photograph of an attractive woman added to the mystery—and created still more idle talk.

Impressions that Arthur was morally lax increased when he attended a garish wedding at the Willard Hotel. The bridegroom was the fabulously rich Colorado Senator H. A. W. Tabor, a vulgarian who buttoned his waistcoat with huge diamonds and was given to language unacceptable in polite drawing rooms. The bride was Tabor's mistress, whom he and his disreputable friends called Baby Doe. Few upright individuals attended the wedding, and exclusive eyebrows all over Washington elevated at the very idea that a President of the United States would countenance such a union.

Arthur, apparently, was unaware that his reputation was threatened, until a close friend told him about the gossip that he had a mistress. The President cried, "Why, this is worse than assassination!" Shortly thereafter, he shattered one rumor by making it known that the picture before which he placed a daily bouquet of flowers was of his late wife. She had died five months before he was nominated for the vice presidency, and recollections of their twenty-one happy years together haunted him for the remainder of his life. By his order, her room in their New York house was kept exactly as she left it; and, in her memory, two months after he moved into the White House, he presented a stained-glass window to St. John's Church, across Lafayette Square.

The President's official performance was much more laudable than anyone had expected, but it irritated those who had counted on his compliance with entrenched political practices. He broke with Senator Conkling early and established himself as a chief executive who would run his office without partisan dictation. He alienated former President Grant when he failed to appoint one of his close friends to a diplomatic post. He urged civil service reform and signed the first Congressional Act to enforce it; and he ordered the prosecution of several of his underlings who were accused of post office graft. Also, he proposed reciprocal trade treaties toward smoother international dealings and vetoed a rivers-and-harbors bill because it favored special interests.

The general public gradually came to appreciate the fairness and efficiency of his administration, and his trips to the West during his last year in office were particularly successful. Newspapers throughout the area praised his accomplishments. Mark Twain wrote: "I am but one in fifty five million; still, in the opinion of this one-fifty-five millionth of the country's population, it would be hard to better President Arthur's administration. But don't decide till you hear from the rest."

Arthur approached the 1884 Republican national convention with high hopes that he would win the nomination on his official record. In addition to strong backing in the West and South, he had the support of New York business. But his opposition was formidable. James G. Blaine twice before had sought the nomination, and he had been subtly campaigning for it by denouncing administration policies ever since Arthur replaced him in the Cabinet. Wayne MacVeagh, who had been Garfield's Attorney General, brought many undecided Republicans into Blaine's camp at the national convention with a public reminder: "Guiteau was the original Arthur man." Grant and his following were already aligned against the President.

Arthur's prospects appeared to be passably promising, however, until censure of his policies was augmented, sub rosa, by personal criticism. Intimations that he had a mistress spread through the convention. The Arthur family coat of arms on his landau was said to be counterfeit. There was talk that he had used government funds to cover his personal expenditures, and much was made of his passion for fancy clothes. Blaine won the nomination. Young Representative Joseph Gurney Cannon, of Illinois, capsulized the outcome of the contest in a remark, quoted across the nation: "Arthur was defeated by his trousers." The general public did not know that the vanquished incumbent already was suffering from Bright's disease, which would take his life two years after he left office.

James G. Blaine had charisma before the word was commonly used. He was a magnetic personality; a persuasive speaker, and with his silver hair, mustache and beard, he looked like a statesman. Furthermore, he had demonstrated his extraordinary abilities as Speaker of the House, as a senator and as Secretary of State.

He had been a constant irritant to Democrats since 1876, when he first aspired to the presidency and Robert Ingersoll put his name in nomination at the Republican convention with this accolade:

> Like an armed warrior, like a plumed knight, James G. Blaine marched down the hall of American Congress and threw his shining lance full and fair against the brazen forebears of every traitor in this country!

Blaine lost that nomination to Rutherford B. Hayes, and four years later he lost to Garfield; but the fifty-four-year-old Plumed Knight was riding full tilt to the White House in 1884, when he was toppled by the Democratic nominee, forty-seven-year-old Grover Cleveland, the reform Governor of New York.

The campaign would be remembered as "the dirtiest" in American annals. Actually, it was not as vicious as the one in which Thomas Jefferson defeated John Adams in 1800, or as acrimonious as Andrew Jackson's battle against John Quincy Adams in 1828. Woodrow Wilson's struggle for reelection in

1916 would reek with even more underground vilifications. But the 1884 contest was above-board, with more open mudslinging from both sides than in any other national campaign, before or since.

Independent Republicans, known as the Mugwumps, were outraged when Blaine was nominated. They were suspicious about his amassed wealth—with no visible income except government salaries—and they had long regarded him as a political opportunist. With Carl Schurz and the Reverend Henry Ward Beecher in the vanguard, they supported Cleveland and made morality the main issue by bringing out "the Mulligan letters." The correspondence the Plumed Knight had managed to suppress for years had to do with a Congressional ruling, while Blaine was Speaker of the House, which retrieved several tracts of land for the Little Rock and Fort Smith Railroad and granted the company the privilege of secretly selling its bonds. Blaine had an investment of $339,000 in the bonds. He was believed to have profited handsomely.

While keeping books for Warren Fisher, Jr., of the Little Rock line, James Mulligan, of Boston, ran across letters from Blaine that clearly implicated him. One message, offering the recipient $10,000 to retrieve the entire correspondence, had the postscript, *Burn this letter,* in Blaine's handwriting. Pro-Cleveland newspapers published the letters without comment other than that the originals were held in the office of a prestigious Boston law firm, where they could be read by any respectable individual.

"There is not a word in the letters which is not entirely consistent with the most scrupulous integrity and honor," the Plumed Knight proclaimed in the *Kennebec Journal.* "I hope every Republican paper will publish them in full." Republican editors were less confident. Several suppressed the bulk of the material and published the remainder with biased interpretations. Pro-Cleveland newspapers played the political bonanza to the hilt. The new Democratic campaign cry went up:

Blaine! Blaine
The Continental liar
From the State of Maine!
Burn this letter!

The Republicans retaliated by reviving local gossip that went back ten years. With the headline A TERRIBLE TALE—A DARK CHAPTER IN PUBLIC MAN'S HISTORY, the Buffalo *Evening Telegraph* stated that Maria Halpin, a Buffalo woman, bore Grover Cleveland's child, and that the father abandoned the boy in an orphans' asylum. The bombshell hit full force in New York and reverberated through the country. Religious leaders and church organs urged the defeat of the iniquitious Democratic candidate. The Republican cry went: "Ma! Ma! Where's my Pa?"

Distressed at possible effects on Cleveland's campaign, Charles W. Goodyear asked him how the matter should be handled. "Tell the truth!" was the governor's common-sense reply. He added that the accurate part should be admitted at once, thus dispelling the falsehoods surrounding it.

The Democratic candidate at the same time was infuriated when he learned that Charles W. McCune, a Democratic newspaper editor, planned to whitewash him by printing quondam gossip that Oscar Folsom was the child's father, and that Cleveland, a bachelor, had taken the blame to protect the honor of his married friend. Giving vent to his indignation, Cleveland wrote to Donald N. Lockwood, who had made a nominating speech for him, as follows:

> I learned last night that McCune had started the story and told it to newspaper men (one, at least) that I had nothing to do with the subject of the *Telegraph* story—that my silence was to protect my friend Oscar Folsom. Now is this man crazy or does he wish to ruin somebody? Is he fool enough to suppose for one moment that if such was

the truth (which it is not, so far as the motive for silence is concerned) that I would permit my dead friend's memory to suffer for my sake? And Mrs. Folsom and her daughter at my house at this very time! I am afraid that I shall have the occasion to pray to be delivered from my friends . . . This story of McCune's must be stopped. I have prevented its publication in one paper at least.

As the clamor about Cleveland's morals grew louder, a Boston committee of Democrats sent an attorney to Buffalo to investigate an attack attributed in the Boston *Journal* to the Reverend George C. Ball, a Baptist minister. According to the report, which Ball disclaimed, he had asserted that the governor of New York was "habitually dissipated during his years in Buffalo." About the same time, the Reverend James Freeman Clark, a Unitarian, publicly stated that on the basis of personal acquaintance with Mrs. Halpin he believed she might have falsely named Cleveland the father of her child. Henry Ward Beecher, the eminent Congregationalist minister, asserted that in all the history of politics there had never been "lies so cruel, so atrocious as those concerning Mr. Cleveland." However, Beecher's statement was something less than a windfall to the Democratic candidate, for the eloquent preacher was being sued at the time by Theodore Tilton, one of his parishioners, who charged that Beecher had illicit relations with Mrs. Tilton. Furthermore, *The Independent,* a religious organ of which Beecher had once been editor, took issue with him by editorializing that Cleveland's election "would argue a low state of morals among the people, and be a shame and a never-to-be-forgotten disgrace to the nation."

Conversely, prominent Democrats in Buffalo, after an exhaustive investigation, published this redundant summation of their findings:

Our examination of the general charges which have been made against Grover Cleveland's private character shows that they are wholly untrue. In every instance in which reports and insinuations have been tangible enough to furnish a clue, they have positively proved to be false. The attack upon Grover Cleveland's character is thoroughly discredited when we consider the source from which it comes.

The true story began in 1871, while "Big Steve" Cleveland was the sheriff of Erie County. Even then, with his walrus mustache and overly ample waistline, he looked like a jovial German burgomaster as he quaffed beer with cronies in their favorite saloon. But intimates knew that behind his easy-going exterior the Presbyterian minister's son was a man of rugged character, with an inflexible sense of duty. He did not hesitate to prosecute friends when they were corrupt. He did not shift responsibility even when, as sheriff, he was required under law to serve as hangman if the usual functionary was unavailable. Twice, he had placed the noose around a condemned murderer's neck and had sprung the trap door. After that, his enemies called him The Hangman of Buffalo.

Off duty, the sheriff relaxed on a Niagara Island property with fellow members of The Jolly Reefers, a group of unmarried men who gave parties to which no ladies were invited but accommodating women were always welcome. A new guest in 1871 was Mrs. Maria Crofts Halpin, a pretty thirty-five-year-old widow who arrived in Buffalo from New Jersey, where she had left her two children. She obtained a job as a collar maker and regularly attended St. John's Episcopal Church. In due course she attracted the attention of two or three Jolly Reefers and was soon included in their Niagara Island carousals. Sheriff Cleveland generally was present, and occasionally he brought along some of his married friends, including Oscar Folsom, the Democratic district leader.

Mrs. Halpin worked as hard as she played. She advanced from collar maker to clerk in a department store and then was placed in charge of the cloak section, where she stayed—until she was dismissed because she was pregnant. In September 1874 she gave birth to a son, named him Oscar Folsom Cleveland, announced that the sheriff was the father, and insisted that he marry her.

According to a letter to a Boston friend, the designated parent did not know whether or not the child was his, but he did not deny the paternity, and although he refused to marry the mother, he promised to support her son and implied that he would provide funds for her from time to time.

Within a year Maria was drinking heavily and even in sober moments did not look after the child properly. Cleveland decided that foster parents were indicated, but until suitable ones could be found, he realized something had to be done at once. At his behest, the Buffalo Overseer of the Poor dispatched two detectives to Mrs. Halpin's house, and over her vociferous protest they took the boy to a Protestant orphanage. A few hours later the mother was temporarily committed to a Catholic institution for the mentally unbalanced. Both operations were negotiated without court hearings and attendant publicity.

Cleveland's troubles multiplied as soon as Maria was released—and was insistent on his helping to support her. He gave her enough money to start a modest business in Niagara Falls and continued to pay the five dollars a week required by the orphanage until the boy was adopted.

Maria returned to Buffalo within a few months and employed an attorney to start court proceedings for custody of her son, but before the necessary papers could be drawn up, she tried to kidnap him. Cleveland offered her five hundred dollars to drop the suit; she accepted the money and vanished from Buffalo. He would not hear from her again for nineteen years. Meanwhile, he managed to have the boy adopted by a prosperous couple who promised that he would be educated and launched on a professional career.

Local gossip subsided quickly after Maria left Buffalo and the scandal was rarely mentioned through Cleveland's years as mayor of Buffalo and as governor of New York, until after he was nominated for the presidency. If the story had been published during the convention, he would not have been the candidate, and if the opposition had exposed it later in the campaign, when the defense of Cleveland would have been more difficult to mobilize, Blaine would have been President.

With both the candidates under personal attack, the choice appeared to be between a libertine, whose integrity in public service was indisputable, and a model family man, who betrayed his public trust for personal gain. At a meeting of the Mugwumps in New York, one of the leaders drew the line distinctly in a speech: "We are told that Mr. Blaine has been delinquent in office but blameless in private life, while Mr. Cleveland had been a model of official integrity but culpable in his personal relations. We should therefore elect Mr. Cleveland to public office, which he is so well qualified to fill, and remand Mr. Blaine to the private station which he is admirably fitted to adorn."

Embattled Democrats were prepared to blast even that conception of the Plumed Knight. They sent a resourceful individual to Albany with a bundle of material purporting that "a shotgun" had figured in the marriage of Blaine and Miss Harriet Stanwood thirty-four years previously. Without looking at the contents, Governor Cleveland asked, "Are the papers all here?" Assured they were, he tore the packet into bits and ordered an aide to burn them on the spot. When the last piece was ashes, the Democratic nominee said, "The other side can have a monopoly on all the dirt in this campaign." But the story had already reached an Indiana newspaper editor who published an item to the effect that certain people thought Blaine's marriage to Miss Stanwood was hastened by her father for reasons best known to him. The Plumed Knight instituted a libel suit against the editor but dropped it when other publications did not pick up the story.

As the campaign went on, debates in and out of the press continued. An article in *The Nation* pointed out that "very few benefactors of the human race have been chaste," and added, "The standards by which some ministers now propose to exclude Cleveland would have prevented Washington, Jefferson, Franklin and Hamilton, not to go any further, from taking any prominent part in the foundation of America." Charles Dana in the powerful New York *Sun* retorted: "We do not believe the American people will knowingly elect to the Presidency a coarse debauchee who would bring harlots to Washington and hire lodgings for them convenient to the White House." Young Teddy Roosevelt left his ranch in the West to berate the Democratic candidate. "I think he is not a man who should be put in that office," T.R. proclaimed from a platform in New York. "And there is no lack of reason for it. His public career, in the first place, and then *private reasons as well.*"

Vituperations echoed in slogans at great torchlight parades for both candidates as the campaign proceeded. Supporters of Cleveland invariably reiterated the chant: "Blaine! Blaine! The continental liar/From the State of Maine!" Republicans marched to the refrain, "Ma! Ma! Where's my Pa?" Democrats rejoined, "Gone to the White House, Ha! Ha! Ha!"

A few weeks before the election the Halpin story appeared to have lost its effect. Cleveland wrote to a former law partner:

> I hope now that the scandal business is about wound up that you have a little freedom from the annoyance and trouble which it necessarily brought in its train. I think the matter was arranged in the best possible way, and that the

policy of not cringing was not only necessary but the only possible way.

Shortly afterward, however, Cleveland's election chances dwindled. Tammany Hall had come out solidly against him. Majorities in the Midwest and New England were backing Blaine, and throughout the country he had strong Catholic support (his mother was an Irish Catholic and his sister was mother superior in a convent). The prospect of a Republican in the White House appeared to be assured.

To strengthen that hope, pro-Blaine newspapers rehashed the Halpin scandal and reported that the governor of New York had also consorted with women of easy virtue in Albany. Mrs. Henry Ward Beecher sent Cleveland a clipping and urged him to implement his admonition. "Tell the truth!" by openly denying or affirming the latest aspersion. He replied that he was "shocked and dumbfounded by the clipping because it purports to give what a man actually knows, and not a mere report, as the other four or five lies which I have heard, or read about my life in Albany." Continuing, he insisted that his conduct in Albany had never been anything except "laborious and perfectly correct."

Censure of him escalated and was rising to a new peak about a week before the election when a New York newspaper advertisement invited clergymen to meet the Republican candidate at the Fifth Avenue Hotel. The import was obvious; men of the cloth, in the presence of Blaine, would discuss his opponent's unfitness for the highest office.

The Reverend S. D. Burchard, pastor of the Murray Hill Presbyterian Church, served as spokeman for the assemblage. Directing his remarks to Blaine, he reviewed the morals charges against Cleveland and ended by assuring the Republican candidate that the Protestant clergy would battle to the end the election of the nominee supported by the party of

Rum, Romanism, and Rebellion! Burchard obviously wished to stress that Cleveland and his crowd imbibed liquor excessively, that many were Roman Catholics, and that the Democratic party was on the losing side in the Civil War. Blaine thoughtlessly thanked the spokesman for his remarks and the gathering for its support.

Within an hour after the meeting ended, a shorthand reporter had disclosed Burchard's speech in full at Democratic headquarters. "Write that out!" cried Arthur P. Gorman, New York campaign manager, when he heard Burchard's alliterative catchphrase, *Rum, Romanism, and Rebellion!* It was circulated on handbills and plastered in large print on storefronts all over New York City before the end of the day. And by the time Democratic newspapers across the country had fully publicized it, many people were attributing the slogan to the Republican candidate.

Despite prior instructions from Tammany Hall, the Irish Catholic vote turned to Cleveland. He carried New York State and won by 36 electoral votes. For the first time in twenty-eight years, a Democrat would be President; and the country-wide elation of the party faithful concurred with that of Indiana's Democratic manager, who expressed his delight in widely quoted verse:

> Hurrah for Maria,
> Hurrah for the kid.
> I voted for Cleveland
> And I'm damned glad I did!

Disparaging items in the press and irresponsible talk focused on Cleveland after he moved into the White House. Early rumors that the portly President would wed "a Miss Van Vechten of New York" died when neither her identity nor marriage plans could be adduced. Subsequent reports that he was secretly courting the attractive widow of Oscar Folsom brought up reminders that Folsom, as well as Cleveland, had been ignominiously linked with Maria Halpin. Actually, the President was already engaged to Mrs. Folsom's twenty-two-year-old daughter, Frances, who had called him "Uncle Cleve" as a child, and for whom he became legal guardian when her father died.

The formal announcement that the President would marry his pretty ward in the White House rocked the nation. Base insinuations about the forty-nine-year-old bachelor, whose fiancée was young enough to be his daughter, appeared in a New York scandal sheet, and allusions to his transgressions in earlier years were carried by newspapers in other cities.

Unfavorable press notices faded after the White House wedding, but the President's resentment of journalists who had demeaned him persisted. He expressed his opinion of them in the New York *Evening Post*:

> They have used the enormous power of the modern newspaper to perpetuate and disseminate a colossal impertinence, and have done it, not as professional gossips and tatlers, but as the guides and instructors of the public in conduct and morals. And they have done it, not to a private citizen, but to the President of the United States, thereby lifting their offence into the gaze of the whole world, and doing their utmost to make American journalism contemptible in the estimation of good breeding everywhere.

Cleveland's personal life was not an issue in the 1888 campaign, in which he was defeated by Benjamin Harrison, nor was it an issue four years later, when he defeated Harrison and returned to the White House. During his second term, however, there was intermittent gossip that he drank heavily and was cruel to his young wife, and that her unhappiness caused their children to be born deaf and dumb. The latter rumor was refuted by White House visitors who noted and reported that the youngsters were normal, but recurrent talk that the often inebriated President physically abused his wife eventually prompted curious individuals outside of Washington to seek denial direct from the White House. Mrs. Cleveland's reply to one letter was published stating that she "could wish for American women no greater blessing than that their lives be as happy and their husband may be as kind, attentive, considerate, and affectionate as mine."

The First Lady's marked solicitude for the President after his operation for cancer of the mouth and his devotion to her were noted by Ike Hoover, the chief White House usher; "She would watch over him as though he were one of her children . . . Cleveland idolized Mrs. Cleveland, thought of her as a child, was tender and considerate of her always."

The President heard from Maria Halpin two years before he left office. Remarried and living in New Rochelle, New York, she wrote to him twice, demanding money and threatening to disclose "embarrassing facts" if it was not forthcoming. He did not reply.

Of all our slandered Presidents, William McKinley, last to be elected in the nineteenth century, was the most fortunate; the slime that was aimed at him vanished for lack of substance before it could harm his reputation in even the slightest respect.

Paradoxically, his remarkable devotion to his ill wife was responsible for evil rumors about their relationship. Political adversaries figured that no human being could be so constantly concerned as he was reputed to be about an increasingly indisposed and demanding mate. And when he became a presidential candidate, they tried to expose chinks in his saintly armor.

McKinley had been regarded as a presidential prospect at Republican conventions in 1888 and 1892. In the latter year, with the powerful backing of Marcus Alonzo (Mark) Hanna, the shrewd financier and political kingmaker, McKinley after fourteen years in the United States Congress was elected governor of Ohio. Hanna had not only promoted him for that office but had also rescued him from financial disaster. Representative McKinley was in dire straits when notes that he had countersigned for a friend were called. Hanna arranged payments and described McKinley at the time as "the best man I ever knew." Four years later "Hanna's man" won the presidential nomination on the first ballot.

The Republicans had a candidate whose career in public service had been estimable and whose loving care of his ailing wife had established him as a man of virtually superhuman kindliness. They extolled his fitness for the White House with such emphasis on his personal virtues that Teddy Roosevelt said they were selling him "as if he were patent medicine," and William Allen White observed that they were making him "a statue in the park."

Running against the Democratic nominee, former Nebraska Representative William Jennings Bryan, with free silver the predominant issue, McKinley was soon locked into a tense political battle with an uncertain outcome. Under Hanna's astute direction, he waged his assuasive campaign from the front porch of his Canton, Ohio, home, while his eloquent opponent addressed throngs across the nation. But when innumerable voters whom Hanna transported to Canton appeared to be more impressed with McKinley's low-keyed speeches than with Bryan's effulgent oratory, Democratic workers sought ways to discredit the Republican's personal image. Specifically, and without Bryan's knowledge, they scrutinized McKinley's background for possible evidence that he was not the chaste man, the model husband, he was said to be.

Close inspection of his history turned up nothing that could be used against him. The son of a foundryman of sturdy

Scotch-Irish ancestry, he was born in Niles, Ohio, attended Allegheny College in Pennsylvania, and taught school for two or three terms before he volunteered for the Civil War. After four years in uniform he left military service a brevet major, studied law, moved to Canton, Ohio, and became the prosecuting attorney of Stark County. Democratic investigators learned from one of his old acquaintances that "the courtly Major McKinley was always popular with the girls" and that after he moved to Canton he was thought at first to be "an easy mark for women bent on marriage." But many who had known him in those years remembered that his romantic interests soon centered on beautiful Ida Saxon, a banker's daughter, whose family was prominent in the town and throughout the state. Educated at Brook Hall Seminary in Pennsylvania, she had toured Europe. She was highly intelligent but extremely nervous, and her possessiveness of her ever-affable suitor was noticeable months before they were married.

He was twenty-eight, she was twenty-two, when they exchanged vows in an elaborate church ceremony in Canton. But their happiness was marred within five years by the deaths of their two daughters, and by Mrs. McKinley's subsequent obsession that the tragedies were Divine punishment for sins that she or her husband might have committed in the past. The major's grief was accentuated by her insistence that he spend every possible moment with her, though he willingly complied. He gave up his only diversions, walking and horseback riding, and curtailed his working hours to be with her. The love and allegiance forged by mutual sorrow and the sick wife's complete emotional dependence on her husband would be binding for their twenty-six remaining years together.

They led a quiet life during his years in Congress. Mrs. McKinley rarely left the old Ebbitt House, where they resided, but she rallied enough from time to time to receive a few friends. When well, she was delightful—a stimulating talker with a wide variety of interests. She took pride in her husband's accomplishments in Congress and was an ideal companion in every way. But her recurrent illness—incipient epilepsy, which doctors diagnosed as "a nervous malady"—intensified her irritability and made her increasingly demanding. Her patient husband, worrying incessantly about her deteriorating condition, rushed home from his office every day to look after her, and he wrote her long letters when speaking engagements necessitated his being away from her overnight.

His friends were awed by his undeviating attention to her. Capitol Hill correspondents, assuming that he needed a few diversions, casually mentioned that he sometimes played cards and often tippled with Congressional colleagues. Those reports distressed McKinley, and he set out to end them by informing the journalists that while he enjoyed an occasional game of casino with friends, his card playing generally was restricted to euchre with his wife, and his drinking to a few sips of Scotch now and then at home. News gatherers from then on substituted "inveterate smoker" for "heavy drinker" in their trivial references to Congressman McKinley.

Nothing more damaging than that was uncovered by sleuths in search of evidence that could be used against him in his first presidential campaign. Nevertheless, workers in the opposition camp trumped up and circulated scurrilous stories, purporting that in drunken moments he beat his insane and hopelessly crippled wife and ran after other women.

McKinley ostensibly ignored the slander, while his Canton headquarters released this statement: "Name calling and enmities are below the Republican presidential candidate." But many distressed confidential letters were exchanged by his promoters—until he won the election.

Mrs. McKinley was virtually an invalid in the White House, but with the President's persistent attention and assistance she managed to fulfill many of her social duties. He knew that she doted on being in the limelight and that she was acutely conscious of her prerogatives as First Lady, so he encouraged her to exert her will power to the utmost to receive with him at their parties. Furthermore, he changed protocol for White House dinners so she could sit beside him. By then, she was subject to epileptic seizures, which he called "fainting spells." And when he noted the onset of an attack, which would render her rigid and glassy-eyed for a few seconds, he tenderly dropped a silk handkerchief over her face until she regained consciousness. Then he brought her back into conversations as though nothing unusual had happened. Mark Hanna after one such touching incident remarked, "President McKinley has made it pretty hard for the rest of husbands."

When McKinley was shot by Leon Czolgosz, an American-born anarchist on September 6, 1901, the wounded President's first words to his secretary, George B. Cortelyou, were, "My wife—be careful, Cortelyou, how you tell her—oh, be careful!"

V

Peck's Bad Boy

In 1915–16, American politics was again swept by a virulent
contagion of undercover slander when President Wilson's
prospect for reelection was threatened by innuendos and
falsehoods about his private life. They were to plague him
periodically throughout his fight for the League of Nations.

His romance with Edith Bolling Galt, less than a year after
his first wife's death, fomented poisonous talk that reminded
one of his friends of "George Washington's experience" but,
in reality, it was more venomous than surreptitious attacks on
any previous President.

Ellen Axson Wilson, a victim of nephritis with complica-
tions, died a year and five months after she became First Lady.
Her last words to Dr. Cary T. Grayson, the White House
physician, were, "Promise me that you will take good care of
my husband." Inconsolable when the end came, the President
agonized by her deathbed for two nights afterward. Following
the burial in her native Georgia he returned to the White

House, heartbroken, and for months his depression was so intense his physician became concerned.

Margaret Wilson, the President's unmarried daughter, was absorbed in her musical career. His other daughters, Jessie (Mrs. Francis P. Sayre) and Eleanor (Mrs. William G. McAdoo), had homes and family responsibilities of their own. The President's cousin Helen Bones, who had been his wife's personal secretary, continued to reside at the White House, but she could not comfort him. Dr. Grayson, remembering his promise to Ellen Wilson, sought a realistic way to bring the dispirited fifty-eight-year-old widower back to normal.

A promising thought occurred to the physician one afternoon when he and Wilson, riding in a White House limousine, passed an electromobile driven by a woman. Grayson bowed to her, and the President asked, "Who is that beautiful lady?"

She was Mrs. Norman Galt, the forty-two-year-old widow of a prosperous Washington jeweler and the guardian of Alice Gertrude (Altrude) Gordon, whom Grayson was courting at the time and would marry the following year. Grayson promoted a friendship between Helen Bones and Mrs. Galt, and in April 1915 Miss Bones introduced the President to her. Previously she had glimpsed him from a distance only four times and before her friendship with Miss Bones had never been inside the White House.

Daughter of a circuit court judge, Edith Bolling Galt belonged to an established Virginia family, with an ancestral line going back to Pocahontas and John Rolfe. During her seventeen years in Washington, however, she had not been socially active; a widow since 1908, she resided quietly with two maids in an unpretentious house at Twentieth Street and New Hampshire Avenue. But she had traveled extensively and her fashionable gowns were from Worth.

The President's delight in meeting her was soon confirmed by the regularity with which he began to entertain her at the

White House, at the theater and sports events, aboard the presidential yacht, and on long motor trips. The friendship quickly blossomed into romance; within two months he had asked her to marry him.

As a grief-stricken widower, he had elicited wide sympathy, but as the suitor of the attractive Mrs. Galt, so soon after his wife's death, he quickly became the target of censure. In the Peyton Place atmosphere of Washington, gossip exploded, and as it echoed throughout the country, it took on invidious imputations. Women in the Midwest, particularly, were filled with indignation at the President's swift faithlessness to Ellen Wilson's memory, and as though personally affronted, virtuous matrons and spinsters in many areas deplored his untimely courtship and rehashed old rumors about his excessive fondness for the ladies. Political enemies of both sexes seized on the agitation and promoted it, with pointed reminders that his more recent moral lapse verified suspicions that had floated through his first presidential campaign.

The wave of criticism and distortion soon swelled into a flood of invidious rumors, the most flagrant being that the President and "the Galt woman" were in love before Ellen Wilson's death and had conspired with Dr. Grayson to dispose of her. One fiction had it that the physician poisoned her; another, that when she threatened divorce because of her husband's new emotional attachment, he pushed her down the stairs, causing fatal internal hemorrhages. The malevolent grapevine rustled from Georgia that her unmarked grave was disgracefully neglected, overgrown with vegetation and washed away at the surface while the President was preoccupied with his latest love affair.

Supplementing those obloquies were others: that as "a youthful skirt-chaser," Wilson was given to waiting at stage doors to take accommodating soubrettes to midnight suppers; that Ellen Wilson's constant worries about her husband's infidelities—and, particularly, his destructive romance with "a

Mrs. Peck" over the years—had made his wife a semi-invalid long before she became First Lady; and that a few weeks after her death he received in his White House office a pregnant young woman, who left by a side door with a sizable amount of money.

Furious at the rumors and fearful of their political consequences, Democrats across the country branded them "Republican drivel," while White House acolytes repeatedly explained that the condtion of Mrs. Wilson's grave was due to the caretaker's illness, of which the President was not informed, and that the Carrara headstone he had ordered from Italy was delayed in shipment because of European war emergencies. The White House staff confirmed that he had received in his office a pregnant woman—an impoverished married relation, whom he had financially assisted.

His friendship with the Mrs. Peck to whom some of the stories referred, started in the winter of 1907. As president of Princeton University, Wilson had been engrossed for some time in a fight to democratize the institution. He was disheartened by growing antagonisms and particularly distressed because his closest confrere, Professor John Grier Hibben, had aligned himself with the opposition at a crucial time. Before that, the struggle had already begun to affect Wilson's health. He lost the sight of one eye, and his physician ordered him to retire. He refused and survived a serious operation, but recurrent attacks of neuritis continued to torment him.

His Princeton salary was barely enough to support his family and the constant inflow of relatives who came and stayed months on end. A winter vacation shared with his wife and daughters was out of the question; so, late in January 1907, his physician and Mrs. Wilson and her brother, Princeton professor Stockton Axson, urged him to go alone to Bermuda. They hoped a locale far removed from family responsibilities and academic worries would restore his health and raise his flagging spirits.

In Bermuda he met Mrs. Peck, the leading American hostess. The former Mary Allen, born of well-to-do parents in Grand Rapids, Michigan, and reared in Duluth, Minnesota, she had lived in Europe for several years after her marriage to Thomas Hulbert in 1883. She was amusing, conversant in the arts, and an accomplished pianist. Years after Hulbert was killed in an accident, when their only son Allen was an infant, she married Thomas D. Peck, a Pittsfield, Massachusetts, manufacturer and began to winter in Bermuda. Her house became a gathering place for celebrated visitors. She was said to entertain "everybody worth knowing" who came to the island; and Woodrow Wilson was distinguished on several accounts. His battles at Princeton had attracted considerable attention, and there was much talk of him as a national presidential possibility. The Charlottesville (S.C.) *News and Courier* had hailed him "the most promising Southern candidate for the nation's highest office." Colonel George Harvey, editor of *Harper's Weekly*, had declared in a speech before the Lotus Club in New York: "As one of a considerable number of Democrats who have become tired of voting Republican tickets, it is with a sense of rapture that I contemplate even the remotest possibility of casting a ballot for the President of Princeton University to be President of the United States." The idea was gathering force throughout the nation.

Like most successful hostesses, Mrs. Peck had a flair for making her special guests shine in lively repartee. Wilson, when inspired, was a vividly brilliant conversationalist. He enjoyed the stimulating people Mrs. Peck assembled to meet and talk with him and was delighted that she was avidly interested in his philosophy and aspirations. He especially doted on feminine adulation. With a worshipful wife and three daughters, he had it all the time at home, and for years he had cultivated a number of women friends. Mrs. Peck fitted into the pattern.

He was a prolific letter writer. No previous American notable, with the possible exception of Thomas Jefferson, ever wrote to friends more regularly and at such length. And, like Jefferson, Wilson enjoyed corresponding with sympathetic matrons.

Before he left Bermuda, he wrote his first letter to Mrs. Peck. He had a prompt reply, and the interchange that would cause unconscionable gossip in his presidential campaigns was well under way when he returned to Bermuda in January 1908.

Within six months, he was again discouraged about the way things were going at Princeton and beset by neuritis. Again, he went to Bermuda at the insistence of his physician, his wife and Professor Axson, who remembered that the previous visit had revived him, and again he was drawn into Mrs. Peck's adulatory orbit.

He returned to Princeton, refreshed and full of plans for his wife to meet charming Mrs. Peck. She was a guest of the Wilsons in Princeton a few weeks later and she entertained them in Pittsfield. The two women got on amiably and visiting back and forth continued; but Wilson handled most of the correspondence. Through his remaining years at Princeton and throughout the time he was governor of New Jersey, he wrote regularly to Mrs. Peck.

When he ran for the presidency in 1912 backstairs talk made much of his visits to "that woman in Bermuda" and his constant communications with her. Busybodies had managed to find out her name, somehow had learned about the correspondence, and figured that she was at odds with her husband as early as June 1909, when this item appeared in the New York *Town Topics*:

> Pittsfield, Mass., is now devouring with great glee the contents of little notes which Thomas D. Peck has been sending out to tradespeople, carrying information that he made Mrs. Peck a liberal allowance and hereafter she will pay all bills which she may contract.

Throughout the campaign sly references to Wilson's trips to Bermuda in 1907 and 1908—and again in 1910—added currency to whispers that he was the cause of Mrs. Peck's divorce in 1911. But to the consternation of his political foes, the gossip did not counteract the powerful forces working in his favor. His opposition was split between the candidacies of William Howard Taft (Republican) and Theodore Roosevelt (Progressive—or Bull Moose), with the latter apparently ahead. A number of orthodox Republicans were more apprehensive about T.R. than about Wilson. Furthermore, insinuations that he was a philanderer gave a degree of warmth to his cold professorial visage—which he called "my Scotch-Presbyterian face"—and humanized him to many voters.

The evil talk receded when the President-elect, with his wife and daughters, spent a month at Mrs. Peck's Glencove Cottage in Bermuda. As Mrs. Hulbert—she had resumed her first husband's name after divorcing Peck—she visited the Wilsons in Sea Girt, New Jersey, just before they moved to Washington, and later she accompanied the new First Lady on a New York shopping trip. By the time she was a White House guest in April 1913, gossip about her and the President appeared to be all but forgotten.

Wicked memories were revived with a vengeance, however, to accentuate wide disapproval of his precipitate courtship of Mrs. Galt. What had been abortive rumors about his uncurbed sensuality three years before were given new life in July 1915 and incorporated in an underground drive to degrade him on moral grounds.

From California, where Mrs. Peck was living with her son, came unpublished reports of her indignation that her longtime paramour was involved in another love affair; also, that she was all set to file a breach of promise suit based on Wilson's compromising letters to her, even though he had tried to buy her off with seventy-five hundred dollars. Soon, over card tables, clotheslines and cracker barrels from coast to

coast, the President was Peck's Bad Boy, with the worst implications. And the sobriquet was pay dirt for the Republican
Party, hopefully girding for victory in the next presidential
election.

Distressed Democratic managers bombarded the White
House with pleas that something be done to stop the debase-
ment, but the President refused to dignify any part of it by
denial. His stock answer to reminders that falsehoods could
pose a threat to his reelection was, "Don't worry. The truth is
not a cripple. It can run alone."

When he took Mrs. Galt to visit Margaret Wilson and Mrs.
Sayre at their summer place in Cornish, New Hampshire, in
July 1915, his advisers began to panic. Colonel Edward M.
House, Wilson's alter ego on foreign affairs and confidant on
everything that affected his political career, was particularly
distressed at a report from Director of the Mint Robert W.
Woolley: "The backstairs, sewer gossips are doing deadly
work among the women." House noted in his diary on July 15:
"I am sorry that the President has fallen in love at this time,
for he will be criticised for not waiting longer after Mrs. Wilson's death."

Secretary of the Treasury McAdoo, the President's son-in-
law, and Joseph P. Tumulty, Wilson's secretary, were equally
disturbed about the growing criticism, and they were especially worried about recurring whispers that Mrs. Peck was on
the verge of selling her correspondence from Wilson. They
tried to broach the touchy subject to the President when he
returned to Washington late in July. He refused to discuss it,
and Colonel House was even more disquieted after he boldly
inquired whether the letters, if published, might appear more
endearing than they were meant to be, and the President was
vague about the contents.

From New Hampshire, Mrs. Galt had gone to Geneva, New
York, to visit relatives. After her return to Washington in the
latter part of August, the President's intent to marry her as

soon as possible was obvious to his White House associates. He was usually inaccessible to them because of his long drives with Mrs. Galt. When he was not with her, he spent hours writing her long letters or talking on the direct telephone line between her house and his private office. On September 3 they told his daughters they were engaged.

Word got around, and Democratic leaders in secret conference agreed that someone had to convince Wilson that if he married Mrs. Galt before November 1916, the effects on his campaign for reelection might be disastrous. Frank P. Glass, editor of the Birmingham (Ala.) *News* and Wilson's friend since their undergraduate days at Princeton, undertook the chore. By way of stressing the vulnerability of the President's position, he related to him the substance and extent of the gossip that had already spread about him and Mrs. Peck and hinted that it might be even worse and more injurious to his political future if he planned to marry Mrs. Galt any time before the end of the 1916 campaign. Glass' memorandum, written immediately after the meeting, reads: "Before he got all my story, tears came into his eyes while his voice and demeanor showed he was profoundly moved. He had not imagined that his enemies could be so unjust, so cruel. I reminded him of George Washington's experience . . ." Glass further recalled that the President said in reference to his correspondence with Mrs. Peck, "There is nothing in any letter I ever wrote that I am ashamed to have published."

Later, in a note to the Reverend Sylvester W. Beach, who was his pastor at Princeton, Wilson wrote, "I do not know how to deal with the fiendish lies that are being circulated about my personal character, other than to invite those who repeat them to consult anybody who has ever known me for any length of time . . . Poison of this sort is hard to find an antidote for . . ."

He continued to appear more appalled by the injustice of the slander than worried about its effect on his political career, but he was extremely disturbed by Edith Galt's reaction—she suggested that they postpone the wedding for at least six months. (In her memoirs, published years later, she quoted his reply, "If the people do not trust me, now is the time to find out.")

On September 18 McAdoo made a final attempt to block the marriage. Lunching alone with the President, McAdoo said he had received an anonymous letter stating that Mrs. Hulbert (Peck) was telling everybody about the hush money from Wilson and was consulting lawyers about a breach of promise suit. McAdoo said further that he and House had sounded out newspaper reporters and had found they firmly believed she would sell the incriminating letters to the Republican Party the moment the engagement was officially announced.

Shaken by McAdoo's disclosures, Wilson insisted that the letters contained nothing remotely embarrassing and that Ellen had known everything about his friendship and correspondence with Mrs. Hulbert. Also, he stressed that the seventy-five hundred dollars he had sent her was a loan to rescue her son from financial difficulty, and that it represented nothing more than assistance he would give to any friend in need.

Nevertheless, McAdoo reiterated, the "California friend" might make—indeed, was making—trouble, which not only could pose problems in the 1916 campaign but might also subject Mrs. Galt to the kind of malodorous whisperings that had circulated three years previously.

The effectiveness of McAdoo's argument was borne out a few hours later, when the President asked Grayson to go to Mrs. Galt with the whole story, and to tell her she was released from "any promises." Her answer, in a letter to Wilson, was that she was undeterred by rumors and threats and would "stand by" him—"not for duty, not for pity, not for honour—but for love . . . trusting, comprehensive love."

For three days she waited for a reply; then Grayson telephoned that the President was ill and wanted to see her at the

White House. There they decided to be married before the end of the year.

At last resigned to a prospect they had tried to prevent, House and McAdoo pretended they had been for it all along. The shrewd colonel, in fact, feigned surprise when the President told him, on September 10, about the talk with McAdoo. But in his diary two days later, House wrote the following, as though he hoped all the world would read it at the time:

> He [the President] does not know now that the anony-
> mous letter was not genuine. However he spoke to me
> about it with great concern, telling me it was contrary to
> his idea of Mrs. Hulbert and that he thought she had fallen
> under some evil influence. He did not know that I knew
> the entire story of the money having been sent and of the
> anonymous letter, and in order to protect McAdoo, I
> could not explain.
>
> I have never seen a man more dependent on a woman's
> companionship. He was perfectly happy and contented
> with his wife. They had an ideal married life, as all his
> relatives will testify and have, indeed, to me. But his
> loneliness since her death has oppressed him and if he
> does not marry, and marry quickly, I believe he will go
> into a decline. Dr. Grayson shares this belief . . .

As wedding plans proceeded, House busied himself toward making everything as pleasant as possible for Wilson—and palatable to the country at large. He bolstered the President's spirits by telling him that a quiet canvass of influential Democrats showed they favored the marriage at an early date. Following through, House arranged for Dr. Stockton Axson, at that time on the faculty of Rice Institute, to write an article on his brother-in-law's private life. Then House rounded up testimonies from others who were also eager to vindicate the President. Furthermore, the resourceful colonel worked out a

plan to mollify at least one segment of womanhood—the suff-
ragettes, who were pressing for announced White House support and were grumbling that the President's absorption with
one woman was blinding him to the voting rights of all women.

On October 4 the President wrote a letter to Mrs. Hulbert
(Peck) and kept a copy for the record:

> Before the public announcement is made known, I want
> you to be the first to know of the good fortune that has
> come to me. I have not been at liberty to speak of it
> sooner. I am engaged to be married to Mrs. Norman Galt
> of this city, a woman I am sure you would admire and love
> as everyone does who knows her, and I feel a blessing
> greater than any I can measure in words has come to me
> . . . I am writing this in great haste, amid a pressure of
> clamorous engagements that cannot be gainsaid, but you
> will know in what spirit.
> Helen [Bones] joins me in affectionate messages
> Your devoted friend
> Woodrow Wilson

The engagement was officially announced from the White
House two days later. Mrs. Peck was silent, and public reaction
was more favorable than anyone had dared to hope. The following morning the New York *Times* carried the front-page
headline:

PRESIDENT TO WED MRS. NORMAN GALT, INTIMATE FRIEND OF
HIS DAUGHTERS: ALSO COMES OUT FOR WOMEN'S SUFFRAGE

That evening Colonel House gave a dinner in New York for
Wilson and his fiancée and took them to the Empire Theater
to see Cyril Maude in *Grumpy*. Ovation followed ovation in
rising crescendos as the President escorted Mrs. Galt to his
box. By the time they returned to Washington an extra force

of clerks had been employed to take care of congratulations pouring into the White House.

Axson's article, edited by House, appeared in the New York *Times* on October 8 with the title:

MR. WILSON AS SEEN BY ONE OF HIS FAMILY
Professor Stockton Axson, Brother of the First Wife of the President,
Writes an Intimate Sketch
of Mr. Wilson as He is At Home.

He described Wilson as "the most considerate man I ever knew" and as having "always been so gentle in his home life that he has appeared to some *too* domesticated. In the days of his unfortunate collegiate quarrels at Princeton, one charge that used to be made against him was that he was so shut up in his home life that he did not know men and the ways of men." Axson also recalled the President's devotion to Ellen and his depression after her death, and then touched on the prospective wedding: "His intimate friends often expressed to me the wish that the President would marry again, as he was utterly desolate. We who love him feel that God Himself must have directed the circumstances which brought Mrs. Galt into the White House circle." The article was reprinted in twenty newspapers, and Mrs. Malcolm Forbes, of Boston, underwrote the cost of a million copies for free distribution.

Through press interviews, old friends of Wilson came up with confirmation of his fidelity to his late wife, and several emphasized that his propensity for cultivating other women was constantly encouraged by her. A college classmate recalled Wilson as saying, "My best friends have all been women," and another observed, "His basic shyness vanished in the presence of scintillating females." A former Princeton associate compared him to Disraeli in his extraordinary reliance on women to challenge him in lively conversation. Ellen Wilson was remembered as a wife whose security in her hus-

band's love divested her of all jealously, and of having said
early in their life together, "Since you have not married someone who is gay, I must provide you with friends who are." Also
widely publicized was the fact that he frequently visited and
corresponded with a number of fascinating matrons, including
Mrs. Harvey Fielding Reid, wife of a Johns Hopkins professor;
Mrs. Crawford Toy, wife of a Harvard professor; and Mrs.
John Grier Hibben (even after her husband defected from
Wilson at Princeton and succeeded him as president of the
university).

Meanwhile, still fearful that the letters to Mrs. Peck might
come out as more affectionate in tone than his chief had intended them, Texas-born Colonel House hedged that possibility with a widely quoted confession: "We Southerners like
to write mash notes."

The organized effort to improve the President's image
helped to some extent, despite Republican cries that political
expediency had linked his announced engagement to his declaration for women's suffrage. Meanwhile a typographical error in the Washington *Post* had inadvertently contributed to
the spate of lewd anecdotes already sweeping the nation. Describing an evening at the theater, enhanced by the attendance
of the engaged pair, a reporter wrote that instead of watching
the performance "the President spent most of his time entertaining Mrs. Galt." *Entertaining* came out *entering* in the newspaper's earliest edition. And although copies were hastily retrieved from newstands—after a White House aide detected
the typographical error and wildly telephoned the managing
editor—enough copies had been sold to convulse innumerable readers, even after the wedding took place on December
18, 1915.

When the 1916 campaign went into high gear, Peck's Bad
Boy again activated wagging tongues everywhere, and the
vilification catalog was enlarged by fresh entries. One was that
shortly before the marriage Edith Galt paid Mrs. Peck a tidy

sum—for silence—and the President promised Louis Brandeis
his Supreme Court post (the appointment was made in January
1916) for negotiating the bribe and personally delivering it;
another, that Colonel House stalled Mrs. Peck's threats by
taking her twice to Europe, while McAdoo offered her an an-
nual stipend from the Treasury Department for her promise
that she would destroy her letters from Wilson and would
refrain from divulging anything about her romance with him.
A message from a Boston lawyer to a minister who was actively
working for Wilson's reelection reflected the covert defama-
tions at the height of the campaign as follows:

> It seems strange to me that you as a clergyman would
> urge any man to vote for Mr. Wilson. Half of the people
> in the United States know the general facts about his
> extensive acquaintance with Mrs. Peck . . . In fact, the
> matter is so generally known that you ask any man who is
> Peck's Bad Boy, and, with a smile, you will be told that he
> is Mr. Wilson . . .

The recipient forwarded the letter to Justice Brandeis. He
termed it "vile slander," but its import was augmented by
recurrent whispers that Mrs. Peck was providing the Republican party with material which well might lead to impeachment
of the President.

Eager to present printed proof of Wilson's moral deficiencies, his foes doggedly tried to confirm one sensational rumor
after another, while Democrats countered that any reflection
on his reputation was baseless political gunfire. Significantly
enough, the Republicans were never able to track down anything about the President's character that could be openly
used against him or publicly refuted by the Democratic party.
Anyway, toward the end of the campaign, fears that America
might be more quickly drawn into the European conflict with
a change of leadership eclipsed senseless rumors, and the

Democratic rallying cry, "He kept us out of War!" kept Wilson in the White House.

After his reelection, the President's popularity escalated, as a spirit of national unity pervaded the country at war. To many in America he was little less than a god, and his prestige abroad was monumental. He was the most famous leader in the world when peace was declared.

His power was threatened at home, however, when the Democrats lost their majority in Congress at the midterm elections, and shortly thereafter, indications that he still was anathema to Americans who wanted a strictly moral universe began to appear as ominous clouds on the horizon. At the same time, there were grumblings across the country that the President was taking all the kudos for winning the war, and Republicans in Congress flexed their political muscles to show who would control the aftermath. Prepared to resume chairmanship of the Senate Foreign Relations Committee was Wilson's most powerful political enemy, Senator Henry Cabot Lodge, of Massachusetts.

Disapproval of the President grew in the United States when he announced he would attend the Paris Peace Conference. With his wife and a shipload of notables, he sailed for Europe in December 1918. His renown abroad was still prodigious; he and the First Lady were royally received in England and Italy and wildly acclaimed on their arrival in Paris. As Wilson battled for "peace without vengeance" at the conference, however, European power politics unleashed old venoms, and enemies at home criticized his dabbling in negotiations that should have been left to diplomatic masterminds.

Assigning Colonel House to carry on at the peace table and leaving Mrs. Wilson in Paris, the President returned to Washington to reinforce his political fences before adjournment of the Sixty-fifth Congress. And with the hope of cementing trusted friendships and assuaging old enmities, he entertained

Senate and House leaders at a White House dinner. The evening was something less than a success, for beneath surface politeness, there were foreboding undercurrents. With all the tact and charm he could summon, the President discussed his conception of a League of Nations that would end war for all time, but he was vague when his guests asked pointed questions as to how it could be implemented. Senator Lodge observed afterward that Wilson "was civil and showed no temper" but was generally uninformed about the structure of his envisioned League. "We went away as wise as when we came," the senator said.

Antagonism to the President mounted when he went to France the second time. There the conference was not working out as he had hoped, and other annoyances surfaced. For one thing, the First Lady was nettled at House. During her husband's absence, American journalists in Paris had written glowing articles about the colonel's importance to the President. Mrs. Wilson had questioned House as to how the publicity came about, and when he could not explain she concluded it was self-promoted. Wilson on his own was vexed because House, without consulting him, had made certain concessions that appeared to weaken the American position at the conference. From that point on, the colonel's influence with the President steadily dwindled.

With his vision of lasting peace embodied in the Versailles Treaty—with its Article X, the League of Nations—the President returned to Washington to face the most disheartening battle of his political career. Senator Lodge and his cohorts realistically analyzed the pact and loaded Article X with drastic revisions. Arguing that the amendments virtually nullified the aim of the League, the President rejected them. And when he became convinced that the Foreign Relations Committee would never recommend ratification without insisting on enervating compromises, he determined to arouse nationwide support for the League by personally taking the issue to the people.

He scheduled his crusade through California and the Midwest, with multiple speaking engagements in major cities, and left Washington early in September 1919, accompanied by Mrs. Wilson, Dr. Grayson, and a sizable staff. In the course of the journey, the First Lady for the first time would meet Mrs. Hulbert, the woman would always be "Mrs. Peck" to the gossipy public.

Shortly after the President and his party arrived at the Hotel Alexandria in Los Angeles, he sent his old friend this note: "I am writing for Edith and myself both to beg you to lunch with us here at the hotel tomorrow at one o'clock . . ." Mrs. Hulbert accepted, arrived a few minutes early, and after luncheon, outwaited interruptions of several delegations and lingered on, talking about her troubles until dusk. Mrs. Wilson later described her as "a faded, sweet-looking woman, who was absorbed in her only son" and observed that her extended stay taxed the President, already exhausted from his strenuous schedule. The visitor's account, years afterward, recalled the First Lady as "handsome and Junoesque" and added, "She played well the most difficult role of a third party to the reunion of two old friends endeavoring to relive the incidents of years in a single afternoon." At the end, Mrs. Hulbert wrote, the President escorted her to the elevator, which dropped her "out of sight and out of the life of my old friend—forever."

Five days after the Los Angeles luncheon the President, en route to a speaking engagement in Wichita, Kansas, collapsed on his train and was rushed back to the White House. His return coincided with the Washington arrival of an eminent statesman, Edward Grey, Viscount of Falloden. Lord Grey had served as Britain's foreign minister for eleven years and had written a moving letter to the President after Ellen Wilson died; a warm correspondence had ensued. Furthermore, Lord Grey had been of invaluable assistance to Colonel House on the latter's presidential missions abroad. Although he had retired from public service in 1916, and was old and nearly blind when he was appointed Special Ambassador to the United States, Grey was still internationally recognized as a persuasive negotiator, with great endurance. House urged him to accept the appointment in the hope that he could work out agreements to prevent a naval armaments race and help to bring America into the League.

The President on returning to Washington was too ill to receive any callers, and three days later he suffered a cerebral thrombosis that left him partially paralyzed for some time. (Meanwhile the impenetrable White House secrecy about his condition gave rise to a rash of rumors that he had been stricken by paresis, resulting from the venereal disease that had intermittently incapacitated him since his years at Princeton.) The new British ambassador could not officially function until he had presented his credentials to the President, but nobody appeared willing or able to smooth the way, even after Wilson recovered enough to have a few official visitors. Secretary of State Lansing said he could not help, and so did Grayson and Tumulty. Lord Grey could not ask his old friend House to intercede, for the colonel on his recent return from England had suffered an attack of gallstones so severe he had to be carried by stretcher from the ship to his New York apartment.

Tumulty finally telephoned the envoy that the President hoped to see him within a few days. While he waited and fumed, an unpleasant situation came to light in regard to his secretary, Major Charles Kennedy Craufurd-Stuart, whom he had brought with him from England. Presumably, Lord Grey had been unaware that his aide had incurred White House displeasure in 1918 while serving with the then British ambassador, the Marquess of Reading.

Specifically, the musically gifted but indiscreet major had

enlivened a capital soiree by presenting a pianologue implying that Mrs. Galt managed to become First Lady by paying off her main competition, Mrs. Peck. The stalwart Democratic hostess, Mrs. J. Borden Harriman, was mortified, and so were most of her guests; but the few who were secretly amused repeated the story, and chatter about Peck's Bad Boy permeated Washington. Gossip quickly followed that Craufurd-Stuart compounded the mischief at a dinner some evenings after Mrs. Harriman's party when he recited this riddle:

> "What did Mrs. Galt do when the President proposed to her?
> "Fell out of bed."

Reports of the Britisher's antics quickly reached the White House, and official reaction was forthcoming. Secretary Lansing requested Lord Reading to send the culprit back to England at once. Instead, the envoy dispatched his quaking aide to Lansing's home to plead for mercy. Craufurd-Stuart explictly denied that he had propounded the distasteful riddle. It was attached to him, he said, because he annoyed a prominent woman at a dinner by mentioning an article he had just read in the New York *Tribune* unfavorably comparing the power and ability of the President with those of famous British Prime Ministers. The incensed lady, he went on, had retorted that he would stop at nothing to malign President and Mrs. Wilson, as his performance at Mrs. Harriman's had already proved. However, Craufurd-Stuart insisted, the impromptu pianologue was offered to a sophisticated gathering, merely as light amusement, with no intent to disparage the First Lady. There would be no reoccurrence of his undiplomatic conduct, he promised—indeed, he would make himself socially scarce —if he was allowed to stay in Washington for the remaining weeks of his tour of duty; prior dismissal would ruin his career. Lansing requested him to write his explanation in full for the State Department record.

What happened at the White House after that interview is not clear. The President probably decided that precipitate disposal of the offender would instigate further embarrassing reminders. Anyway, the major stayed on until he accompanied the Marquess of Reading back to England.

Craufurd-Stuart's reappearance on the capital scene in 1919 had naturally infuriated the First Lady, and according to Bernard Baruch's diary, the President "did not see Grey because he had brought back this man who had spoken so scurrilously about Mrs. Wilson." Baruch, head of the War Industries Board, was in a position to know; he had virtually replaced his old enemy, Colonel House, as counselor to the President, and Mrs. Wilson trusted him implicitly.

In any case, Grayson promptly told Secretary Lansing that the First Lady insisted that he remove Craufurd-Stuart without delay. Lansing informed Lord Grey that his secretary's prompt departure "was requested by the White House." The ambassador refused to believe the pressure had emanated from the President and made another effort to see him. When Grey could not get an interview, even with Tumulty, he was furious, and when he gathered that Craufurd-Stuart was about to be dispatched *persona non grata,* the envoy removed his secretary from State Department jurisdiction by making him "a member of the Ambassador's household."

Secretary Lansing was soon acutely conscious of Mrs. Wilson's vexation at his inability to carry out her order. Rumors rippled that she had never cared for him, anyway, and that his days in the Cabinet were numbered because he could never please either her *or* the President.

Prince Edward of England shortly thereafter visited Washington and was escorted to the ill President's bedside, but Lord Grey was not asked to accompany him. (Although still indisposed in New York, Colonel House kept up with what was going on in Washington. He wrote in his diary that the President was not responsible for the slight to the ambassador and that "the commotion about Craufurd-Stuart" was due entirely to the First Lady and without her husband's knowledge.)

Three months after his arrival in the United States, Lord Grey went home. He had never been able to see the President, but he had talked to some of the members of the Foreign Relations Committee; and he wrote a letter to the London *Times* indicating that Senator Lodge's reservations on the League would not impair it and that Britain would accept conditional cooperation of the United States.

Mrs. Wilson's reaction was quoted: "It may be safely assumed that had Lord Grey ventured such utterances while he was in Washington as ambassador, his country would have been promptly asked to withdraw him."

Meanwhile Colonel House from his sickbed in New York worked toward a compromise on the treaty, convinced that otherwise it would never be ratified. Through Stephen Bonsal, the distinguished journalist who had been his interpreter at the Paris peace conference, the colonel managed to get Senator Lodge to agree that his revisions might be modified until they would be acceptable to Wilson. House immediately wrote to the President, urging him to discuss possible amendments with the Foreign Relations Committee. There was no reply. House then emphasized in a letter to Mrs. Wilson that compromise on the treaty was its only hope for ratification and enclosed a similar letter to the President. When silence from the White House persisted, the colonel presented his views in yet another letter to Wilson; still there was no reply. (House never knew whether any of his messages ever reached the President. When Wilson's correspondence was sent to the Library of Congress in 1952, several unopened letters from House were in the collection. One was an urgent plea for compromise on the League.)

Senator Lodge, annoyed that his gestures toward modification brought no response from the White House, introduced a Senate resolution for ratification of the treaty—with his original revisions. Obeying the President's instructions, loyal Senate Democrats voted against the resolution, and they were joined by enough Republicans to defeat it.

The President was still convinced that an awakened public would in time go along with him; and he looked to the 1920 campaign as "a grand and solemn referendum on the League." He was totally unaware of the temper of the country, disillusioned by the aftermath of war, with little comprehension of what the League was all about, and fearful that it would lead America into further European entanglements.

Senator Lodge, keynote speaker at the 1920 Republican National Convention, lambasted the Wilson administration and heralded its repudiation at the polls as follows:

> Through long years of bitter conflict, moral restraints were loosened and all the habits, all the conventions, all the customs of life which even more than law hold society together, have been swept aside . . . Mr. Wilson and his heirs and assigns, or anybody who with bent knee served his purpose, must be driven from all control of our government and all influence in it . . .

When McAdoo three weeks later emerged as a leading contender for nomination at the Democratic convention, his father-in-law declined to endorse him or any of the other presidential aspirants. Many people thought Wilson himself cherished the hope that a deadlock might result in his being drafted for a third term.

Ohio's Governor James M. Cox, who finally got the nomination, with Franklin D. Roosevelt as his running mate, had no choice but to campaign on Wilson's record. Ratification of the League was in the Democratic platform, but it aroused little interest. No public issue did. The majority voted not for the Republican nominee, and not against Cox, but against Woodrow Wilson, and the GOP landslide swept into the presidency

Warren G. Harding, who promised to bring the country "back to normalcy."

Ray Stannard Baker, who had known Wilson intimately since 1910 and was in charge of press relations for the American Peace Commission in Paris, began organizing the President's private papers and official documents at the White House in 1920 and continued the work after his retirement at the S Street, Washington, home of Wilson and his wife. Nine days before the former President died he gave Baker, in writing, "the first and if necessary exclusive" access to all his papers, but was too weak to sign the letter. The following January Edith Wilson turned over the entire collection to Baker without reservations.

In his eight-volume *Life and Letters of Woodrow Wilson,* published between 1927 and 1939, Baker used portions of Wilson's correspondence to amplify the continuing story. An understanding of Wilson's complex personality and the factors and individuals who contributed to his fluctuating political fortunes can be gleaned from the perceptive biography that resulted, as well as from several other exhaustive works published within the past fifty years. Even more revelatory are the intimate glimpses of Wilson in memoirs of relatives and friends who observed him closely over a long period.

Irwin H. (Ike) Hoover, in his 1934 recollections of his years as chief White House usher, commented on the adoration Wilson had from his first wife and daughters: "They pampered him and petted him and looked up to him as their lord and master."

Ellen Wilson McAdoo discussed her father's fondness for women in *The Woodrow Wilsons* (1937): "Father enjoyed the society of women, especially if they were what he called 'charming and conversable' . . . He had several deep and lasting friendships with women, writing them long letters and spending hours in their company. These friendships he shared

with Mother, and I never saw her show a trace of jealousy."
And she recalled that her father once said, "No man has ever
been a success without having been surrounded by admiring
females."

"Mrs. Peck" does not appear in the book, but Mrs. Hulbert
is mentioned, along with Mrs. Hibben and Mrs. Reid, as
among "father's friends I liked the most." And there is an
enlightening account of a visit to the family at Sea Girt, New
Jersey, after Wilson's 1912 election:

> Mrs. Hulbert, whom father had met in Bermuda, came
> . . . to stay with us. She was a charming woman, with great
> intelligence and humor, and particularly fascinating to
> me. Watching her daintily puffing one cigarette after an-
> other, I decided it was a mistake to think it wrong for a
> woman to smoke, since it was so becoming, and neither
> Father nor Mother seemed shocked. We all enjoyed her
> immensely, but her constant suggestions about improving
> our appearance got on our nerves at last . . .

Edith Gittings (Mrs. Harvey Fielding) Reid in *Woodrow Wilson: The Caricature, the Myth and the Man* (1934) observed that
while Wilson liked "essentially feminine women, he was not
attracted to pretty girls, nor they to him, and a fast woman
bored him as much as he bored her." The writer expressed her
admiration for the first Mrs. Wilson in several passages;
among them, this: "Any man or woman who cared for him
could be sure of Ellen Wilson's devotion." In another section,
Mrs. Reid stated: "So long as his first wife lived, there was
perfect harmony of action and understanding between them,"
and she quoted Wilson's description of Ellen: "Tactfully persuasive, not coercive . . . receptive, not aggressive. A man
could read her a treatise or a long essay and she would never
interrupt until the end: she had what I call a speaking silence."
The book ignored "Mrs. Peck," and the writer's sole reference

to Wilson's second wife had to do with the President's illness, as follows: "She and Dr. Grayson tried to keep him from serious worries, at the same time convincing him that he was still in control of the government."

Edith Bolling Wilson in *My Memoir* (1937) stressed that the barrier she raised around the President after his stroke was on the advice of Dr. Francis K. Dercum and other physicians, who warned her that there was no hope for her husband's recovery unless he could be kept from every disturbing problem. The book also brought out her reasons for disliking both House and McAdoo. She recalled that some time after the marriage she asked House how he got the "erroneous impression about the President and Mrs. Peck" and he confessed he never got it from anybody; he said he and McAdoo merely thought a second marriage so soon after Ellen's death would impair Wilson's chance for reelection. Mrs. Wilson wrote also that McAdoo denied his part in the intrigue; he told her, "It was entirely House's idea." In her opinion, both men feared that a new First Lady could be a threat to their White House influence, and she made it clear that she never forgave either of them.

Her disaffection with McAdoo ostensibly made little impression on him, for he did not mention it when he covered his Cabinet career in *Crowded Years,* which came out seven years after Wilson died. But he wrote of his father-in-law, "I never knew anyone who had a more ardent love for humanity than Woodrow Wilson"; he noted further that Wilson was "a many-sided, complex man," and observed, "His first wife was the only human being who knew him perfectly."

Mary Allen Hulbert's *The Story of Mrs. Peck* (1933) recounts in full her ordeal stemming from a warm friendship that was never anything more. The book points out that she and her second husband were estranged before she met Wilson and that the relationship, instigating so much gossip later, was based solely on her sympathetic interest in the brilliant man's accomplishments and aspirations. She remembered he once said to her, "You have a genius for friendship," and that he later wrote, "Your friendship gives me pleasure not only but some subtle help also." She further recalled that her visit to the White House after Ellen's death was on Helen Bones' invitation, that she hardly saw the President during her brief stay, and that his loan of seventy-five hundred dollars a month later was to enable her recently ill son to buy a ranch in California. The amount, half the face value of mortages she held, was "paid back in full," she wrote.

A resumé of the harassment she endured from July 1915 until the President was reelected follows: California news reporters constantly hounded her, even after she told them that Wilson had never asked her to marry him ("so a breach of promise suit was out of the question"), and that nobody at the White House had tried to bribe her. She was visited and grilled by a lawyer who said he was sent by "those boys in Washington"—he later identified them as "the President and Mr. McAdoo"—to find out whether she planned to "make trouble" about his forthcoming marriage. She dismissed the impertinent caller without telling him anything. Her son's recurrent illness depleted her bank account. She eked out a small income by writing magazine articles and a cookbook, then sold encyclopedias from door to door and worked briefly as a motion picture extra in Hollywood. Meanwhile anonymous messages poured in, with offensive questions about her letters from Wilson, and her California cottage was ransacked by persons presumably in search of them.

Returning East early in 1916, she was shadowed for weeks in New York City. Strange individuals sought her out and urged her to assist in a clandestine movement to impeach the President, and although she was in dire need of money, she turned down substantial offers for her letters when she discovered the Republican party planned to use them in the campaign. Finally she wrote to the White House, requesting that a responsible person be sent to carry a confidential message to the President. Her intent, she emphasized, was to inform him about the New York cabal against him without describing it in a letter.

Mrs. Wilson wrote back that she was "so sorry" there was no such messenger to send from the White House. "She suggested," Mrs. Hulbert recalled, "that I write out my information. But I did not choose to do so."

She did not mention that Bernard Baruch paid her $65,000 for her letters from Woodrow Wilson and allowed her to retain them on the promise that she would not allow them to be published during the 1916 campaign. Later, he took possession of them at Ray Stannard Baker's request and turned them over to him. According to Mrs. Hulbert's recollection, she kept the correspondence hidden for some time in her cottage at Nantucket, and when she finally had to sell the house and had arranged to dispose of its contents at auction, her letters "were seized and sent to the White House." She added that Baker paid her for the use of them while he was writing his Wilson biography. And the last sentence of her life story reads: "The publication of them [the letters] would be the final death of base attacks, made primarily on Mr. Wilson, and incidentally on me, which the reader has glimpsed here."

Her correspondence from Wilson has never been published in full, but more than two hundred letters, which she received from him from February 1907 to October 1915, are accessible today in the Library of Congress. They are in no sense compromising. Rather, they are outpourings of a man absorbed by his own thoughts, expressing them to a sympathetic friend. Affording exceptional insights into Wilson's warmth, wit and philosophy, they are, in fact, running commentaries of everything that affected him at the time—trivial happenings, individuals, trials and triumphs. They include memories of his visits to Bermuda "and the long talks with my good and inspiring friend," his uncertainty in 1913 "at leaving a settled way of life of a sudden and launching into a vast sea of Ifs and Buts," his daughters' romances and marriages, his worries about Mexico and the war in Europe, and his recreations ("I play ten or eleven holes of golf every day and twice every week I go to the theatre").

The letters also include innumerable references to his first wife: ("Ellen is delighted with the beautiful lace collar. She sends her love—and will write to you at once" . . . "Ellen looks forward to seeing you" . . . "Ellen so much enjoyed your visit, as did we all!" . . . "Ellen was pleased that you like her paintings. She has great talent."). The postscript "With warm regards from all" often appears. His distress because of his wife's deteriorating health is repeatedly expressed. His letter after her death reads: "Of course you know what has happened to me; but I wanted you to know it direct from me. God has stricken me almost beyond what I can bear."

Some of the letters are in longhand; a few are in pencil; many are neatly typewritten. The earlier salutations are "My dear Mrs. Peck," and the endings "Yours in respect and admiration." Later and briefer messages are to "My dearest friend" from "Your devoted friend." All are signed, "Woodrow Wilson."

The correspondence is not comparable in any way to the tender letters he wrote to Ellen, beginning in 1883, when the Virginia-born son of a Presbyterian minister fell in love with the Georgia-born daughter of a Presbyterian minister, and continuing through their almost thirty years of marriage. The collection clearly shows that he was never separated from her for more than a day without sending her long, ardent letters.

Shortly after Wilson's death more than fourteen items of the correspondence was found in the S Street house and were given to Eleanor McAdoo, the only living daughter. She culled the best for her book, *A Priceless Gift: The Love Letters of Woodrow and Ellen Axson Wilson,* published in 1962.

Ellen's writings are warm but comparatively brief; she was

not an inveterate correspondent. But with pen or typewriter at hand, Wilson had a way of going on and on, commenting on everything and everybody around him. This is exemplified in all of his personal correspondence. His writings to Ellen, however, invariably expressed his deep affection for her. Typically, he wrote from Bermuda in 1908:

> Mark Twain has been down here between boats, and I have seen a good deal of him. He seems to like being with me. Yesterday, Mrs. Peck gave him a lunch at her house and gathered a most entertaining group of garrison people to meet him. He was in great form and delighted everybody.
>
> There is quite a household (at Mrs. Peck's), all of whom I enjoy: her mother, a fine old lady with the breeziness of the West about her, a stepdaughter, her son by a first marriage . . . It is a lively and engaging household, in the midst of which your husband is as young and gay as the youngest member.
>
> I brought two pictures of you with me, and Mrs. Peck is so charmed with them that she insists upon keeping them on the mantel-piece in her drawing room, so it seems almost as if my darling was there . . . and all the while my thoughts follow my darling . . . Ah, how intensely and passionately, how constantly I love you . . . if you were not there to think of and return to, how flat and empty everything I enjoy would be!

Every one of his letters in this collection has an endearing salutation: "My darling sweetheart," or "My precious Ellie," or "My own darling." The usual ending is, "Your own, *Woodrow*."

If all his letters to Mrs. Peck had been made accessible to the public in July 1915 and could have been compared with any one he wrote to Ellen, disapproval of his hasty second marriage might not have stopped, but at least the slander could not have been amplified by snide allusions to Peck's Bad Boy.

VI

Miasma of Dishonor

Warren G. Harding's administration would go down in history as a catastrophe, and he would be remembered as a President who consorted with a mistress in the White House, but in 1920 to a vast majority he appeared to be a leader who could restore normalcy to the postwar nation.

He was a Midwest conservative with a background in business and experience in the United States Senate, and he was not tarred with the intellectual ambitions and global idealism that had disenchanted many with Woodrow Wilson. A delegate at the convention nominating Harding boosted him as "The kind of President we need, a man with no highfalutin' ideas on how to change the world." More to the point in that particular era, his own reiterated campaign assertion, "The less government control over business, the better," suited the big moneymakers.

Harding was monumentally impressive on the platform. He had a resonant voice and his florid phraseology was effective both in arousing acclaim from devotees and in annoying opponents. At the 1916 Republican National Convention, his keynote address electrified the audience. Later, his Senate speech castigating the high-pressured Liberty Bonds drive so thoroughly irritated Secretary of the Treasury McAdoo that he ridiculed the Ohioan's "bow-wow style of oratory" and added, "His speeches left the impression of pompous phrases moving over the landscape in search of an idea. Sometimes these meandering words would actually capture a straggling thought and bear it triumphantly, a prisoner in their midst, until it died of servitude and overwork."

Nevertheless, Harding's oratory was in tune with the times, and it was notably enhanced by his appearance. With a massive but well-proportioned frame, classic features and a bronzed complexion set off by silvering hair, he commanded respect and evoked admiration without saying anything significant. And he was the first presidential candidate for whom women had a chance to vote.

Friends who had grown up with him in Marion, Ohio, affectionately called him W.G. and made much of his good points. He was unfailingly courteous and convivial. He had a flair for getting along with people. He appeared to be properly circumspect; with normal regard for surface appearances in keeping with the moral standards of the day. He was an all-around good citizen.

When pressed, acquaintances might also reveal that W.G. was undiscriminating in his choice of intimates and loyal to even the undeserving. He could not bear to hurt anybody's feelings; he could not say No. Probably apocryphal, but illustrative of his innate compliancy, was the story that his father, while giving young W.G. a thrashing for a minor offense, said, "I guess I ought to be thankful you're a boy. If you'd been a girl, every young scalawag in town would have had his way with you by now!" And W. G.'s faith in the integrity of his fellow-man later prompted a college classmate to tease him, "The difference between you and George Washington is he couldn't tell a lie, and you can't tell a liar!" Time was to prove that these flaws in his character, plus an immature desire to please everyone around him, made him at once fair game for predatory females and a pawn of stronger-willed individuals of either sex.

His susceptibility to feminine wiles had caused casual clothesline gossip in Marion for years—and whispers in Washington during his terms in the Senate. Rumors about it raised some questions at the 1920 Republican Convention in Chicago.

In the light of what was to come out years later, an evening at that convention had special significance. The tight race betwen the two leading contenders, General Leonard Wood and Illinois Govenor Frank O. Lowden, induced a group of powerful men to press for a late-afternoon adjournment; they wanted to foregather quietly and select a candidate to break the imminent deadlock. Colonel George Harvey, an apostate from the Democratic fold after Woodrow Wilson failed to appreciate him, asked three senators to dine with him in his suite at the Blackstone Hotel—Henry Cabot Lodge, of Massachusetts; Charles W. Curtis, of Kansas; and Frank Brandegee, of Connecticut. Eleven other prominent individuals joined the group in the course of the evening.

It was not by accident that Warren G. Harding was discussed as the candidate who could win. One man who was not present had been steadily promoting that idea for some time; and early in the convention he had predicted that before its end a conclave of leaders "in a smoke filled room" would decide on Harding as the next President "at 2:11 A.M."

The prophet was Harry Micajah Daugherty, a Columbus, Ohio, lawyer and political finagler who, after serving in the state legislature and then running unsuccessfully for other offices, had decided he could do better by promoting other men. He liked to recall that he had known Harding since the turn of the century and that after his first glimpse of the impressive man he had mused, "What a great President he'd make!" The Senate was a step toward that goal. Daugherty had persuaded Harding to run for it in 1914, and had managed that successful campaign and also the one in which he was reelected in 1918.

Although generally undistinguished, Harding's Senate career was satisfactory enough to the Republican party and big business, and Daugherty set out to make him President. The initial difficulty was in getting Harding to go along; he insisted that he preferred to stay in the Senate. But Daugherty knew he had Mrs. Harding on his side; a crystal-gazer had predicted that the Ohio senator's wife would one day be First Lady.

Her reliance on clairvoyants had been stimulated in Washington by a "Madame Marcia," who professed that given the date and time of birth she could produce a character profile of any person without even knowing the name. Mrs. Harding provided the required statistics about her husband—November 2, 1865, at 2 P.M.—and the seeress came up with this:

> "Sympathetic, kindly, intuitive, free with promises and trustful of friends; enthusastic, impulsive. Perplexed over financial affairs. Many clandestine love affairs; inclined to recurrent moods of melancholia."

During her husband's remaining years in the Senate, Mrs. Harding consulted one fortune teller after another, and a "higher goal" for Warren G. Harding was firmly set in her mind when Daugherty enlisted her forceful assistance in 1920. The two finally persuaded Harding to allow his name to go into presidential nomination as Ohio's favorite son. Daugherty then moved swiftly from one group to another, reminding every convention delegate he contacted that Harding would be the propitious choice if a deadlock developed between the leading candidates.

It was no surprise to Daugherty, therefore, that the conferees at the Blackstone reached that conclusion after hours of deliberation. Even then, there were some misgivings about Harding. Exactly what they were has never been revealed, but they may have evolved from vague rumors that he was something less than a faithful husband. And, certainly, the Republicans wanted no repetition of the kind of gossip that had haunted Woodrow Wilson's presidential campaigns.

Anyway, at 2 P.M., Harding was summoned. Colonel Harvey met him in a separate room, and with characteristic pomposity, said, "We think you may get the nomination tomorrow. Before acting finally, we think you should tell us, on your own conscience and before God, whether there is anything that might be brought up against you that would embarrass the party, an impediment that might disqualify you and make you inexpedient, either as candidate or as President."

Harding was stunned. He asked for time to consider an answer, and Harvey left him alone. His reflections during the brief interval that followed can only be surmised, for there were several things that might have perturbed him. According to later disclosures, he had been involved with a married woman for years, and the mother of his illegitimate child was in Chicago at the time. But he probably reasoned that both affairs could always be kept secret. Or he might have wondered whether or not his friends were worried about suspicions that there was Negro blood in his family line. He was not overly bothered about that imputation; it had come up repeatedly but ineffectually in his races for the Senate. More than likely, the prospective candidate assumed that his promoters merely wanted routine confirmation that he felt himself adequate to winning the election and serving creditably as President. At any rate, after ten minutes of solitary meditation, Harding emerged and assured Harvey that there was "Nothing, no obstacle" to his candidacy. He won the Republican nomination the following day.

Senator Boies Penrose, of Pennsylvania, was one powerful Harding enthusiast who was not at the convention; he was ill in Philadelphia. But by direct communication lines between his home and Chicago he followed every development. And when his informant on the scene telephoned that the Ohioan had been nominated but added lightly that everybody hoped his "weakness for women" would not be brought up in the race, Penrose retorted, "No worries about that! We'll just throw a halo around his handsome head and everything will be all right!"

While Harding, with Daugherty as his personal manager, waged his campaign, mainly from the front porch of his Marion, Ohio, home, news reporters converged on the maple-shaded county seat of twenty-eight thousand inhabitants and started tracking down details about the candidate's background and personality. Neighbors and other friends willingly came up with favorable facts but were reluctant to discuss anything remotely questionable about W.G., the leading citizen in the town where he had lived for forty-five years. Everyone knew him and almost everyone liked him extravagantly. The only resident who had ever openly hated him for any length of time was his father-in-law, Amos Kling.

A Pennsylvania Mennonite, Kling had moved to Marion during the Civil War and had prospered in the hardware business. Then he dabbled in real estate, became a banker and the richest man in town. His only daughter, Florence (Flossie), attended a fashionable school, finished a course at the Cincinnati Conservatory of Music, and at nineteen enraged her father by eloping with a neighbor, Henry De Wolfe. He was a wealthy man's son, but he was a spendthrift and he drank heavily. Finally, he deserted his wife and their son, who was born six months after the marriage, and Kling refused to support them. De Wolfe's father provided groceries and shelter until Flossie could establish herself as a piano teacher; then Kling relented and invited his daughter and grandson to live with him. Later he adopted the boy and called him Eugene Marshall Kling.

After being unmarried for a decade, Flossie fell in love with W. G. Harding, the good-looking young editor of the Marion *Star*, and made up her mind to marry him. Her father did everything he could to prevent the match, but Flossie was determined. The wedding took place in Marion on July 8, 1891.

Amos Kling did not speak to his daughter for seven years, and for fourteen he was her husband's bitter enemy. In time, however, he mellowed and visited the Hardings, and during his later years the old man came to like his son-in-law.

Meanwhile, acquaintances could not quite figure out why W. G. ever married Flossie. She was eight years his senior, a divorcée with a child, and no beauty. Was it money? She had none of her own, and at the time of the marriage no prospect of inheriting anything. Was it social position? Hers was better than his, and social lines are never more clearly defined than in a small town, but snobbery was not in Harding's makeup. The general conclusion was that Kling's waspish opposition figured strongly in bringing off the marriage; that, coupled with Flossie's fixation on Harding and the latter's characteristic aversion to hurting anybody's feelings. Certainly, it was believed, he had never been deeply in love with her.

A vital woman of principle and purpose, Flossie did her energetic best to make her marriage and the Marion *Star* successful. Perceiving at once that her husband's business methods were slipshod, she took over the newspaper's circulation department and ran it for fourteen years. The enterprise prospered, but employees were loath to credit that to her. They grumbled that her prime reason for being around all the time was that she wanted to keep a sharp eye on every other woman who entered the office. Later, one of her husband's friends recalled that Mrs. Harding was officious in the operation and "at all times jealous and at most times suspicious of Harding

who, with his placid disposition and reluctance to face unpleasant situations, let her have her own way, or appear to
have it, oftener than most men would have . . ."

Others insisted that but for her participation the *Star* would
never have been a moneymaker, and but for her constant
prodding, her husband would never have been anything more
than a small-city newspaper publisher and editor.

With Normalcy for the Nation as its theme, Harding's low-
keyed presidential campaign went smoothly for three months.
Talk about his romantic entanglements was muted. A few individuals in Marion suspected that he had occasionally enjoyed an extramarital fling—or, as William Allen White put it,
"a primrose detour from Main Street"—but they attributed his
errancy to his prosaic marriage. And the general public was
unaware that he had ever been anything but a model husband.

Toward the end of the race, rumors about the ethnic discrepancy in Harding's lineage reverberated through the Deep
South, and the candidate considered the wisdom of issuing a
formal testimonial that he had only white blood in his veins.
Fearful that any such assertion would deflect the sizable Negro
vote, however, Republican managers ruled against such a
statement and warned the nominee to refrain from any discussion of the subject. Harding complied, except on one occasion.
When James M. Faulkner, a political reporter for the Cincinnati *Enquirer*, asked him point-blank, "Do you have Negro
blood?" Harding replied with a smile, "How do I know, Jim.
One of my ancestors may have jumped the fence."

A week before the election, "An Open Letter to the Men and
Women of America" came out, with a genealogical chart al-
legedly tracing Harding's bloodline to "a West Indian Negro
of French stock" who lived in Blooming Grove, Ohio, in the
early nineteenth century. Among five affidavits was one stating, in part, "Warren Gamaliel Harding is not a white man; he
is not a creole, he is a mestizo . . . May God save America from

international shame and a domestic rule." The broadside bore the facsimile signature, "W. E. Chancellor." Dr. William Estabrook Chancellor, an admitted white racist, was a professor at Wooster College, in Ohio. Wooster trustees, concluding that he was unbalanced, demanded his resignation and announced that it had been enforced after he admitted authorship of portions of the diatribe.

Some 250,000 copies of the leaflet were discovered in the San Francisco post office, and the government, under Democratic administration, seized and destroyed them and forbade further dispersal of such material through the mails. Copies continued to get around; many were slipped under doorways or furtively passed from hand to hand.

The Republican party promptly publicized a Harding family tree, showing distinguished roots in the Eastern United States and impeccable branches in Ohio. Edward L. Doheny, an oil multimillionaire who left Democratic ranks to support the Republican nominee, contributed twenty-five thousand dollars for campaign advertisements with full-page portraits of Harding's parents; they had no Negroid features.

News correspondents for months had been on the trail of clues in connection with the candidate's controversial ancestry but had uncovered nothing tangible for publication. However, in tracing the story's origin to the early nineteenth century when Warren Harding's antecedents lived in Blooming Grove, they had learned that one Harding had a dark-complexioned wife, and a man whom he castigated for theft had charged that she was a "nigger." Shortly afterward, two blacksmiths in another Ohio community quarreled and one berated the other for having "a nigger wife." Her maiden name was Harding. Her husband killed the defamer and was sent to prison. When he was released two years later, relatives of the slain man unsuccessfully tried to prove that his accusation was true. From then on, innuendos about miscegenation in the Harding family had come up only when W.G. ran for public office.

Last-ditch efforts by Democrats to revive the story in the 1920 campaign were futile. The roorback ricocheted into the impression that ruthless enemies were trying to victimize Harding, and a number of registered Democrats voted Republican. Harding won the election by an overwhelming majority.

The new President and First Lady got off to a popular start. He ordered that the White House gates be opened—they had been closed and barred during Woodrow Wilson's illness— and he reinstated public tours through the executive mansion. Mrs. Harding announced that she and her husband were "just folks," although news correspondents noted that he generally referred to her as The Duchess. Her freshness and verve as she negotiated a crowded social calendar inspired the Washington *Post* to report, "No President's wife in the memory of the Capital had displayed such endurance."

A series of stag breakfasts and evening poker sessions drew the President's closest men friends to the White House, and he played golf in a male foursome almost every day. He rode horseback on Sunday mornings, returning in time to escort his wife to the Cavalry Baptist Church.

He named some highly able men to his Cabinet, among them Charles Evans Hughes, Secretary of State; Andrew W. Mellon, Secretary of the Treasury; John W. Weeks, Secretary of War; and Herbert C. Hoover, Secretary of Commerce. As expected, Will H. Hays, Republican national chairman, became Postmaster General, and several other appointments appeared to be plausible, including that of Albert B. Fall as Secretary of the Interior. Fall of New Mexico and Harding of Ohio had occupied adjoining seats in the Senate; they were intimate friends; and Fall had forcefully supported Harding's presidential campaign. Also understandable was George Harvey's reward. He became ambassador to Great Britain, the post he had expected to get from Woodrow Wilson.

Wide disapproval emerged, however, when questionable

politicians odiously known as the "Ohio gang" converged on Washington. In the vanguard was Daugherty and trailing him was his constant companion, Jess Smith. Powerful Republicans already regarded Daugherty as a liability, and when it became known that he was slated to be Attorney General, editorial criticism exploded from coast to coast. Particularly vituperative was an attack in the New York *World* pointing out that Daugherty's legal credentials were inadmissible, as he was nothing more than a lobbyist and a political fixer.

"Harry Daugherty is the best friend I have on earth," declared the President. "He can have anything he wants from me." The next week Daugherty became the chief law officer of the United States. Later, he would figure in the disgrace of the administration, as would Fall and two others whom Harding placed in high office. One was Charles R. Forbes.

While on a senatorial junket to Hawaii, Harding had met Forbes and had been impressed with his magnetism and aptitude for pleasurable pursuits. Forbes was adept at promoting himself, and he quickly got across the highlights of his wartime service, from which he said he emerged as colonel with a Distinguished Service Medal and the Croix de Guerre. He was a Democratic appointee in a minor territorial position at the time he met Harding, but he turned Republican in time to be prominently active in the Ohioan's presidential campaign. Forbes expected due recompense, and he got it. Harding made him head of the Veterans Bureau, which annually disbursed $450 million.

Another who had worked effectively toward Harding's election was Thomas W. Miller, a former member of Congress from Delaware and a lawyer who professed to be experienced in handling cases of international importance, Harding appointed him Alien Property Custodian, in charge of handling multiple foreign interests which had been taken over by the government during wartime.

Daugherty, Fall and Forbes became regular members of the

President's intimate group known as his "poker cabinet," and frequently included in the gatherings were Thomas Miller and Jess Smith.

On K Street, a few blocks from the executive mansion, was the Little Green House, a haven for lobbyists with dubious connections and grafters with obscure purposes. Forbes and Miller occasionally dropped in there. Smith was there often, and among other habitués were William J. Burns and Gaston B. Means. Daugherty made Burns head of the Bureau of Investigation, the detective division of the Justice Department, which in reality was something of a medium of political blackmail. Burns hired Means in November 1921 as his assistant. Within two years, Means would be unmasked as a criminal.

At the beginning of the administration Daugherty and Smith shared living quarters in an H Street residence lent to Daugherty by Harding's golf-playing crony Edward Beale (Ned) McLean, publisher of the Washington *Post.* Later, when there was so much gossip about goings-on in the nearby Little Green House, Daugherty took an apartment at the Wardman Park, and Smith moved with him.

In April 1921 Daugherty quietly asked Colonel Edmund W. Starling of the Secret Service if he would act as intermediary for some correspondence between the President and a "young friend in New York." Starling declined. He said his job as chief of the White House detail did not cover his handling private matters; besides, he was too busy guarding the President's safety. James Sloan, Jr., another Secret Service agent, took the assignment and served as a go-between for Harding and his "young friend." Talk soon spread that he was spiriting her in and out of the White House. Democrats who had winced at the gossip about Woodrow Wilson were delighted, and often repeated with chuckles at their dinner tables was Mrs. Bainbridge Colby's summation of Harding: "A handsome josher . . . straddling a Presidential and a primrose path, splitting rapidly."

*   *   *

Mrs. Harding became seriously ill in the spring of 1922 and for six months was under the constant care of Dr. Charles E. Sawyer, the Marion homeopath who lived at the White House and by executive appointment held the rank of brigadier general.

While Mrs. Harding was secluded in her room, and twice near death, portentous developments in and around the administration began to disturb the President. Colonel Starling late in March showed him a letter a friend had received to the effect that the government had secretly leased one of its naval oil reserves to a private corporation. On reading the message the President was visibly upset; and he appeared relieved, and grateful, when Starling assured him that it would not be shown to anyone else.

An oil operator informed Wyoming Senator John B. Kendrick in April that Interior Secretary Fall had leased the naval oil reserve in Wyoming to Harry F. Sinclair's Mammoth Oil Company. (The property was known as Teapot Dome because of the oddly shaped butte that was its landmark.)

Senatorial queries finally brought from the Interior Department confirmation of the Teapot Dome negotiation and also the announcement that the government would soon lease its Elk Hills Reserve in California to the Pan-American Petroleum and Transportation Company, headed by Edward L. Doheny. The official explanation was that drillings on adjoining oil lands were draining supplies from the government properties, and that immediate utilization by private companies would protect the reserves for future U.S. Naval needs. The negotiations were secret "acts of executive discretion," according to Secretary Fall, because "national security" was involved.

Senator Robert M. (Fighting Bob) LaFollette, of Wisconsin, promptly put through a resolution calling for a formal inquiry and requesting Fall to produce "all materials pertaining to the entire subject of leases upon Naval oil reserves." Senator

Thomas J. Walsh, of Montana, was named chairman of the investigating committee. He was to spend eighteen months gathering data that would rock the country for years—and dishonor the Harding administration for all time.

Fall did not provide the requested material; he consistently held to his official explanation and stated that he had the full support of the White House in keeping further details secret. Walsh sought confirmation from the President and on June 7, 1921, received a letter which read in part: "I think it is only fair in this connection to assure you that the policy . . . in dealing with these matters was submitted to me prior to the adoption thereof, and the policy and the subsequent acts have at all times had my entire approval. Warren G. Harding."

Since several senators already believed that somebody in the government had profited by the questionable transactions, the President's endorsement of them aroused suspicions that he himself was culpable. As the Walsh committee intensified its probing, the scandal mills were energized. For a long time to come, grist would be supplied from several administration areas.

Corruption within the Veterans Bureau was brought to light in the spring of 1923. Dr. Sawyer learned that Forbes, the bureau chief, was maneuvering contracts in the extensive hospital-building program for which Congress had appropriated $36 million; also, that he was selling medical supplies left over from the war and pocketing the proceeds. Sawyer told the Attorney General, and the latter advised Harding that a full investigation of Forbes should be launched. Whatever Daugherty's defects were, he was not stupid. Sawyer's information indicated that public exposure of Forbes was inevitable, and Daugherty was well aware that it would reflect on the administration if executive action did not precede Senate inquiries.

The lack of tough fiber in Harding's character showed up as it always did when the sensitivities of a friend were at stake. He told Daugherty he would handle the matter, but even after he had questioned Forbes and was reasonably sure that he was guilty, the President could not bring himself to initiate an inquiry that would disgrace his card-playing crony. He arranged for Forbes to go abroad and to send back a letter that he was resigning from his position "for business reasons."

On February 15, 1923, the resignation arrived in Washington. A Senate investigation started on March 2, and twelve days later Charles F. Cramer, legal counsel for the Veterans Bureau, committed suicide. The obituary mentioned that Cramer was Forbes' top assistant in the agency under investigation; also, that Cramer was a personal friend of the President and had purchased from him the house in which he had lived as senator.

Forbes was summoned back from Europe and indicted. His trial brought out startling facts about his background; he had abandoned his wife, deserted from the Army and served a jail term. Later, successfully concealing his past, he reenlisted for wartime military service and was a lieutenant colonel when he left the Army the second time. Within two weeks after he was charged with defrauding the government during his tenure at the Veterans Bureau, he was found guilty and sent to prison.

The President was vacationing in Florida as a guest of Mr. and Mrs. Edward Beale McLean when his Interior Secretary resigned on March 4, 1923. Knowing little or nothing about Fall's troubles with the Senate, the general public attached no special significance to his departure, but a later report that he was in Russia on oil business caused a stir on Capitol Hill; Senator Walsh had discovered that he had gone under the employment of Harry F. Sinclair.

Multiple worries began to impinge on the President's health later in the spring. His golf games exhausted him and he was dispirited even while playing poker. Arthur Brooks, his valet, had a premonition. "Something is going to happen to our boss," he told another member of the White House domestic staff. "He can't sleep at night. He has to keep propped up on a pillow. If he tries to lie down, he can't breathe." About that time, a clairvoyant warned Mrs. Harding that "dark clouds around the President" portended that he would not live until the end of the year. She was frantic. She urged Captain Joel T. Boone, the President's personal physician, to order Harding to take a vacation somewhere as remote as possible from the pressures of Washington.

The President decided on a summer trip to Alaska, where he could combine business with relaxation. Federal agencies were in disagreement on policies for handling mineral, timber and fishing rights in the Territory and he could visit pertinent areas; he could also officiate at the opening of the Alaskan Railway in July. The schedule called for a return route by ship, down the California coast and through the Panama Canal, with a stop in Puerto Rico.

He planned to take along a large group of officials and personal friends. Daugherty was consulted on the list, but this time there was no question as to whether or not Jess Smith would be included as he had been on several presidential vacations in the past. Talk that he was getting rich by graft had made him an encumbrance to the administration, and Daugherty had suggested that he spend less time in Washington.

Smith committed suicide in Daugherty's apartment on May 30. There was no autopsy. The Justice Department immediately took over and details were hushed up. But Washington pulsated with speculations that Daugherty had either hired an assassin to take care of Smith because he had a loose tongue and knew too much about the Attorney General's operations, or that Smith took his own life to avert some other scandalous exposure. Senator Tom Helfin, of Alabama, broadly hinted at both theories in a speech on the Senate floor.

Smith's guilt in at least one case would come out later and would implicate Daugherty. Those disclosures would be revealed after the President's death, but the oil scandals already were beginning to break when he left for Alaska on June 20.

Throughout the journey, Harding was despondent and ill. With increasing apprehension, Dr. Sawyer, Captain Boone and a trained nurse noted his deteriorating condition, and Mrs. Harding was so distracted in Alaska that she urged a hasty return to the White House. The President insisted, however, on keeping to the planned schedule.

As his ship was nearing Seattle an airplane delivered special mail, including a lengthy coded message. After reading it, he collapsed, and he was bedridden and in a coma much of the time as the ship proceeded down the West Coast. The physicians, meanwhile, had diagnosed his malady as ptomaine poisoning from eating tainted crab. He rallied before the ship reached San Francisco, but later at the Palace Hotel he developed pneumonia. In periods of semiconsciousness, he repeatedly muttered something about "false friends."

When he died on August 2, Mrs. Harding forbade an autopsy, but Sawyer, Boone and two noted consulting physicians, Dr. Ray Lyman Wilbur and Dr. C. M. Cooper, signed a statement that death resulted from a cerebral hemorrhage.

Harding was the first President since McKinley to die in office, and mourning engulfed the country as the funeral train rolled from San Francisco to Washington. The national display of sorrow until after the burial in Marion on August 10 was described in the New York *Times* as "The most remarkable demonstration in American history of affection, respect and reverence for the dead."

Throughout the ordeal, Mrs. Harding's composure was surprising. Nobody saw her shed a tear. Evalyn Walsh McLean, who spent the night with her after the memorial service at the White House, felt that grief had unhinged the widow's mind. At one-thirty in the morning, Mrs. Harding asked Mrs. McLean to go with her to the East Room. "I want to see Warren," she said. For two hours she sat by the casket, gazed at her dead husband's face and talked. "The trip has not hurt you one bit, Warren," she said at one time, and at another, "No one can hurt you now."

Colonel Starling noted that at the funeral two days later in Marion Mrs. Harding "did not weep. Her face was lifted and her eyes shone with a light I had not seen in them before." She died at Dr. Sawyer's sanitarium in Marion fifteen months later.

Administration scandals coming to light within two years after Harding's death indicated that had he lived he would have been impeached. While he was alive one suicide and a jail sentence had already blemished his administration. Another suicide had kindled invidious suspicions about his Attorney General. Montana's freshman Senator Burton K. Wheeler in time would introduce a resolution requesting President Coolidge to ask for Daugherty's resignation because he had "failed to prosecute corruption in high places." Albert Fall was already under scrutiny for his questionable actions as Secretary of the Interior, and even more shocking revelations in that regard came out shortly after Harding's burial when the Walsh committee turned up evidence that Fall had received substantial payments for the Teapot Dome and Elk Hills leases. But years would pass before there would be conclusive proof that Fall got $328,000 in securities from Sinclair and $100,000 "in a little black bag" from the oil multimillionaire Doheny. Fall would finally be sentenced in October 1929 for accepting bribes and fined $100,000; after many delays, he would go to prison in July 1931.

Meanwhile the huge amount of a settlement put through by Thomas W. Miller, the Alien Property Custodian, in September 1921 had aroused Senate suspicions, and an investigation had gone on for many months. The scandal exploded near the end of 1923. Miller had approved reimbursement to the original foreign-born owners of the American Metal Company, which was appropriated by our government and sold during wartime, with the money going into Liberty Bonds. The settlement, signed by the Attorney General, cost our government more than six and a half million dollars. The exhaustive Senate inquiry eventually uncovered evidence that the German bankers who initiated the claim paid a sizeable sum to facilitate it. with $50,000 going to Miller for his recommendation and a duplicate amount to Jess Smith for obtaining Daugherty's signed approval. Miller was convicted for taking the bribe, fined $5,000 and sent to jail. The dead Smith was also adjudged guilty, and the money he received was traced to one of the three accounts still held in his name in the Ohio bank run by M. S. Daugherty, Harry's brother. The Senate investigation then focused on the Attorney General, to determine the extent of his involment in the deal.

Harry Daugherty had a ready answer for everything. To probing senators he declared that his only connection with the Alien Property case was his perfunctory signature on a decision made by another government official. He insisted that he knew nothing about Smith's role in the negotiation, but under pressure he admitted that the money had gone into his brother's bank in an account designated "Jess Smith Extra No. 3." It was initially opened, he said, to receive contributions for Harding's campaign. He stated further that he had never made a personal deposit in the account, although he was empowered to handle disbursements from it. He recalled, however, that Smith had been in debt to the bank for some time and had deposited fifty thousand dollars to reduce the deficit.

When Senate investigators demanded records from the bank, Daugherty destroyed the ledger sheets. A New York grand jury indicted him for conspiracy to defraud the government and faithlessness to his office as Attorney General. He declined to take the witness stand. Instead, he presented a penciled statement, mentioning his long association with Harding as his personal attorney and also Mrs. Harding's, his "most confidential relations with them," and his Cabinet tenure under both Harding and President Coolidge. The final paragraph invoked the Fifth Amendment.

By bringing Harding's name into the statement in such veiled terms, Daugherty left the impression that he was concealing something that would reflect on the character of his late chief. Daugherty's lawyer, Max D. Steuer, fortified this by asserting, "If the jury knew the real reason for destroying the ledger sheets, they would commend rather than condemn Mr. Daugherty; but he insisted on silence."

After long deliberation the jury failed to find the Attorney General guilty. Even without testifying under oath, he had managed to project the idea that the late President's integrity was at stake, and that Daugherty had acted in the only way possible to protect the memory of his old friend.

That idea was not acceptable to senators who had known Harding. Despite the opprobrium surrounding the late President's administration, they were convinced that he had never personally shared in ill-gotten gains, and they concluded that Daugherty had refused cross-examination by the grand jury because he knew it would bring out proof of his own fraud. He had claimed he spent all his savings on Harding's campaign and was insolvent when he entered government service at twelve thousand dollars a year. Yet, he had been living high in Washington, and senators suspected that the ledger sheets could have shown sudden and substantial affluence. Daughtery knew that his Cabinet days were numbered and that President Coolidge wanted him out of office. He resigned in April 1924 and returned to Ohio.

However, he left a plethora of questions about his vaunted "protection" of Harding's memory. Was there something in Harding's private life that might have been revealed by the ledger sheets? Had the controversial bank account been held to handle payments to a paramour or to ensure the silence of those who knew about her? How much had Fall or Forbes or Daugherty or Miller known about Harding's personal transgressions? How much had his wife known?

Before leaving the White House, Mrs. Harding had asked friends to help her round up all correspondence from her late husband. Later she had burned all his official and personal letters that she could collect. Her excuse was that some of the contents might be misconstrued to his discredit. Exactly what had the letters contained? Had any of them or Daugherty's burned bank records contained material having to do with the "woman stories" about the late President?

The public was prepared to believe almost anything about him when a book entitled *The President's Daughter*, published in 1927, alleged that Harding had a mistress from 1917 until 1923 and that he fathered an illegitimate daughter. The author was Nan Britton; the account, her life story.

It was put out by the Elizabeth Ann Guild, Inc., and since nobody had ever heard of such a publishing firm and advance advertising signified the volume's sensational content, reputable booksellers refused to handle it, and responsible reviewers were reluctant to pass public judgment on it. But copies were sold under counters and were surreptitiously circulated by hand, and in three weeks, the book reached almost a hundred thousand readers. Within the next month it became the second best seller in the country.

The frontispiece featured a photograph of a six-year-old girl; the dedication was: "With understanding and love to all unwedded mothers and to their innocent children whose fathers are not usually known to the world."

The gist of the narrative was that Warren Harding was editor of the Marion *Star* when fourteen-year-old Nan Britton, daughter of a physician, began supplying school items for the newspaper. She was thirty years younger than Harding and she doted on him, in the manner of many teen-agers who fasten their romantic hopes on handsome older men. Her obsession continued without his knowledge until two years after he entered the Senate. Then, from New York, where she was living, she wrote to him, asking his help in getting employment. Harding promptly replied that he would see her on his next trip to New York. Shortly afterward, he met her in a hotel there, and the affair began. Subsequently he obtained a job for her with the United States Steel Corporation at sixteen dollars a week. He visited her many times in New York and she saw him often in Washington, at the Ebbitt House or in apartments he borrowed from friends or in his private office on Capitol Hill. During Senate recesses, they met in Ohio and Illinois, and she once accompanied him (as his "niece") to Indiana. He wrote her lengthy love letters during their entire courtship. (None are in the book.) On October 22, 1919, she gave birth to a daughter in Asbury Park, New Jersey, and named her Elizabeth Ann Harding. The mother was twenty-three at the time; the father, fifty-four.

The account continues: Harding arranged for Nan to work as a clerk at headquarters during the Chicago convention in 1920, and she saw him at her sister's apartment several times before and one time after he was nominated for the presidency. He was generous with her. He sent her $100 or $150 every week or so, and in Chicago he gave her three $500 bills in one lot. He promised to look after her and their daughter always. During the campaign she left the child with her sister in Chicago and stayed with friends in the Adirondacks. Harding never saw the child, but Nan met him secretly in Marion just after he was elected President, and she visited him several times thereafter in Washington—sometimes at the White House. He paid her way to Europe in 1923, and she was in France when he died.

Her story goes on and on: Nan married a Swedish ship captain in January 1924, but separated from him within a short while. She was destitute. She returned to New York and tried to find out whether or not Harding had left any funds for her. The Secret Service agent—she gave him the pseudonym Tim Slade—knew of no such legacy; and in the autumn of 1925 she contacted Harding's sisters, Miss Daisy Harding and Mrs. Heber Votaw. The latter would not listen to Nan's story, but Miss Harding was sympathetic and sent her checks totaling $890. Dr. George T. Harding, Warren's younger brother, then intervened and ordered his sister not to dispense any more funds until he talked to Nan.

She traveled to Marion to see Dr. Harding. During the four-hour interview, she insisted that her dead lover had promised to provide for her and their child, and she asked $50,000 for a trust fund for Elizabeth Ann and $2,500 for herself. Dr. Harding posed many pointed questions and made painstaking notes of her answers. He ascertained that she had no letters from his brother, and that she was unable to recall definite dates and places in answer to many queries. Finally, he said he would talk to her later, but she was never able to see him again.

The book is replete with sordid details, and one farcical episode after another gives a comic-opera touch to many passages. An example has to do with a New York hotel bedroom tryst that was interrupted by a ringing telephone. Harding answered, "You've got the wrong party!" but he had hardly replaced the receiver when there was a rap on the door; two men unlocked it, entered the room and began asking questions.

The account continues in Nan's words:

"One man asked my name. I whispered to Mr. Harding. 'What shall I say to them?'

" 'Tell them the truth,' he said. 'They've got us!' "

The questioning went on until one of the intruders, intimating that he was about to send for the police patrol, picked up Harding's hat and noted the name in gold lettering on the inner band. Then, again in Nan's words: "They became calm immediately. Not only calm, but strangely respectful, withdrawing very soon. Mr. Harding remarked, 'Gee, Nan, I thought I wouldn't get out of that under $1,000!' "

The memoir also recalls that Harding's child was conceived

during a love-making session on a couch in his private office at the Senate. When the White House became their trysting place, Harding insisted that they had to be "very circumspect because people seemed to have eyes in the sides of their heads." The one hideaway where they could "share kisses in safety" was a small clothes closet off the anteroom of his office. ("We repaired there many times in the course of my visits to the White House . . .").

The melodramatic outpouring, on the heels of disclosures of blatant dishonesty in Harding's official family, was a catalyst for follow-up verbal reports and writings that further blackened his name and also Mrs. Harding's.

A former White House maid attributed Mrs. Harding's "icy calm" at her husband's funeral to their constant quarrels during the last year of his life. Another described Mrs. Harding as "a nagger" who tried to dominate her husband. A White House mail clerk said that President Harding ordered him to destroy a stack of letters from Nan Britton before his wife found them. A fortune teller divulged that Mrs. Harding's serious illnesses were brought on by distress about her husband's affair with "that woman," and also by painful memories of an earlier attachment to a matron in Marion.

Gaston B. Means added his slimy touch to the odium. In 1922 his employment in the Department of Justice and his contacts at the Little Green House on K Street paid off handsomely—until it became widely known that he was a facile liar and a grafter. He was convicted and imprisoned for illegally obtaining permits for withdrawal of liquor from government-sealed distilleries and selling them to bootleggers, but he got out of jail just in time to cash in on what he knew or could fabricate about Harding and his wife, both deceased.

Somehow, Means managed to get a reputable writer, May Dixon Thacker, to collaborate with him on *The Strange Death of President Harding*, published in 1931. The fantastic account provided readers with fresh tidbits about Harding's liaison with Nan Britton ("a most attractive young woman, blonde, fresh and vital") and raised questions about the President's peculiar illness and sudden death.

According to Means, Mrs. Harding knew about her husband's affair with Nan Britton and hired Means to shadow her. He stole a packet of Harding's letters from her sister's apartment in Chicago and took them to the First Lady. She poured out her troubles to Means, complaining that Harding was impotent but still subject to the wiles of designing women; meanwhile she made life miserable for him. Just before the trip to Alaska, she told Means about the fortune teller who had predicted the President's death and asked whether an autopsy would be imperative if he passed away suddenly. Means informed her that there could be no postmortem examination without her consent, and so Means wrote she appeared "greatly relieved." With that buildup, the book then clearly insinuates that Mrs. Harding's insane jealousy led her to poison her husband.

The incredible exposé had enormous circulation, and Means' mention of several odd circumstances surrounding the death raised morbid speculations. Why was Harding the only one poisoned by crab when it was served to everybody in his party? Why had Mrs. Harding refused an autopsy? Why was she so singularly composed at the funeral? Why did she destroy Harding's correspondence? How much did she know about corruption in his administration?

Rumors fed on rumors and took off in all directions. There were wild and conflicting whispers: that Harding committed suicide because he knew the oil scandals would disgrace his administration; that Mrs. Harding mercifully killed him to save him from impeachment, and that Dr. Sawyer helped her to place poison in the crab which made Harding ill. The reference to Sawyer brought up more speculations. Mrs. Harding was a patient at his sanitarium in Marion when he was found dead there, in September 1924. Food poisoning was designated the cause. Could Mrs. Harding, completely unbalanced at last, have been responsible?

A few months after Means' book was published, it was repudiated at the source. Mrs. Thacker, in an article in *Liberty* magazine (November 7, 1931), revealed she had found that much of the material which he had provided was false, and she disclaimed responsibility for any part of the account. But corrective explanations rarely catch up with malicious innuendos. The book continued to sell, and many readers continued to accept it as factual.

The portions about Nan Britton did contain scattered grains of truth. A number of capital residents had glimpsed her in Washington and some knew that she had visited the President at the White House. Furthermore, Means' statement that Harding and Nan sometimes met "in the house of a very accommodating lady who was supposed to be Mrs. Harding's friend but appears to have played both sides" could be verified by several individuals. They were well aware that "the accommodating lady" was a veiled reference to Evalyn Walsh McLean, in whose home Harding and Miss Britton occasionally met. Washingtonians had gossiped about that for some time, and as recently as 1970 Mrs. A. Mitchell Palmer, widow of Woodrow Wilson's Attorney General, recalled in an interview published in the Washington *Star:* "I did not know Warren Harding, but I remember him well, not under the best circumstances either. He used to drop by Evalyn McLean's house to visit that woman [Nan Britton]. He would just walk in and go right upstairs. Evalyn completely ignored him. I was appalled the first day I saw him there. 'I think we should rise when the President enters,' I said. 'Tut, tut,' said Evalyn, 'he doesn't want to be noticed.' I should think not—when I realized what was going on!"

Nan Britton's autobiography had left no doubts as to what was going on, and the effects on her for some time after its publication were unpleasant. Harding still had a few friends left and some tried to uncover proof that the lurid romance never took place—at least, not over a long period of time; also, that Miss Britton magnified the connection simply to extort money from a dead man's relatives. Others who had known Harding for many years recalled that doctors at Battle Creek, Michigan, where he had gone for treatment several times, had repeatedly told him he was sterile. Concurrently, there were countercharges that Nan was victimized by a lecher, bore him a child, and then was heartlessly left to fend for herself.

In November 1931 she sued for a share of Harding's estate. The court found "no cause for action." She instituted a libel suit to clear her character. Again, there was "no cause for action." A second book with her name on the spine appeared in 1932, entitled *Honesty in Politics*. It was primarily a rehash of her first memoir, but it contained several photographs of the child, bearing a remarkable resemblance to those of Harding which were included.

The publicity for the second book described the Elizabeth Ann Guild, Inc., as the publishing firm for the Elizabeth Ann League, which Miss Britton professed that she set up to benefit illegitimate children. Her plan, she wrote, was to support it with proceeds from her books and motion picture sales. (*The President's Daughter* was made into a film, *Children of No Importance*, in 1928.) The reason she gave for destroying Harding's letters was that he had feared they might fall into the hands of vicious persons who would use them for blackmail.

Shortly after the second book appeared, Harry M. Daugherty in *The Inside Story of the Harding Tragedy* declared that he had never heard of Nan Britton before *The President's Daughter* came out and that he did not believe a word of it. He called attention to ridiculous features of the book: the only Harding signature in it appeared on a campaign portrait, with the impersonal inscription: "To Miss Nan Britton, with the good wishes of a Marion friend and neighbor. Sincerely, Warren G. Harding"; and a snapshot of Harding was shown with a fragmentized, unreadable autograph and the underline: "Received by the author in June, 1921, with a forty-page letter from Mr. Harding." Daugherty's book also pointed out that no affectionate letters were quoted in the account. And, Daugherty asked, in effect, Why did Harding never see the child, who was reputedly born in 1919, while he was a senator and free to travel without Secret Service surveillance?

Daugherty's attack on Nan Britton was supplemented by several concurrent disclosures besides those connected with Harding. The most forceful was that the *The President's Daughter* was actually written by a Richard Wightman, whose wife sued him for divorce in March 1928, on grounds of abandonment and his morally incriminating association with Nan Britton.

The charges against Nan Britton comprised only a small part of Daugherty's opus, however, for the book was obviously meant to be a whitewash of his own role in Harding's administration. The emphasis, in fact, was on the shortcomings of other appointees: Harding's Attorney General came through the account as a dedicated servant of the people, beleaguered by jealousies and cut down by enemies—but a loyal friend of his President to the end. That fealty he offered as explanation enough for his refusal to take the witness stand when he was brought to trial.

Three years after publication of that book, Mark Sullivan, a distinguished Washington journalist and author, visited Daugherty in his Columbus, Ohio, home and asked him specifically if he declined to testify because he feared cross-examination would bring to light some "woman story" about Harding. Daugherty said, "If there was any woman scrape in Harding's life, I never knew it, and if there had been one Harding would have told me." Sullivan pressed him further. If there was no "woman scrape," was there an improper romance? Daugherty answered, "I never talk about dead men or living women." Once again, Harding's Attorney General left the late President's conduct open to question.

Colonel Starling, who was on Secret Service duty at the White House for thirty years and had Harding under surveillance from the moment of his election until his death, was convinced that imputations about Harding's sexual depravity were spurious. Starling wrote in his autobiography, "His acts are things to which I can swear. He never did anything more reprehensible than curse mildly at a golf ball and play poker with his friends. He was the kindest man I ever knew. But he was weak, and he trusted everyone."

The general public did not know until long after Harding died that he speculated heavily in the stock market. Under an account name, he was $180,000 in default to the Washington branch of a Cleveland brokerage house at the time of his death. James M. Sloan, Jr., the local manager, had acted as intermediary for Harding and Nan Britton. The company quietly reached a compromise with the late President's relatives and received $30,000 in settlement from his estate.

Despite the miasma of dishonor that clouded the aftermath of his death, nothing ever surfaced to indicate that Harding financially profited from any of the operations that scandalized his years in the White House. His public tragedy was recognized as resulting from his faith in unworthy acquaintances to whom he felt indebted. "Friendship in politics undermines more principles than fraud, and gratitude is a worse poison than graft," Samuel Hopkins Adams observed, in his novel about the disgraceful administration.

Harding's personal image was shattered by indications, however inaccurate or reprehensible, in Nan Britton's books, Gaston B. Means' network of falsehoods, and suspicions flowing in their wake within a short time after his death. However, still other evidence that Harding was immoral has come to light in recent years. While collecting material for a biography of Harding in 1960, an established author, Francis Russell, found a cache of two hundred and fifty love letters that Harding wrote from 1909 to 1920 to an Ohio merchant's wife. They had been in possession of the Marion lawyer who was her guardian during the latter part of her life. A recluse for several years, she died in 1960.

Russell planned to bring out his book in 1965, the hundredth anniversary of Harding's birth, but Dr. George T. Harding, III, a nephew of the late President, filed a million-dollar suit in 1964 to prohibit public disclosure of the letters. Russell's biography, *The Shadow of Blooming Grove,* appeared four years later without quoting the letters in full. However, the book clearly shows that Harding and Mrs. James E. Phillips had an illicit liaison, beginning in 1905 and continuing over a period of fifteen years.

According to this account, attractive Carrie Phillips, wife of a partner in the Uhler-Phillips department store in Marion, became close friends with Harding and his wife while he was lieutenant governor of Ohio. Carrie's son died, and some time thereafter—while Mrs. Harding was in a Columbus hospital and Phillips was under medical treatment at Battle Creek— Harding comforted the bereaved mother. The sexual intimacy started then, but the principals managed to keep it secret for years, with neither of their lawful mates suspecting anything. In fact, the Hardings and the Phillipses spent much time together. They toured the Mediterranean and Egypt in 1909. Later the four went to Bermuda. But as early as 1908 Carrie asked Harding whether or not he was prepared to leave his wife for her. When his answer was not forthcoming, she wrote him that she planned to take her daughter to Germany for an extended stay. She did, and during her three years abroad, Harding became involved with Nan Britton. Meanwhile, Phillips joined his wife and daughter in Germany.

When they returned, home, Carrie resumed her affair with Harding. But as a member of the Senate, he was increasingly uncomfortable because she was pro-German and was trailed by Secret Service agents. Furthermore, she insisted on his voting against America's entry into the war.

Mrs. Harding, presumably, and Phillips, certainly, learned about the illicit liaison before Harding was nominated for the presidency. By then, both Carrie and Harding realized that nothing more could come of their romance, and the break was complete by the time he ran for the highest office. The few residents of Marion who had known about the relationship discreetly refrained from mentioning it to prying newspaper reporters who covered Harding's campaign, and the reestablished surface friendship between the candidate and Mrs. Phillips gave no hint to strangers that there had been anything irregular between them. Yet, Will Hays feared that the scandal might be uncovered; he sent Albert Lasker to Mrs. Phillips, with an offer of twenty thousand dollars plus a monthly sum so long as Harding held office, provided she and her husband would take an expense-paid trip around the world. They complied—and stayed abroad until after Harding's death.

The letters from Harding to Mrs. Phillips will be concealed at the Library of Congress until July 29, 2014, and copies will also be guarded from public perusal by the Ohio Historical Society until that date. The American Heritage Publishing Company, which had the microfilm copies, returned them to Dr. Harding and paid him ten thousand dollars for giving the originals to the Library of Congress. Concurrently, he dropped his million-dollar suit against the company, Francis Russell and the publishing firm that brought out his book, and Glenn Thompson, retired editor of the Dayton *Journal Herald*, who also had copies of the letters (which he returned to Harding's heirs).

Russell observed in the preface of his biography:

> The letters if they can be considered shocking—and some of them can—are more so because they were written by the President of the United States, than through the tumescence of their content. When I first read them, I felt

a sense of pity for the lonely Harding, for Carrie Phillips was clearly the love of his life, and he was more loving than loved.

The general public can eventually learn the complete story through the letters, but what more is there to know about Harding's immoral conduct with women? Certainly, enough documentation already is at hand to indicate that Chief White House Usher Ike Hoover was not far wrong when he assessed the thirty-fourth President as "a sporting ladies man."

VII

The Capital
Gossip Mill

Within a short time after President Franklin Delano Roosevelt took office, Washington whispers started that he was mentally and morally deficient. The New Deal, already shaking up the country, was clearly the product of a disordered mind, it was said, while his "eye for the ladies" was more obvious and reprehensible than it had been when he was the philandering young Assistant Secretary of the Navy during the Wilson administration.

The executive mansion had been the despair of gossip-mongers for ten years before F.D.R. was inaugurated. Presidents Coolidge and Hoover personified rectitude, conducted themselves with the dignity expected of those who bore the burden of national responsibility, and were invulnerable to character assaults. Only two episodes relieved the tedium for purveyors of White House gossip throughout the decade, and neither one suited their purposes.

The first, a hinted reflection on Mrs. Coolidge's reputation rather than on that of her husband, occurred in June 1927, when Game Lodge in the Black Hills of South Dakota was the Summer White House. Early one morning, the First Lady and James Haley of the Secret Service set off for an announced short hike. President Coolidge was distressed when she had not returned for lunch, and he was frantic hours later when she was still missing. He had sent out a searching party before his wife and her escort appeared, exhausted. Haley explained that after conducting Mrs. Coolidge far into the unfamiliar area, he had difficulty in finding the return path. "Silent Cal" emerged from his monosyllabic shell long enough to berate the agent at some length, and then ordered his prompt replacement on the White House detail. Newsmen at Game Lodge, on an otherwise dull day, filed reports that the President was visibly angered because the fifty-year-old First Lady and handsome Jim Haley had lost themselves in the Black Hills for many hours. The innuendo that a romantic tryst might have prompted the prolonged absence activated many wagging tongues—but not in Washington, D. C., where Grace Coolidge was known to be as far above suspicion as was Caesar's wife. Yet, the gossip was aired enough elsewhere to be mentioned years later in biographies of Calvin Coolidge.

President Hoover probably never knew that a wild-eyed woman stormed through a White House gate in 1929 and insisted that he was the father of her unborn child. The guards dispatched her quickly, and though the incident was noised around the capital city, it was concluded that only a demented woman would try to impugn the honor of Herbert Hoover.

The high moralistic tone and the stilted, elegant and starchy customs that characterized much White House entertaining through the years vanished the moment Eleanor Roosevelt appeared, gloveless and in a trainless evening gown, at her first formal reception, and the President began booming first-name greetings and pleasantries to the presentation line.

Then and there, practices that had often reflected George and Martha Washington's stiff levees in Philadelphia were liquidated, and Thomas Jefferson's break with cumbersome formality was revived, with a fresh accent: guests in the highest quarter would no longer be expected to conduct themselves with solemn dignity—they could relax and enjoy themselves, in the manner of the convivial President.

From then on, flippancies rippled through White House parties with the unrestraint of banter at a company-town picnic. Now and then an anecdote would be conveyed to F.D.R, and he would toss back his head and roar with delight. Particularly choice stories were sometimes repaid with invitations to impromptu White House dinners or to the Sunday-night suppers at which Mrs. Roosevelt scrambled eggs in a chafing dish for from a dozen to twenty persons and everyone except the hosts was addressed by first name.

The President's flair for establishing easy fellowship on a social basis enlivened all his parties, but his "familiarities" with some of his pretty guests were grist to the anti-New Deal gossip mill. Typical of the criticism that poured through staid Republican circles was a mangled account of his repartee with a newspaperman's wife at a state function. The carpers perhaps did not know that at a small White House dinner the week before, she had switched her legs from under the table to show the President she was wearing one of the first pairs of nylon stockings in Washington. "Well, Betty," he chortled, as he spied her at the formal reception, "how are the nylons holding up tonight?" Her tittered reply was unaudible to virtually everyone around except F.D.R., and his rejoinder was muffled in laughter. But the story as it buzzed around the capital went that she answered, "They're holding up as well as usual, Mr. President," and that he came back, with a guffaw, "Well, if they fall, be sure to let *me* know!"

A result of this kind of report was a rush of gossip that F.D.R.'s flirtations had caused Eleanor much anguish during their earlier years in Washington. She managed to keep him reasonably in line, old-timers said, until he was attracted to her beautiful social secretary, Lucy Page Mercer. Exactly what happened after that came out in several different versions, but the general inference among those who had known Miss Mercer was that the devastatingly handsome, self-indulgent Franklin Roosevelt was "a wolf" in those days; Lucy, a devout Catholic, was his conscience-stricken prey; and Eleanor was the one who put an end to the affair as soon as she learned about it. Anyway, as Lucy's friends happily pointed out, the socially secure but needy young woman went on to become the contented wife of Winthrop Rutherfurd, a wealthy widower. Eleanor's lot had never been easy, the gist of the chatter usually continued, but as First Lady she might well stop gadding around the country and spend more time keeping close watch on the unstable President, for even though he could rise from a wheelchair only with help, his rakish compulsions seemed to be as strong as ever.

There was no middle ground on attitudes about Franklin Roosevelt. In Washington, as elsewhere, many people admired him to the point of worship and completely trusted his leadership. Others, who believed the New Deal to be a force foisted on the country to destroy individual initiative and responsibility, despised its chief architect and criticized everything he did. Deep-seated hostility to his policies intensified after his landslide reelection in 1936, and from then on, antagonism to his administration carried a steady undercurrent of polemics about his megalomania, along with incessant and invidious conjectures about his private life.

For several years much of the gossip focused on his relationship with Miss Marguerite (Missy) LeHand, the handiest target. In her thirties when F.D.R. became President, she had been his private secretary since the early 1920s. Tall and slim, with prematurely silver hair and gray eyes, she was attractive, and had a low-keyed personality and a sense of humor that responded to Roosevelt's levities. She traveled with him, supervised his executive staff and the running of his establishment at Warm Springs, Georgia, lived in the White House, and spent many evenings alone with him in his study ("I knit, while he talks on—and on," she once said). Furthermore, when Mrs. Roosevelt was away from Washington, Miss LeHand frequently entertained friends whom she and the President found amusing, although some of these people seldom were guests at intimate White House dinners when the First Lady was there.

Whether or not Eleanor Roosevelt was as devoted to Missy as she appeared to be puzzled many people who knew both women and often saw them together. Newspaper correspondents who met weekly with the First Lady got an inkling, in 1938, that she was jealous of some of the secretary's prerogatives, at least. Doris Fleeson's profile on Miss LeHand, describing her as the President's indispensable aide, had just been published in *The Saturday Evening Post.* A reporter at Mrs. Roosevelt's next press conference asked her what she thought of the article. Her secretary, Miss Malvina (Tommy) Thompson, frowned. Mrs. Roosevelt was also obviously annoyed. Her only comment, as she cut off further discussion, was, "I just wish somebody would write a piece about Tommy, who makes life possible for *me.*"

After Miss LeHand suffered a stroke in June 1941—she died the next year—her duties were taken over by her assistant, Miss Grace Tully. By that time, Washington whispers were to the effect that the President was romantically interested in Crown Princess Martha of Norway, the lovely and lithe young matron who would spend most of the war years in the United States. Shortly after she and her small son and two daughters took up residence at Pook's Hill, a Maryland estate on the outskirts of the capital, rumors began that F.D.R. had ordered U. S. agents not only to protect her safety but also to see that nothing marred the tranquillity of the publicity-free haven he had personally selected for her. During her four and a half years in America, Crown Prince Olaf, her husband, came over from time to time to be with his family and to confer with the President. On every visit, the prince and his wife were entertained by the Roosevelts, either in Washington or at Hyde Park. In the many interludes between Olaf's visits, however, busybodies reported that the princess and her children spent much time at the White House, sometimes staying a week at a time; also, that she often lunched or had tea with the President when the First Lady was absent; that he occasionally rode out to Pook's Hill to see her in the evenings; that she called him "dear godfather," at his request; and that she stayed near him at White House parties, flirting with him and monopolizing his attention as much as possible. On several such occasions, observers thought that Mrs. Roosevelt, who was equally gracious to everyone, conducted herself more like royalty than did the princess.

As usually happens under such circumstances, there were constant levities about Mrs. Roosevelt ("Princess Martha's lady-in-waiting"), the President and his reputed favorite. For example, at a high-level dinner in Washington, F.D.R.'s infatuation with the princess was being discussed at some length when Republican Senator Arthur Vandenberg, of Michigan, was asked what he thought about it. He replied, with mock seriousness, "Oh, I doubt Roosevelt's very much interested in her, or anyone else, except himself. Since he now regards himself as the King of America, he probably just figures he and Princess Martha are royalty together, and can do as they please, let the commoners think what they may." After that story made the rounds, there were many sly allusions to "F.D.R.'s royal affair" over capital dinner tables.

If any of the tales about his devotion to the princess ever got to F.D.R., he must have been highly amused, because, for some time before Martha went home, in October 1944, he was spending much time with Mrs. Rutherfurd, the former Lucy

Mercer. Presumably, the news correspondents who traveled with him during his 1944 campaign (the one he called "the meanest of all") were unaware that when F.D.R.'s train stopped one morning in New Jersey so that he could visit "personal friends" at Allumachy, the main friend he had in mind was Mrs. Rutherfurd. Residing that summer at Tranquility Farm, one of her three homes, the fifty-three-year-old widow, whose husband had died a few months before, was still beautiful and even more charming than she had been when young Roosevelt fell in love with her.

For the remainder of his life, he was with Lucy Rutherfurd as often as possible. She frequently lunched or dined with him at the White House when Mrs.Roosevelt was not there, though always in the company of others—his cousins, Daisy Suckley and Laura Delano, or his daughter, Anna, or his secretaries. Furthermore, since all movements of the wartime President were closely covered by security, he was able to be with Mrs. Rutherfurd many times outside of Washington. These meetings were successfully shielded from the press and from most other people, including his wife. As would be revealed later, only the few trusted people who were with him at Warm Springs through his last days knew that Mrs. Rutherfurd was there when he was fatally stricken, and that she left shortly before Mrs. Roosevelt arrived to be with him during his final hours.

Several books in recent years have dealt with the story of F.D.R.'s enduring love for Lucy Mercer Rutherfurd. At least two have given the public more understanding of his emotional makeup, and of his wife's role in keeping together a marriage that apparently lasted only as a realistic working relationship. If the exhaustive accounts of his long romance had appeared just after he died, the general public might have been shocked by the disclosures. But many years later, moral standards had become less constrictive, and mortal weaknesses more understandable and forgivable.

Oddly enough, considering they were individuals of national importance, only veiled references to the near breakup of the Roosevelts' marriage appeared in print for many years. The first book to mention it was *Washington Tapestry* (1946) by Olive Clapper, widow of the noted news correspondent, Raymond Clapper. Alluding to "persistent rumors" that the union was almost disrupted in 1918, she wrote: "Mrs. Roosevelt was supposed to have called her husband and the enamored woman to a conference, at which she offered her husband a divorce if the woman would marry him. A Catholic, the woman could not marry a divorced man. When she expressed these sentiments, Mrs. Roosevelt issued an ultimatum that they must stop seeing each other, to which they promptly acquiesced."

Grace Tully's *FDR—My Boss* (1949) was the first book to reveal that when the President suffered the stroke that would soon result in his death, Lucy Rutherfurd had been at Warm Springs for three days, along with Madame Shoumatoff (whom she had commissioned to paint a portrait of F.D.R.) and others. Miss Tully's account also makes it clear that Mrs. Rutherfurd left some hours before Mrs. Roosevelt arrived.

Jonathan Daniels, F.D.R.'s last press secretary, mentioned the Mercer–Roosevelt romance in *The End of Innocence* (1954) and, again, in *The Time Between Wars* (1966). His *Washington Quadrille* (1968) was the first book to go into the story at some length, with the accent on Lucy's background. Joseph Lash's *Eleanor and Franklin* (1971) gives an even more detailed account of the attachment that almost disrupted the marriage, with emphasis on Mrs. Roosevelt's heartbreak and her determination then to find fulfillment of her own.

The most sensational disclosures yet, however, are in *An Untold Story: The Roosevelts of Hyde Park* (1973) by Elliott Roosevelt and James Brough. Working from the stated premise that Franklin and Eleanor Roosevelt after the birth of their youngest son, John, in 1916, "never again lived together as man and wife" because she did not want to bear any more children, the book goes on to describe circumstances, as they were known to a member of the immediate family, about F.D.R.'s intimacy with Lucy Mercer and, later, over a period of many years, with Miss LeHand.

"I feel that the truth is better told than alluded to in veiled sentences," Elliott Roosevelt gave as his prime reason for bringing out his version of his parents' marriage and the course of their lives as their union held together as a working rather than a romantic relationship.

The other sons and the only daughter of Franklin and Eleanor Roosevelt "disassociated" themselves completely from Elliott's account. However, Anna Roosevelt Halstead earlier threw some light on the dissension between her parents. As quoted in Lash's *Eleanor and Franklin,* Mrs. Halstead recalled, "If Father became friendly with a princess or a secretary, he'd reach out and pat her fanny and laugh like hell and was probably telling her a funny story at the same time, whereas to Mother that was terrible . . . He loved to outrage Granny, to tease her. He could never do that with Mother. She was much too serious. Mother was inhibiting to him. She would never go along. That's why he turned elsewhere."

Lash's book also gives an insight into Mrs. Roosevelt's feelings about Princess Martha by including a personal letter Eleanor wrote shortly before Mme. Chiang Kai-shek's White House visit in 1943. The final portion of the letter reads in part: "I think she is going to surprise Franklin a good deal but she will charm him. She won't lean like Martha of Norway though!"

In *This I Remember* (1949), Eleanor Roosevelt's recollection of her White House years, most of the allusions to Crown Princess Martha are highly complimentary. But one may guess at some between-the-lines meaning in this passage: "During the war she spent a week or more with us each spring and autumn, on her way to some place for the summer or back to Washington for the winter." More significant, perhaps is a comment about Miss LeHand: "Missy was young and pretty and loved a good time, and occasionally her social contacts got mixed with her work and made it hard for others." Also, this: "As Miss LeHand lived at the White House, she very often, when I was not there, invited people she thought my husband would enjoy, or whom she personally wanted, but he never gave this type of social gathering a thought."

Mrs. Roosevelt also recalled that after her husband's inauguration in 1932 she made a tentative suggestion to him: "Perhaps merely being hostess at the necessary formal functions would not take all my time and that he might like me to do a real job and take over some of his mail. He looked at me quizzically and said he did not think that would do, that Missy, who had been handling his mail for a long time, would feel that I was interfering. I knew he was right and that it would not work, but it was a last effort to keep in close touch and to feel that I had a real job to do."

Referring to that passage just after the book came out, a long-time Washington resident said, "No wonder Franklin didn't want his wife to handle his mail. She was doing that in 1918, when she came across his letters from Lucy Mercer. Actually, Eleanor must have suspected for some time that he and Lucy were in love, but one letter, at least, gave her an excuse to have the matter out with them, once and for all."

The person making those comments to an intimate friend in 1948 is now a nonagenarian, who professes that she "knew more about that affair when it was going on, and how it was called off, than anyone else living today." This woman has long been reticent about saying much more than that about the romance. Some time ago, she recalled, "While Franklin Roosevelt was President, and there was as much misleading talk about what went on in 1918, I kept quiet for I promised Lucy I would." Although she has been distressed about disclosures she feels "are unfair to Lucy's memory," she said recently "Even now, when so many lies and half-truths are coming out, I'm not about to capitalize, personally, on facts she told me in confidence." However, on the promise that her name would not be revealed ("I don't want writers and other curious people hounding me in droves, at this late date," she said), the old-timer agreed to recount the story as she got it direct from Lucy Mercer. The verbatim recollections follow:

"Lucy and I became close friends about the time Eleanor Roosevelt employed her as a social secretary. She was socially prominent, with a background as distinguished as that of any Roosevelt, but she needed the job. She was a beautiful young woman, gay and stimulating, so naturally she had many suitors. Nigel Law of the British Embassy was one of many who were seriously interested in her, but her mother discouraged that courtship; he wasn't rich, and Minnie Mercer, who had run through a fortune, wanted Lucy to marry a man with lots of money.

"Law's best friend was Franklin Roosevelt, the handsomest man who ever hit Washington. He had great charm, and he was attracted to good-looking women, but he wasn't a skirt-chaser—out after every pretty thing he saw. He never had to chase anybody! But he did chafe at the marriage bit, because he liked to have a good time, and Eleanor was always too serious to be any fun. He and Lucy started going around together—at first, always with Law and other people—one summer when Eleanor was at Campobello with the children. When she returned to Washington in the fall, Franklin had already told Lucy he wanted to get a divorce and marry her. Over the next few months she put him off, told him time and again she could never break up a home. He kept assuring her that he and Eleanor had ceased to have anything in common except their children. They absorbed most of her time and she spent the rest on any do-good thing that came along.

"Franklin had convinced Lucy that he could get a divorce without too much trouble, and they were seriously discussing marriage when she went into the Navy as a yeoman (F), in

1917, and was assigned, at his request, to work with him in the Navy Department. By then, they were going around together enough, and without other people, to cause a lot of talk. You may be sure Eleanor heard some of it; she was always jealous of Franklin and suspicious of friends he enjoyed. But she didn't show her hand; she continued to be as gracious as ever to Lucy. However, when Lucy was unexpectedly released from Navy duty in October 1917 with no explanation except that it was 'by special order of the Secretary of the Navy,' she worried considerably that Eleanor might have had something to do with the dismissal. Yet, immediately afterward, Eleanor took her back as social secretary and was so kind to her that Lucy became conscience-stricken about her overpowering love for Franklin. Most people who knew Lucy well at the time thought her religion would never have permitted her to marry Franklin, even if a divorce could have been smoothly arranged. That was not true. She was a devout Catholic, but she loved Franklin so much, she would have married him if things could have been worked out as they hoped. Things did not work out, as time went on. Lucy sensed that Franklin was having second thoughts about Eleanor's willingness to give him a divorce, and also about his mother's possible reaction. Lucy had been having second thoughts for some time. She bothered constantly about hurting Eleanor, but what disturbed her most was that Franklin had five children who might one day hold her responsible for coming between their parents.

"The utter hopelessness of anything good ever coming of the romance struck her full force while Franklin was on a trip to Europe in the fall of 1918. She took refuge in her religion then, and prayed for Divine guidance. Franklin wrote to her every day, repeatedly reassuring her that everything would be all right, in time. Her letters to him more and more poured out her worries, and finally she wrote that because of her religion she doubted she could ever bring herself to marry a divorced man with children. When he returned home, he fell ill with double pneumonia. Eleanor took charge of his mail. It was then that she found Lucy's letters—he had kept every one—that showed beyond all doubt the seriousness of the romance. Shortly after Franklin recovered, Eleanor summoned him and Lucy to a conference, and that was when the showdown came.

"Shaken and in tears, Lucy came to my apartment straight from the meeting. She said Eleanor had told her and Franklin that she had found out they were in love and had warned them of the serious consequences on his children and his career if the affair continued. She did not offer to give him a divorce; Lucy told me divorce was never mentioned. Anyway, after Eleanor finished talking, she (Lucy) did not wait for Franklin to speak up. She simply said she had already resolved to end the romance because of her religion; and then she solemnly promised she would never be alone with Franklin, again. Eleanor then said that she could continue as her social secretary, and that ended the meeting.

"One thing I know for sure—Lucy kept her promise for many years. Franklin communicated with her after he became President, and tried to arrange to be with her during her several visits to Washington to see her mother during his first term. But she refused to meet him until after Wintie Rutherfurd died. Then, Franklin called on her at Tranquility Farm. After that, as everybody knows now, she saw him many times. Why not? Theirs was a truly great love; and their being together, often, warmed his last years and was equally rewarding to her. But I've always been convinced that their romance was never a sexual thing; Lucy was too high-minded ever to have carried on like that with a married man. And if she had, I don't think Franklin Roosevelt's love for her would have lasted all those years. I just hope accounts from now on will be as good as Daniels' and Lash's—and never make the romance one of those dirty affairs."

Some accounts will, of course. A recent magazine article referred to Lucy Rutherfurd as Franklin Roosevelt's "long-time mistress" and stated that the "illicit affair" was resumed after he became President, and that he "died in her arms" at Warm Springs. Fortunately for Franklin Roosevelt and the woman whom he probably loved more than any other, reliable biographies show them in a better light.

Having honed their scalpels on Franklin Roosevelt's character, slanderers would have slashed out at his White House successor, Harry Truman, in the same way—if that had been possible. However, Truman's conduct as a faithful husband had never been questioned while he served in the Senate and the vice presidency, nor could it be when he moved up to the supreme post. After his retirement, he said, on his seventy-fifth birthday in Springfield, Missouri, "Three things can ruin a man—money, power and women. I never had any money, I never wanted power, and the only woman in my life is up at the house right now." The country had been well aware that Bess Truman was up at Harry's house throughout his many years in Washington.

President Nixon is another public servant whose conduct with women has never been questioned. His character in that respect was unassailable during his terms in the House, the Senate and the vice presidency, and it is equally so today. Throughout his entire political career, he has been fortunate in that his detractors have been consistently deprived of at least one stick that flayed the reputation of so many of his White House predecessors.

That fewer people rushed to make moralistic judgments after World War II was shown when Dwight D. Eisenhower ran for the highest office in 1952.

There had been much wartime gossip about the general's purported intimacy with a young Irish divorcée, Kay Summersby. Mrs. Summersby had been his civilian driver and, later, one of his secretaries, while he was based in London as commanding general of the U. S. forces in Europe. On the basis of fragmentary reports from abroad, Washington rumors ran that he took "the good-looking Summersby woman" everywhere, and that she was hostess at all his parties and a constant guest at Telegraph Cottage, his retreat on the outskirts of London. Subsequent tales around Washington had it that Army wives throughout the city were incensed at the example the supreme general was setting for their husbands overseas, and that Mamie Eisenhower was "fed up" with his infidelity and might divorce him as soon as the war ended.

After he came home in a cloud of glory and it was apparent that his marriage would remain intact, the gossip receded. But suspicions boiled up again in 1948, when Eisenhower resisted overtures from powerful elements in both major parties and put an end to a drive to draft him at the Democratic National Convention. Meanwhile, reports that Kay Summersby's tell-all memoirs would be published before the end of the year revived many of the wartime tales—and started more. The worst one was that she had turned down substantial sums from two of Eisenhower's friends not to finish the book, and that when she refused both the money and suggestions that she tone down all personal references to the general, two of his pals arranged to purchase all the copies before they could be made available to the public.

The book, *Eisenhower Was My Boss,* was on sale throughout the country, however, in September 1948 when Mrs. Summersby arrived in Washington, D. C., on the first lap of her book-promotion tour. Reporters who rushed to interview her observed that the tall, rangy woman appeared to be the antithesis of a *femme fatale.* Passably attractive but not pretty, she had an almost boyish exuberance, with a sense of humor that was understandably offset by nervousness. But she was composed and clever enough to sidestep every searching question about her friendship with her former boss. "Everything is in the book," she said again and again.

Readers seemed to like the book; they gathered from Mrs. Summersby's chatty recollections that the writer had been the general's dedicated aide for three and a half years; had seen him through the tensions of war; and with his trusted officers who were also constantly around him, had shared his occasional amusements.

According to her account, she met General Eisenhower in May 1942, when she was assigned to drive him and General Mark Clark during a ten-day visit to London; when Eisenhower, shortly thereafter, took over the European command, he requested that Kay be his regular driver. From then on, she was the fourth member of his inner circle, which included his naval aide, Commander (later Captain) Harry C. Butcher; his army aide, Captain Ernest Lee; and Sergeant Mickey McKeogh (whose many chores Mrs. Summersby remembered, took in the writing "of a personal report each week to Mrs. Eisenhower"). She dined with them frequently, went horseback riding with the general several times a week, occasionally entertained him and the others at dinner and bridge, and was his "favorite bridge partner" at Telegraph Cottage. However, according to Mrs. Summersby, everyone in the group knew that she was engaged to Colonel Richard Arnold ("my own, my very special American"), and that they planned to be married in June 1944. Meanwhile he was dispatched to the fighting front in Africa, and not long afterward he was killed at Oran.

She was inducted into the Women's Army Corps, and as Captain Summersby, became General Eisenhower's personal secretary and military aide. Thereafter, she accompanied him on his trips around Europe, North Africa and the Middle East. With plans to visit her dead fiancé's mother in Florida, she flew to the United States in June 1944, stopped in Washington, and called on Mrs. Eisenhower ("an attractive, petite woman, her bangs the hint of a vivacious, friendly personality"), and thoroughly enjoyed the visit. But all her experiences in Washington were not so pleasant, judging from this recollection:

Some of the most social army wives made it clear—crystal-clear—that they regarded any uniformed female overseas as a mere "camp follower." Being human, I was even more upset at learning that my own reputation was lost. In addition to being a woman overseas, I was a *foreign* woman—and I traveled with the Big Brass. Therefore I was a Bad Woman. This was a fact, gleefully acknowledged and established fact. These women didn't—and don't—leave any loopholes for doubt; they didn't—and don't—give any opportunity for defense. Nothing I could say or do would change their attitude. I was classified, labeled and filed . . . This all-out assault on my character hurt; it hurt terribly. After the hurt came resentment; after the resentment, anger.

Solace finally came, she went on, with the realization that "practically every woman who served abroad was slandered." Yet, she added, there remained "echoes of a small wicked voice: 'Next war, My Girl, you may as well do all those things of which you're accused; they'll *say* you did, anyway.'"

In April 1952, Eisenhower announced that he would seek the Republican nomination for President. Scattered whispers about his "London love affair" went around once again but they amounted to nothing. He was exactly what the Republican majority wanted, a military hero and a knowlegeable internationalist with a personality that appealed to people in all walks of life. He had strong support from women, just as Clare Boothe Luce predicted, "because," she said, "he exemplifies what the fair sex looks for—a combination of father, husband and son."

After he won the nomination, a new wave of surreptitious rumbles went round that Kay Summersby "might make trouble for Ike, yet," and the report spread that some of his rich friends (Joseph P. Kennedy was mentioned among them several times) had paid Mrs. Summersby a handsome sum and packed her back to England, to stay until after the election. That canard stopped when she was found to be working in a New York dress shop. Then the story started that she had "been paid—just to keep her mouth shut." Finally, whispers floated around that the Republican presidential nominee was "just plain lucky" because his Democratic opponent, Adlai Stevenson, was the first divorced man ever to try for the highest office.

Anyway, as though by gentlemen's agreement, the morals of the opposing candidates played no part in the campaign. Worries about the possible damaging effects of Stevenson's divorce had been quelled in a Massachusetts caucus of Roman Catholics when one man, expressing the opinion of many, declared, "Hell, half our wives would divorce us if they could!" and got an ovation. Meanwhile, Republicans easily discredited as "Democratic propaganda" the incipient revival of innuendos about Eisenhower "and that British woman."

The cry "I like Ike!" caught on throughout the country and throttled everything that was said against him. He won with a vast majority. Another huge victory at the polls retained him in the White House four years later, and throughout his presidency references to "Ike's wartime love affair" were as negligible as they had been in his 1952 campaign.

There were those who thought that President John F. Kennedy was delighted that youth and the media made him a vigorous sex symbol, because the image counteracted the 1960 campaign talk that he was physically unable to run the country (he had a lame back and was under treatment for Addison's disease). Others thought that J.F.K. was not concerned about being any kind of "symbol"; that he just wanted to be an outstanding President; and that if he had any spare time, he would make good use of it—perhaps by writing another book. Skeptics believed that since woman-chasing was a normal way of life with the Kennedy boys, as it had been with their father, the young President as a matter of course would follow his dark urges when and where he pleased, so long as they did not interfere with his official duties.

If the skeptics were right, J.F.K. reached the supreme post at a propitious time, for after more than two decades of alternating world tension and actual war, people—particularly those in urban areas—seemed amused rather than distressed at tales about the White House that would have shocked their ancestors.

In any case, much of the gossip that titillated sophisticates on the Washington cocktail circuit while J.F.K. was President seemed to bear out Theodore Sorenson's prediction shortly after the 1960 election: "This administration is going to do for sex what the last one did for golf." Certainly, a strong accent on sensuality pervaded the nation's capital during the Kennedy years. There was hardly a moment when gossip about sex was not either in action or in a kind of holding pattern until the next juicy tidbit about boudoir intimacies at the highest level could be worked out.

The President's background gave some impetus to what might be expected of the youngest man ever elected to the supreme office. Beginning shortly after he entered Congress in 1947, the general impression among his hard-working colleagues on Capitol Hill was that he spent more time dallying around Palm Beach than on legislative problems. His friends insisted that was not true; Jack Kennedy, they said, was brilliant and well-organized and could get things done a lot quicker than the average Congressman and, therefore, had some time to relax from the grind. At any rate, during his six years in the House, newspapers and magazines frequently referred to him as one of the nation's richest, most eligible bachelors, and made much of his attraction to pretty debutantes and motion picture starlets.

Intimations that he was a playboy while holding public office never seemed to bother him, and they certainly did not when he successfully ran for the Senate against Henry Cabot Lodge in 1952. In the midst of his heated campaign, for instance, the story got around that his opposition might make use of a snapshot of Representative Kennedy and a girl reposing in the nude on a Florida beach. His insouciance to the possible damage if the picture was publicized was shown when his perturbed aides brought it to his attention. He studied it with evident interest for a moment and then said with a smile. "Yes, I remember her. She was *great.*"

After Senator Kennedy married Jacqueline Bouvier in 1953, gossipers turned their attention elsewhere until he became a contender for the Democratic nomination for the presidency. Then talk circulated that Mrs. Kennedy's distaste for the political life and her increasing annoyance at her husband's philandering would have led her to divorce him if Joseph P. Kennedy had not given her a million dollars—the sum increased as the story was repeated—to maintain the marriage until after the election, at least.

Conjectures about J.F.K.'s morals spread through Republican ranks during his presidential campaign, but they were of little political consequence. The main issue was his religion, but Kennedy very effectively laid that issue to rest and won the election with 303 electoral votes over Richard Nixon's 219. (However, he won by less than one-tenth of one percent of the popular vote.)

Through his slightly more than a thousand days as President, talkative Washington circles buzzed with tales about Jack Kennedy's uncurbed sex life, with names, places and intimate details, as though the purveyors themselves had pulled up chairs and watched the proceedings. With the evidence generally inferential—and never conclusive—small scandals seemed constantly on the verge of breaking, while story after story was related as though it was wildly entertaining.

The only tale that appeared to be based on anything but hearsay became common talk in the capital some time before it spread elsewhere. Its genesis was *The Blauvelt Family Genealogy*, written by Louis Blauvelt and published by the Association of Blauvelt Descendants in East Orange, New Jersey, in 1957. Tracing the bloodline of Gerrit Hendricken (later known as Blauvelt), a Hollander who settled in New York in 1638, the book for some time was of little interest to anyone except the family. However, it became a sensation after an amateur genealogist, thumbing through the single copy at the Library of Congress, came across this paragraph:

> Durie (Kerr) Malcolm . . . We have no birthdate. She was born Kerr but took the name of her stepfather. She first married Firmin Desloge, IV. They were divorced. Durie then married F. John Bersbach. They were divorced, and she married, third, John F. Kennedy, son of Joseph P. Kennedy, one time Ambassador to England. (There were no children of the second and third marriage. One child, Durie, by the first.)

Photostats of the passage quickly circulated around the capital and created a stir with what appeared to be evidence that the first Roman Catholic in the presidency had an ex-wife. News correspondents who questioned Pierre Salinger, White House press secretary, were generally satisfied when he quoted the President's terse reaction, "There's nothing to it, of course." However, a few reporters looked further for facts that might either confirm or discredit the genealogical note. They discovered that Louis Blauvelt had died in 1959, and that although he was said to have worked on his book over a period of thirty years, his sketch of Durie Malcolm was not only inaccurate as to the chronology of her first and second marriages but also in its failure to mention that she married Thomas H. Shevlin in 1947. When reporters located her at her summer home in Newport, Rhode Island, and questioned her about the Blauvelt reference to John F. Kennedy, she said, "It's all too ridiculous! Why, everyone knows the President has been married only once."

Despite that statement, along with a flood of gossip about the President's sexual indiscretions in and out of the White House, talk about his secret "first marriage" persisted in Washington; and in time the rumor was used by arch-conservative and racist publications in efforts to denigrate Kennedy politically. *The Realist,* a Greenwich Village sheet, carried the Blauvelt item. *The Thunderbolt,* an organ of the National States Rights party, dilated on it in an article entitled "The White Man's Viewpoint." *The Winrod Letter,* sent out by the Reverend Gordon Winrod, a Protestant rightist of Little Rock, Arkansas, gave exposé treatment to the "secret marriage" of the Catholic President, and according to later disclosures, a hundred thousand copies reached mailbox holders in Massachusetts alone.

Parade magazine, the first major publication to touch the story, denied the report; its gossip-quiz column by Walter Scott (Lloyd Shearer), on September 2, 1962, carried a letter, asking whether or not the Blauvelt statement about the President was true. The answer, based on a quote from J.F.K., was a categorical denial. (Years later, Shearer recalled, "We got 12,000 letters on whether or not Kennedy had been married previously. Finally I called Pierre Salinger and said we are going with this one, one way or the other. Almost immediately, he got a verbatim answer from the President. He admitted taking out the girl, but flatly denied ever marrying her.")

Newsweek, two weeks after the *Parade* paragraph appeared, further labeled the Blauvelt story erroneous and observed that it might have been drawn from a Miami gossip column to the effect that Jack Kennedy and Durie Malcolm were frequently seen together in 1947. *Newsweek* also quoted "a Blauvelt in-law" as saying that Louis Blauvelt's reference to Kennedy was "a colossal mistake . . . It is likely that the old man formed the idea in his head, seeing that clipping . . . and the family hadn't had anyone that famous for a long time."

Mrs. William Smith, Blauvelt's daughter, told a reporter that while her father was generally meticulous in collecting and organizing his material, "he must have made a mistake." Mrs. Shevlin, the former Durie Malcolm, interviewed while vacationing in Montecatini, Italy, said the story was "absolutely false" and that she was not "even sure" how it began. She continued, "I've been married to Mr. Shevlin for many years, and previously I was married for a short time to John Bersbach, and then Firmin Desloge by whom I had a daughter who's now twenty. I know the President's family well and have known them for a long time, and I saw him years ago in Palm Beach and went with him and his family to an Orange Bowl game in Miami. I've rarely seen him since."

London's *Sunday Telegraph* and *The Observer* carried *Parade*'s question and answer. Yet, on September 20 the New York *Times* quoted James N. Blauvelt, president of the Association of Blauvelt Descendants: "I am sure that Louis Blauvelt could not have put it [the report] in his book unless he was sure of the facts. Where he got his information, I would not know."

The list of sources in Blauvelt's book cited as basis for the Malcolm passage a letter from Howard Ira Durie, of Woodcliff, New Jersey, and a newspaper clipping, neither of which could be found in Blauvelt's files. Subsequent investigation turned up as the probable source of the questionable impression a society column in the New York *World Telegram* (January 20, 1947), reporting that Massachusetts Congressman John F. Kennedy was being seen constantly, in Palm Beach and Miami, with Durie Malcolm Desloge, daughter of the George H. Malcolms, of Palm Beach and Chicago. "She is beautiful and intelligent," the account went on. "Tiny obstacle is that the Kennedy clan frowns on divorce. Durie has said 'Good morning, Judge' to F. John Bersbach. A similiar situation in St. Louis with Firmin V. Desloge, makes it two."

Meanwhile, queries about the President's "first marriage" poured into the White House. For some time the stock answer was: "We have an affidavit from the Blauvelt Family Association in New Jersey saying there is no material in the files about the President marrying Miss Malcolm." Finally, a form letter went out in reply to the persistent question stating simply: "The President has been married only once—to his wife, Jacqueline Kennedy."

The immediate result of the agitation was a new harvest of tales about the President's illicit escapades. One line of the gossip was that the Secret Service and buddies from Jack's college days were spiriting women of easy virtue into the White House by day, and wayward wives he fancied, out late at night. He was said to spend many evenings with a Georgetown matron, whose husband was frequently out of town. He appointed the husband of a former amour to a plushy diplomatic post, according to the whispers, and placed one of his "girls" on the White House staff. Converse rumors had it that the latter was not and never had been J.F.K.'s mistress, that she was a one-time intimate of Aly Khan and that she had been put on the staff at Jackie's insistence. But the usual addendum alleged Jack did enjoy the blandishments of at least two other young women who worked at the White House—and sometimes shared them with his cronies.

There were also fantastic accounts of the President's weekends in Palm Beach, where he was said to be surrounded by New York models and film celebrities and protected by his aides and reporters who drank his liquor and enjoyed the same entertainment he did. Marilyn Monroe's name came up repeatedly in backstairs talk about J.F.K. Rumors flew that Jackie's frequent trips away from Washington were generally prompted by her disgust with her husband's attentions to other women—particularly film starlets; but, the story went, the only one of whom she was truly jealous was Odile Rodin, the delectable blond actress who was Porfirio Rubirosa's delight in his last days. "I know for a fact," said one of Mrs. Kennedy's reputed friends, "that Jackie was more openly annoyed with Jack's absorption with Odile Rodin, one night at the White House, than she has ever been about any of his other carryings-on."

If even a tenth of the whispers about President Kennedy's erotic activity had been true, he would have had no time to contend with the constant series of crises that bedeviled his administration, or to travel, as he did, on the nation's business to Canada, South America, Mexico, and twice to Europe, or to work out proposals for sweeping civil rights legislation and a $10 billion tax cut to bolster the country. Some of his aides, distressed at last about the incessant innuendos about his private life, tried to counteract the mounting talk by citing his accomplishments, his courage, and—always—his charisma, in the original Greek sense, the "gift of grace." With all he was doing for the country, his devotees implied, those who were doing nothing had little right to chatter about how he spent his well-earned spare time. At the very least, his defenders went on, he had made Washington an infinitely livelier and more stimulating city.

Yet, suggestions that J.F.K.'s administration had exhilarated the nation's capital brought unpleasant reactions, some of which was reflected by Victor Lasky in his nationally syndicated column, appearing in the Washington *Star*, March 17, 1963:

> President Kennedy says since he's been in office the capital is jazzier. The growth rate in parties has trebled since JFK took over the ship of state. By day the New Frontiers-men call for sacrifices, but at sundown the sacrifices are forgotten as the bubbly begins to flow. Prime Minister Macmillan marvelled that President Kennedy is always on his toes during discussions but in the evening there will be music and wine and pretty women. Inevitably such goings-on have led to the circulation of wild stories concerning the White House . . . The Presidency is more

than a political office. The President is the leader of the people. He sets the moral tone.

Looking to the 1964 campaign, Kennedy's cohorts worked hard to elevate the moral tone of the White House. A spate of press reports pictured him as a devoted husband and family man. There was much less emphasis on "the beautiful people" who flocked around the Kennedys and the gaiety of White House parties.

The vision of Camelot on Pennsylvania Avenue seemed idyllic by the time the President left for Texas accompanied by Mrs. Kennedy in November 1963. However, on the last day of his life, *The Thunderbolt* circulated in Dallas with a front-page headline "Kennedy Keeps Mistress" and a salacious story implying that what was told was a mere indication of his many sexual transgressions.

After he became, at forty-eight, the fourth American President to be assassinated, nation-wide distress, tremendous shock, and sympathy for his bereaved family drew around his memory a laudatory cordon that would last for many years. How history will treat John F. Kennedy in the years to come is conjectural at this point. Results of a survey conducted by Louis Harris and published in January 1973 showed that J.F.K.'s rating as an administrator who inspired confidence and had an appealing personality was higher than that of any of the past six chief executives. Mr. Harris' summation was: "By far the strongest showing for President Kennedy and perhaps the explanation for his high standing across the boards, along with the fact that he was martyred by assassination while in office, was evident on the dimension of 'most appealing personality.'"

His wit, charm and grace have been mentioned in every definitive discussion of him since his death. Several recent accounts in the revisionist genre of history, however, have raised serious questions about his capabilities. At the same time, others have stressed the probability that he would have proved to be a great leader if he had been given enough time. In the long run, unbiased assessments of his actual administration, and not extracts from the gossip columns, will determine his stature among our Presidents.

As this is written, not enough time has elapsed since Lyndon Baines Johnson's death for him to be viewed in valid perspective. Strong indications now are that he will finally fare better in history than he did in his last years in the White House. He bore then the brunt for prosecuting an unpopular war that he had inherited. Objective appraisals in the future may judge him less harshly on that, but they cannot fail to give him high marks for bringing about a richer yield of humanitarian legislation than did even Franklin D. Roosevelt.

Biographers in the future may have difficulty in delineating Johnson as a man, for he was a complex, volatile individual, with idiosyncrasies that sometimes obscured his finer qualities. He set a frenzied pace for himself, kept at it, and expected everybody else around him to do the same. He was quick to anger, and also quick to forgive. He could be blunt, and often was, but he was also compassionate. He was one of the most gregarious men who ever lived in the White House. He freely admitted that one of the things he hated most was to be alone, so even on his off-duty hours he kept himself surrounded as much as possible with trusted aides and long-time friends, who appreciated his ability and charm, and shared his likes and dislikes. He also admitted that he had "a weakness for beautiful women." He once refused to take a highly able woman on his staff because, he said, "She's got everything but good looks." Another time, he spied a lovely reporter at one of his press conferences. "You're the prettiest thing I ever saw," he told her afterward; the next day, she was employed as a writer in one of his offices.

Many of the insinuations about President Johnson's inordinate interest in the opposite sex stemmed from gossip that had circulated around Capitol Hill for many years. As the six-foot-three, extraordinarily handsome twenty-three-year-old secretary to a Texas Representative, L.B.J. was said "to take a shine to every pretty girl that came along—and to enchant every one who held his interest for more than five minutes." He had been married for almost three years when he became a member of Congress. Over the next decade, as his position skyrocketed in the House, intermittent speculations that his charming wife might well be worried about his flirtations were downgraded by the Johnsons' friends of long standing. In their opinion, Bird (she was rarely called Lady Bird in those days) understood her impulsive mate better than anyone else ever could; she was confident of his love for her, and she knew that his roving eye was propelled more by vanity than sensuality. She held him by the loosest of reins, catering to his whims and never complaining about anything he did. ("She always knew how to handle me," Johnson remarked years later. "She is my strength.")

"I do everything intensively," he often said and anyone who had his admiration was well aware of that characteristic. His obvious devotion to some of his female employees—one, particularly—was viewed with some suspicion after he began to wield tremendous power in the Senate. His success in getting passed every important bill he espoused created resentment of some of his methods ("everything from wheedling to arm-twisting," was a common complaint), and, in time, that criticism was joined to charges that he was "a ruthless politician" and to whispers that he was a philanderer on Capitol Hill.

At the height of the gossip, House Speaker Sam Rayburn, Johnson's political mentor and one of his close friends, told him some of the things that were being said and subtly suggested that he might be more guarded in displaying his affections. "The talk won't help you," the Speaker went on, "and it might be bothersome to Bird." Johnson pondered the matter for a few moments and then replied, "Bird knows every-thing about me, and all my lady friends are hers, too. So I'll be damned if I try to shut up babbling mouths! Besides," he added, with characteristic irony and a wry smile, "I wouldn't want to deprive them of their dearest enjoyment."

As President, L.B.J. yearned for popular acclaim. He strove for total approval of the press, an impossible feat for any chief executive. He wanted everyone to regard him as a lovable, paternalistic leader, who would bring about innovations and reforms redounding to the good of all. Medicare, the Civil Rights Act and the Voting Rights Act would be among the epic measures achieved in his program toward his envisioned Great Society. But he would be less successful in establishing himself as a warmly appealing President, particularly among the Kennedy devotees, who constantly contrasted L.B.J.'s explo-sive temperament and "crude" mannerisms with the coolly detached, elegant "style" of his predecessor.

Innuendos about President Johnson's obsession with women generally filtered through old impressions that tied in with his gregarious nature and folksy habits. In the presidency, as before, he liked to relax and forget the cares of the day with aides and former Capitol Hill colleagues. Lady Bird was always around; the men usually brought along their wives, and some of them were beautiful. Naturally, then, suspicions occasion-ally surfaced that the President was interested in one or an-other of them, and vice versa, but such gossip never seemed to get anywhere. His custom of kissing his feminine friends ("by the wholesale," it was said) at social functions brought adverse comments from some people, but certainly not from the women thus saluted—they loved it. His ever-courtly man-ner toward women in the press seemed a bit overdone to some of their male colleagues. "The Lochinvar of the Pedernales," as they sometimes snidely referred to him, was up to his old tricks, as they saw it, and they took an especially dim view of his attentions to a comely columnist and a television personality, both of whom had capitalized earlier on impressions that they were special favorites of John F. Kennedy.

Actually, however, President Johnson provided gossips with far less material than most people who had long known him expected. Busybodies perked up each time they saw him dancing with an attractive woman. But he also danced with so many others, and appeared to be so interested in each one at the time, that he baffled even resourceful scandalmongers throughout most of his administration.

Yet, during his final months in the White House, rumors began to spread that Johnson's emotional interests had finally centered on a Harvard graduate student in her early twenties. Specifically, the talk went, he was "often closeted away" with her in his White House office or at the LBJ Ranch in Texas. It all sounded more sensational than it turned out to be, but the talk persisted even after he retired from office.

The young woman was Miss Doris Kearns, and she first met the President in 1967, a few weeks after she had written an article, "How to Dump LBJ in 1968" for the *New Republic*. He did not know about the magazine piece when he teased her for arriving half an hour late at a White House party, where she and other nominees for White House fellowships were scheduled to be photographed with him. "You're the woman who kept me waiting," he said with a broad smile. Then he asked her to dance. Before the evening was over, he had not only danced with her several times but after learning that she was active in the peace movement he had also given her his views on the value of intelligent dissent.

A front-page item next day in the Washington *Evening Star* played up the President's attention to the young lady who had written a sharp criticism of him for a magazine. The Associated Press picked up the story, and soon readers across the country were interested in Miss Kearns, particularly those on the West

Coast; the San Francisco *Chronicle* had developed the AP report into a feature story, with the headline "Johnson Wants Woman in Boudoir."

The President was not deterred by the publicity. Characteristically, he was determined that Miss Kearns, who had obviously disapproved of him when she wrote the "dump Johnson" piece, would be brought into his camp, or, at least, that he could change her opinion of him personally. Miss Kearns was assigned to the Labor Department, where she stayed for several months. Then, when L.B.J. decided not to run for reelection, he asked her to work with him at the White House. Her initial assignment was somewhat vague. "What I think he really wanted was just somebody to talk to," she said later. She would go and talk to him in the evenings two or three times a week, when he wanted to relax. They discussed the war a lot, argued about it, presumably never did agree; and he also talked a great deal about his family, and the memoirs he had already begun to write. After her White House fellowship expired, Doris Kearns stayed on at the White House to work on the book. After he retired from the presidency, she spent a good deal of time at the LBJ Ranch, devoting herself to the project until she began teaching at Harvard in the autumn of 1969. After that, she flew to Texas to continue helping L.B.J. with his writing on weekends, during Christmas and Easter vacations, and a full month in the summer of 1970. She was the only woman among six persons whom he mentioned in the preface of his book, *The Vantage Point* (1971), as those to whom he was particularly indebted for help in research, editing and writing. Apparently he did, after all, persuade her to change her opinion of him.

Relatively few people were deeply disturbed as insinuations, half-true stories and falsehoods that made the Washington rounds and in some instances reached other sections of the country during the Kennedy and Johnson administrations. Certainly, there were no outraged reactions from the press or the general public such as there were to tales of similar nature in the early days of our national history. Americans in general finally had come around to the view that presumed or actual weaknesses of the flesh are not related to a President's ability to run the country.

Yet, responsible citizens today are as eager as were their forefathers to regard the holder of the highest office as an individual who is superior in every respect. Whispered conjectures or overt charges that he is morally lax may not destroy the majority's confidence in a strong President—they never have, at any time in our history—but joined with the inevitable criticisms that assail any man in the White House, they can be politically threatening at the time, and they may deflect attention from his accomplishments indefinitely.

Two hundred years ago, John Adams, complaining about the rancor in the Continental Congress, wrote: "Politics are an ordeal path among the red-hot ploughshares. Who then would be a politician for the pleasure of running barefoot among them?" Twelve years later Adams was running barefoot for the presidency as, it seems, will any man to this day who has even a remote chance of attaining that office. Adams, like most other Presidents, was constantly assailed by partisan censure, but only once was his character attacked; and the attempt then to besmirch the morally rigid image of Adams was so ridiculous that nobody believed the calumny. Abigail Adams said at the time, "That is because my husband, all his life, has obeyed St. Paul's admonition, 'Abstain from all appearance of evil.' "

Even in our times, which have been called "permissive," the avoidance of "all appearance of evil" seems to any President the only possible insurance against scandal. Still, malicious attention to either the presumed or actual personal peccadilloes of exceptionally able chief executives has seldom affected their efficiency in office. Otherwise, our country might have been deprived of the services of its most illustrious leaders.

ℬibliography

Abernethy, Arthur T. *Did Washington Aspire to be King?* New York, 1906

Adams, Henry. *History of the United States of America During the Administration of Thomas Jefferson* (10 vols.), New York, 1889

Adams, James Truslow. *The Living Jefferson*, New York, 1936

Adams, John Quincy. *Memoirs of John Quincy Adams* (Portions of his diary from 1795 to 1849; edited by Charles Francis Adams, 12 vols., Philadelphia, 1874–77)

Adams, Samuel Hopkins. *Incredible Era: The Life and Times of Warren Gamaliel Harding*, Boston, 1939

Agar, Herbert. *The People's Choice*, Boston, 1933

Alden, John Richard. *General Charles Lee, Traitor or Patriot?* New York 1951

Alexander, Holmes. *Aaron Burr, The Proud Pretender*, New York, 1937

Allison, John Murray. *Adams and Jefferson*, Norman, Okla. 1966

Amory, Cleveland. *Who Killed Society?* New York, 1960

Anderson, Isabel. *Presidents and Pies: Life in Washington* (1897–1919), Boston, 1920

Angle, Paul M. "The Miner Collection: A Criticism," *Atlantic Monthly*, April, 1929

Bacheller, Irving, and Herbert S. Kathes. *Great Moments in the Life of Washington*, New York, 1932

Bacon, Edmund. *Jefferson at Monticello*, New York, 1862

Baer, James A., Jr. *Jefferson at Monticello*, Charlottesville, Va., 1967

Baker, Ray Stannard. *Woodrow Wilson: Life and Letters* (8 vols), New York, 1927–39

Barber, James David. *The Presidential Character*, Englewood Cliffs, N. J., 1927

Barton, William E. *The Women Lincoln Loved*, Indianapolis, 1927

Baruch, Bernard. *Baruch: My Own Story*, New York, 1957

Bassett, John Spencer. *The Life of Andrew Jackson*, Boston, 1967

Bell, Jack L. *The Splendid Misery*, New York, 1960

Bellamy, Francis Rufus. *The Private Life of George Washington*, New York, 1951

Benedict, Michael Lee. *The Impeachment and Trial of Andrew Johnson*, New York, 1973

Betts, Edwin Morris, and James Adams Baer, Jr. *The Family Letters of Thomas Jefferson*, Columbia, Mo., 1966

Beveridge, Albert J. *The Life of John Marshall*, New York, 1927

Billias, George Athan. *George Washington's Generals*, New York, 1964

Birney, Catherine H. *The Grimké Sisters*, Boston, 1885

Blauvelt, Louis. *The Blauvelt Family Genealogy*, East Orange, N. J., 1957

Boorstin, Daniel J. *The Lost World of Thomas Jefferson*, New York, 1948

Bowers. Claude G. *Jefferson and Hamilton—The Struggle for Democracy in America*, Boston, 1925

――――. *The Young Jefferson*. Boston, 1945

――――. *The Party Battles of the Jackson Period*, New York, 1922

Boyd, Thomas. *Light-Horse Harry Lee*, New York, 1931

Bradford, Gamaliel. *Saints and Sinners*, Cambridge, 1931

Brandt, Irving. *James Madison* (5 vols.), New York, 1941–61

Britton, Nan. *The President's Daughter*, New York, 1927

――――. *Honesty in Politics*, New York, 1932

Brown, Ray, *Madame Jumel*, Jamestown, Va., 1965

Bruberger, R. L. *The Image of America*, New York, 1959

Bullock, Helen Duprey. *My Head and My Heart,* New York, 1945

Burns, James MacGregor. *Roosevelt: The Lion and the Fox,* New York, 1956

_____. *Roosevelt: The Soldier of Freedom.* New York, 1970

_____. *The Embattled Presidency,* Urbana, Ill., 1964

Cable, Mary. *American Manners and Morals,* New York, 1969

Calhoun, Arthur W. *A Social History of the American Family,* (3 vols.), New York, 1945

Carpenter, Frank G. *Carp's Washington* (arranged and edited by Frances Carpenter), New York, 1960

Carroll, J. A., and M. V. Ashworth. *George Washington,* New York, 1957

Carruthers, Olive. *Lincoln's Other Mary,* Chicago–New York, 1946

Catchings, Benjamin S. *Master Thoughts of Thomas Jefferson,* New York, 1907

Channing, Edward. *History of the United States* (Vol. IV), New York, 1938

Chapin, Elizabeth M. *American Court Gossip or Life at the Nation's Capital,* Marshalltown, Iowa, 1887

Chinard, Gilbert. *The Literary Bible of Thomas Jefferson—His Commonplace Book of Philosophers and Poets,* Baltimore, Md. 1928

Clapper, Olive. *Washington Tapestry,* New York, 1946

Clinch, Nancy Gager. *The Kennedy Neurosis,* New York, 1973

Cloud, A. J., and Vierland Kesey. *Episodes in the Life of George Washington,* New York, 1932

Commager, Henry Steele. *America in Perspective,* New York, 1947

_____. *A Search for a Usable Past,* New York, 1967

_____. *The Spirit of Seventy-Six,* Indianapolis, 1958

Coolidge, Harold Jefferson. *Thoughts on Thomas Jefferson,* Boston, 1936

Corbin, John. *The Unknown Washington,* New York, 1930

Cunliffe, Marcus. *George Washington, Man and Monument,* Boston, 1958

Current, Richard N. *The Lincoln Nobody Knows,* New York, 1958

Curtis, William Eleroy. *The True Abraham Lincoln,* Philadelphia, 1903

_____. *The True Thomas Jefferson,* Philadelphia, 1901

Daniels, Jonathan. *Washington Quadrille,* New York, 1968

_____. *The Ordeal of Ambition,* New York, 1970

Daugherty, Harry M., and Thomas Dixon. *The Inside Story of the Harding Tragedy*, New York, 1932

Dos Passos, John. *The Head and Heart of Thomas Jefferson*, New York, 1954

———. *Mr. Wilson's War*, New York, 1962

Duncan, William Cary. *The Amazing Madame Jumel*, New York, 1935

Eaton, Clement. "A Dangerous Pamphlet in the Old South," *Journal of Southern History*, Vol. II. Baton Rouge La., 1936

Eaton, Margaret (O'Neale) Timberlake. *Autobiography of Peggy Eaton*, New York, 1932

Everett, Edward. *The Life of George Washington*, New York, 1860

Falkner, Leonard. *Painted Lady, Eliza Jumel*, New York, 1962

Fäy, Bernard. *George Washington: "Republican Aristocrat,"* Boston, 1931

Fishwick, Marshall. "The Man in the White Marble Toga," *Saturday Review*, February 10, 1960

Fitzpatrick, John C. *The Autobiography of Martin Van Buren* (edited) Washington, S. C., 1920

———. *Diaries of George Washington* (edited) Boston, 1925

———. "The George Washington Scandals," *Scribner's* magazine, April, 1927

———. *George Washington Himself*, Indianapolis, 1933

Fleming, Thomas J. *Affectionately Yours, George Washington*, New York, 1967

———. *The Man from Monticello*, New York, 1969

Flexner, James Thomas. *The Forge of Experience (1732–75)*, Boston, 1965

———. *George Washington in The Revolution*, Boston, 1967

Ford, Paul Leicester. *The Writings of Thomas Jefferson* (Vols. I–X), New York, 1897

———. *The True George Washington*, Philadelphia, 1896

Ford, Worthington Chauncey. *The Spurious Letters Attributed to Washington*, New York, 1889

———. *George Washington*, Boston, 1910

Freeman, Douglas Southall. *George Washington* (6 vols.) New York, 1946–52

French, Allen. "The First George Washington Scandal," *Massachusetts Historical Society Proceedings*, Vol. 65, Norwood, Mass. 1940

Furman, Bess. *White House Profile*, Indianapolis, 1951

Furnas, J. C. *Goodbye to Uncle Tom*, New York, 1956

Garraty, John A. *Woodrow Wilson: A Great Life in Brief*, New York, 1956

Graham, Pearl M. "Thomas Jefferson and Sally Hemings," *The Journal of Negro History*, Washington, D. C., April, 1961

Grayson, Cary T. *Woodrow Wilson*, New York, 1960

Green, Constance McLaughlin. *Washington: Village and Capital, 1800–1878*, Princeton, N. J., 1962

———. *Washington: Capital City, 1879–1950*, Princeton, N. J., 1963

Grimké, Angelina E. *Letters to Catherine E. Beecher*, Boston, 1838

Griswold, Rufus Wilmot. *The Republican Court: or, American Society in the Days of Washington*, New York, 1867

Headley, John Tyler. *Washington and His Generals*, New York, 1888

Helm, Katherine. *The True Story of Mary, Wife of Lincoln*, New York, 1928

Herndon, William H., and J. W. Weik. *The True Story of a Great Life*, Chicago, 1890

Hoover, Irwin H. *Forty-two Years in the White House*, Boston & New York, 1934

Howe, George Frederick. *Chester A. Arthur: A Quarter-Century of Machine Politics*, New York, 1934

Hughes, Rupert. *George Washington* (3 vols.) New York, 1933

Hulbert, Mary Allen. *The Story of Mrs. Peck*, New York, 1933

Irving, Washington. *Life of George Washington*, New York, 1857

Isaac. *Memoirs of a Monticello Slave* (as dictated to Charles Campbell in 1840), Charlottesville, Va., 1951

James, Marquis. *Andrew Jackson: The Border Captain*, Indianapolis, 1933

———. *Andrew Jackson: Portrait of a President*, Indianapolis, 1937

Jefferson, Thomas. *The Life and Morals of Jesus of Nazareth*. New York, 1902

Jellison, Charles A. "That Scoundrel Callender," *The Virginia Magazine of History and Biography*, Virginia Historical Society, Richmond, Va., July 1959

Johnson, Gerald W. *Andrew Jackson*, New York, 1927

———. *American Heroes and Hero Worship*, New York, 1941

———. *Woodrow Wilson*, New York, 1944

Jordan, Winthrop D. *White Over Black*, Chapel Hill, N. C., 1968

Kelley, Frank K. *The Fight for the White House: The Story of 1812*, New York, 1961

Kitman, Marvin. *George Washington's Expense Account*, New York, 1970

Kimball, Marie. *Jefferson: The Road To Glory*, New York, 1943

———. *Jefferson: War and Peace*, New York, 1947

———. *Jefferson: The Scene of Europe*, New York, 1950

Knollenberg, Bernhard. *George Washington: "The Virginia Patriot,"* Durham, N. C., 1964

Lamon, Ward Hill. *The Life of Abraham Lincoln*, New York, 1872

La Rochefoucauld-Liancourt, Duc de. *Travels Through the United States of North America*, London, 1797

Lash, Joseph P. *Eleanor and Franklin*, New York, 1971

Lasky, Victor. *JFK: The Man and the Myth*, New York, 1963

Lawrence, David. *The True Story of Woodrow Wilson*, New York, 1924

Leary, Lewis. *That Rascal Freneau*, New Brunswick, N. J., 1941

Lee, Henry. *Observations on the Writings of Thomas Jefferson*, Philadelphia, 1839

Leech, Margaret. *Reveille in Washington*, New York, 1941

Link, Arthur S. *Wilson: Confusion and Crisis, 1915–1916*, Princeton, 1964

———. *Wilson: Campaigns for Progressivism and Peace*, Princeton, 1965

Little, Shelby. *George Washington*, New York, 1929

Lodge, Henry Cabot. *George Washington* (Vol. I, II), Boston and New York, 1889

Longworth, Alice Roosevelt. *Crowded Hours*, New York, 1933

Lorant, Stefan. *The Glorious Burden*, New York, 1968

Lossing, Benson J. *Life of Washington* (3 vols.), New York, 1860

McAdie, Alexander. *Thomas Jefferson at Home*, Worcester, Mass., 1931

McAdoo, Eleanor Wilson. *The Woodrow Wilsons*, New York, 1937

———. *A Priceless Gift: The Love Letters of Woodrow Wilson and Ellen Axson Wilson*, New York, 1962

McAdoo, William G. *Crowded Years*, Boston, 1931

McCalley, Robert. *Slavery and Jeffersonian Virginia*, Urbana, Ill., 1964

McElroy, Robert McNutt. *Grover Cleveland: The Man and the Statesman* (2 vols.), New York, 1923

McLean, Evalyn Walsh, with Boyden Sparks. *Father Struck it Rich*, Boston, 1936

McPherson, Harry, *A Political Education,* Boston, 1972

Malone, Dumas. *Jefferson The Virginian* (Vol. I of *Jefferson and His Time*) Boston, 1948

―――. *Jefferson and the Rights of Man* (Vol. II), Boston, 1951

―――. *Jefferson and the Ordeal of Liberty* (Vol. III), Boston, 1962

―――. *Jefferson, The President—First Term, 1801–1805,* Boston, 1970

Marshall, John. *The Life of George Washington* (5 vols.) London, 1804–07

Mayo, Bernard. *Jefferson Himself,* Boston, 1942

―――. *Thomas Jefferson and His Unknown Brother Randolph,* Charlottesville, Va., 1942

―――. *Myths and Men,* Athens, Ga., 1959

Means, Gaston B., with May Dixon Thacker. *The Strange Death of President Harding,* New York, 1931

Milton, George Fort. *Abraham Lincoln and the Fifth Column,* New York, 1942

Moore, Charles. *The Family Life of George Washington,* Boston, 1926

Moore, George H. *The Treason of Charles Lee,* New York, 1858

―――. *Libels on Washington,* New York, 1889

Morison, Samuel Eliot. *The Oxford History of the American People,* New York, 1965

Morgan, James. *Our Presidents,* New York, 1924

Mott, Frank Luther. *Jefferson and the Press,* Baton Rouge, 1943

Nevins, Allan. *American Press Opinion: Washington to Coolidge,* New York, 1928

―――. *American Social History,* New York, 1931

―――. *Grover Cleveland: A Study in Courage,* New York, 1934

Nicolay, Helen. *Andrew Jackson, The Fighting President,* New York, 1929

Nicolay, John G., and John Hay. *Abraham Lincoln, A History,* New York, 1890

Nock, Albert Jay. *Jefferson,* New York, 1926

Padover, Saul A. *Jefferson,* London, 1942

Parker, George F. *Recollection of Grover Cleveland,* New York, 1909

Parmet, Herbert, and Marie B. Hecht. *Aaron Burr: Portrait of an Ambitious Man,* New York, 1967

Parton, James. *Life of Andrew Jackson* (Vol. I), New York, 1858

―――. *Life of Thomas Jefferson,* Boston, 1874

Patton, John S., and Sallie J. Doswell. *Monticello and Its Master*, Charlottesville, Va., 1925

Paulding, James K. *A Life of Washington* (Vol. I), New York, 1858

Peterson, Merrill D. *The Jefferson Image in the American Mind*, New York, 1960

————. *Thomas Jefferson: A Profile*, New York, 1967

————. *Thomas Jefferson and the New Nation*, New York, 1970

Pierson, Hamilton Wilson. *Jefferson at Monticello: The Private Life of Thomas Jefferson*, Charlottesville, Va., 1967

Pollard, James E. *The Presidents and the Press*, New York, 1947

Prussing, Eugene E. *George Washington In Love and Otherwise*, Chicago, 1925

Randall, Henry S. *The Life of Thomas Jefferson* (3 vols.), Philadelphia, 1858

Randolph, Sarah N. *The Domestic Life of Thomas Jefferson*, New York, 1871

Reid, Edith Gittings. *Woodrow Wilson: The Caricature, the Myth and the Man*, New York, 1934

Robins, Edward. *Romances of Early America*, Philadelphia, 1902

Robins, Sally Nelson. *Love Stories of Famous Virginians*, Richmond, 1923

Roosevelt, Elliott, and James Blough. *An Untold Story: The Roosevelts of Hyde Park*. New York, 1973

Ross, Ishbel. *Charmers and Cranks*, New York, 1965

Russell, Francis. *The Shadow of Blooming Grove*, New York, 1968

Sandburg, Carl. *Abraham Lincoln, The War Years*, New York, 1939

————. *Mary Lincoln, Wife and Widow*, New York, 1932

Schachner, Nathan. *Thomas Jefferson*, New York, 1951

Schlesinger, Arthur M., Jr. *The Age of Jackson*, Boston, 1946

————. *A Thousand Days: John F. Kennedy in the White House*, Boston, 1965

Seymour, Charles. *The Intimate Papers of Colonel House*, Boston, 1941

Shelton, William H. *The Jumel Mansion*, New York, 1916

Shepard, Edward M. *Martin Van Buren*, New York, 1899

Sinclair, Andrew. *The Available Man: The Life Behind the Masks of Warren Gamaliel Harding*, New York, 1965

Smith, Gene. *When the Cheering Stopped*, New York, 1954

Smith, Harrison. "Human Under Stone, Paint and Ink," *Saturday Review*, September 18, 1948

Smith, Margaret Bayard. *The First Forty Years of Washington Society*, New York, 1946

Sparks, Jared. *The Life of Washington*. Boston, 1842

Starling, Edmund W. *Starling of the White House* (as told to Thomas Sugrue), New York, 1946

Stetson, Charles W. *Washington and His Neighbors*, Richmond, 1956

Stone, I. F. *In a Time of Torment*, New York, 1967

Sullivan, Mark. *Our Times: The Twenties*, New York, 1937

Summersby, Kay: *Eisenhower Was My Boss*, New York, 1948

Tebbel, John. *George Washington's America*, New York, 1954

"Thomas Jefferson's Negro Grandchildren," *Ebony* magazine, Chicago, 1954

Tully, Grace. FDR—*My Boss*, New York, 1949

Tumulty, Joseph. *Woodrow Wilson as I Knew Him*, New York, 1921

Turner, Justie C., and Linda Levitt. *Mary Todd Lincoln*, New York, 1972

Tugwell, Rexford G. *Grover Cleveland*, New York, 1968

Van der Linden, Frank. *The Turning Point: Jefferson's Battle for the Presidency*, Washington, D.C., 1962

Walworth, Arthur. *Woodrow Wilson: American Prophet*, New York, 1958

Wecter, Dixon. *The Saga of American Society*, New York, 1937

———. *The Hero in America*, New York, 1941

Weems, Mason L. *The Life of Washington* (edited by Marcus Cunliffe) Cambridge, Mass., 1962

Weik, J. W. *The Real Lincoln*, New York, 1922

Wharton, Anne Hollingsworth. *Social Life in the Early Republic*, New York, 1902

White, William Allen. *Woodrow Wilson: The Man, His Times and His Task*. New York, 1924

———. *Masks in a Pageant*, New York, 1928

Wicker, Tom. *Kennedy Without Tears*, New York, 1964

Williamson, George C. *Richard Cosway, R. A.*, London, 1905

Wilson, Edith Bolling. *My Memoir*, Indianapolis, 1937

Woodward, W. E. *George Washington: The Image and the Man*, New York, 1946

INDEX